Looking *at the* Personal Diaries *of*

William F. Dusenberry

of Bloomingdale, (Cabell County) Virginia/West Virginia
1855 and 1856 Plus Parts *of* 1862, 1869, 1870, and 1871

by *Carrie Eldridge*

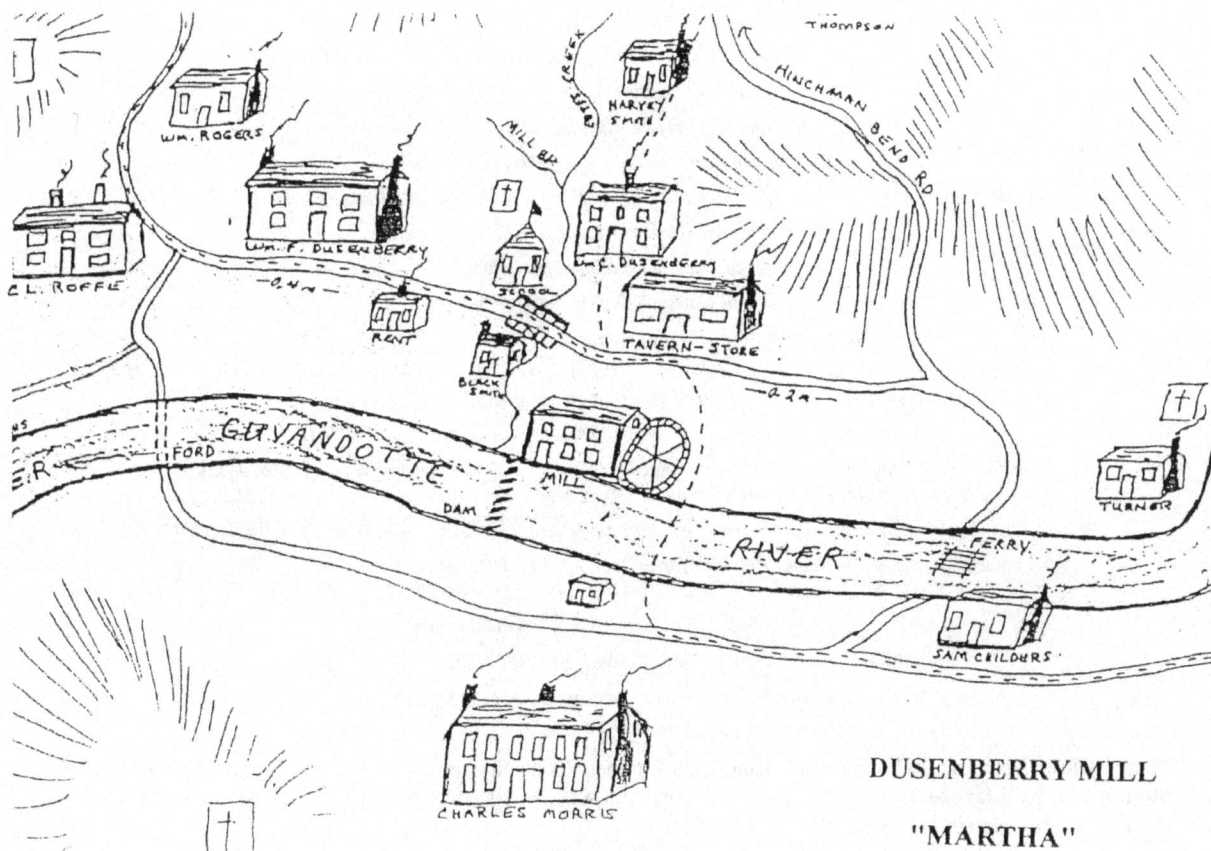

DUSENBERRY MILL

"MARTHA"

HERITAGE BOOKS
2020

HERITAGE BOOKS
AN IMPRINT OF HERITAGE BOOKS, INC.

Books, CDs, and more—Worldwide

For our listing of thousands of titles see our website
at
www.HeritageBooks.com

Published 2020 by
HERITAGE BOOKS, INC.
Publishing Division
5810 Ruatan Street
Berwyn Heights, Md. 20740

Heritage Books by the author:

An Atlas of Appalachian Trails to the Ohio River

An Atlas of German Migration and America

An Atlas of Northern Trails Westward from New England

An Atlas of Settlement between the Appalachian Mountains and the Mississippi/Missouri Valleys: 1760–1880

An Atlas of the Southern Trails to the Mississippi

An Atlas of Trails West of the Mississippi River

Cabell County's Empire for Freedom

Cabell County, Virginia/West Virginia, Superior Court Records, 1843–1848

*Looking at the Personal Diaries of William F. Dusenberry of Bloomingdale, (Cabell County),
Virginia/West Virginia, 1855 and 1856, Plus Parts of 1862, 1869, 1870, and 1871*

Minute Books: Cabell County, [West] Virginia Minute Book 1, 1809–1815

*Miscellaneous Cabell County, West Virginia Records: Order Book Overseers of the Poor, 1814–1861;
Fee Book, 1826–1839; 1857–1859 (Rule Book); Cabell Land for Tax Purposes, 1861–1865*

Nicholas County, Kentucky Property Tax Lists, 1800–1811 with Indexes to Deed Books A & B (2), and C

*Nicholas County, Kentucky Records: Stray Book 1, 1805–1811; Stray Book 2, 1813–1819;
Stray Book 3, 1820–1870; and Execution Book A, 1801–1878*

On the Frontier of Virginia and North Carolina

Owen County, Kentucky Stray Books 1 & 2: 1819–1830, 1830–1864

Torn Apart: How Cabell Countians Fought the Civil War

These "Dusenberry Diaries" are found in the Fred Lambert Collection in the Special Collection Department of Morrow Library, Marshall University, Huntington, West Virginia, and used by permission. Special thanks to Special Collections staff for aid in this project.

International Standard Book Numbers
Paperbound: 978-0-7884-0379-8

CONTENTS

APPROXIMATE LOCATION OF HOMES MENTIONED IN DUSENBERRY DIARY

NOT TO SCALE

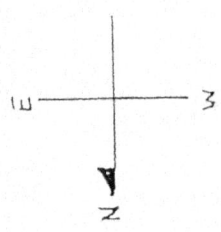

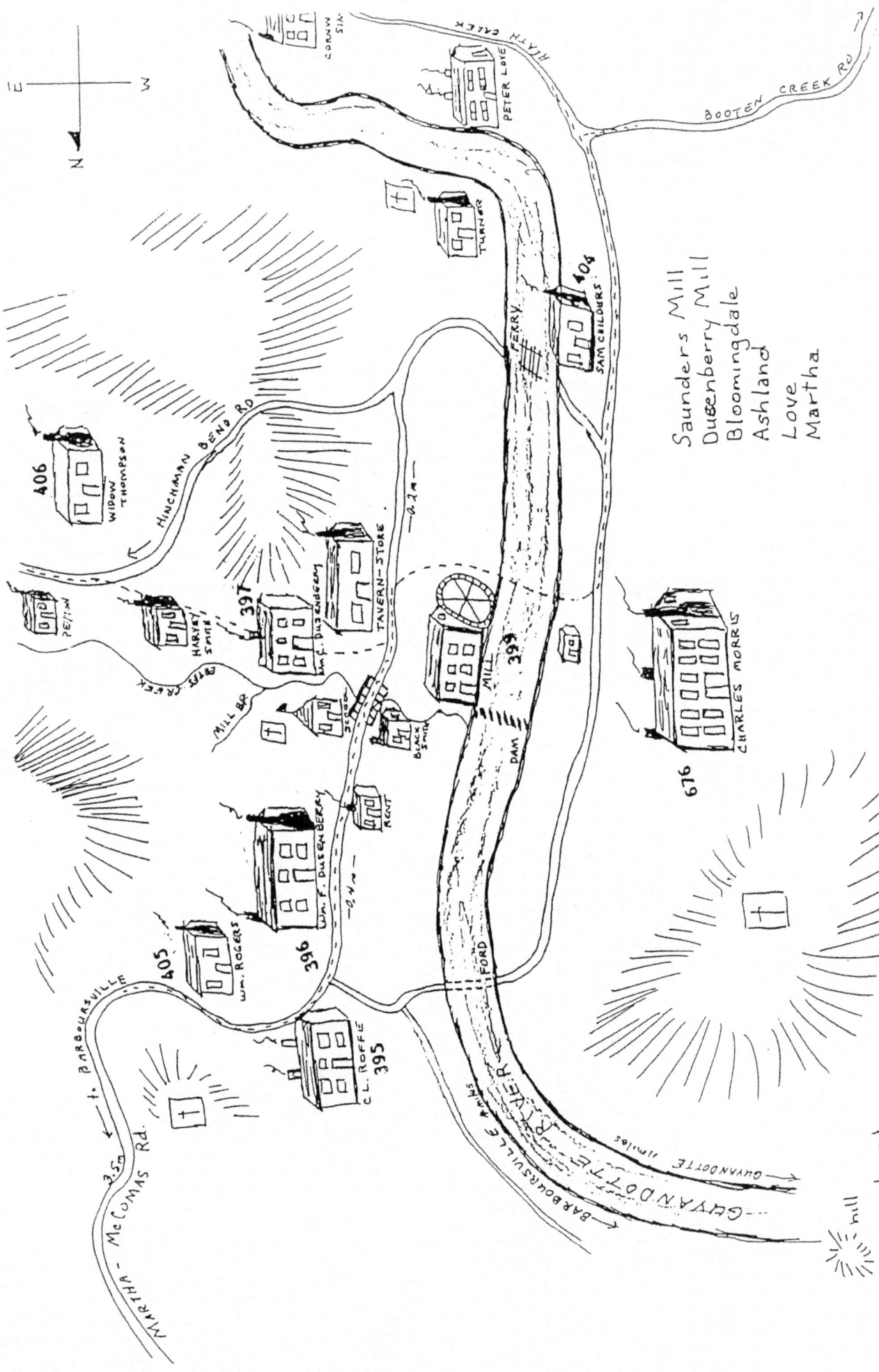

Saunders Mill
Dusenberry Mill
Bloomingdale
Ashland
Love
Martha

BOOTEN CREEK RD.

HEATH CREEK

PETER LOVE

CORNW SIX

TURNER

SAM CHILDERS

404

FERRY

WIDOW THOMPSON

406

HINCHMAN BEND RD.

PETTON

HARVEY SMITH

WM. F. DUSENBERRY

TAVERN-STORE

397

BETS CREEK

MILL BR.

SCHOOL

BLACK SMITH

AGENT

WM. F. DUSENBERRY

396

WM. ROGERS

405

C. L. ROFFE
395

t. BARBOURSVILLE 3.5

MARTHA — McCOMAS Rd.

MILL

DAM

FORD

399

676

CHARLES MORRIS

GUYANDOTTE RIVER

BARBOURSVILLE 4 MILES

GUYANDOTTE 10 MILES

hill

present road

E

N

W

The Personal Diaries of Wm.F.Dusenberry
Bloomingdale,Virginia

1855,1856,1862,1869,1870,1871

copies of orginals made by Fred B.Lambert about
1925 and part of the F.B.Lambert collection
MS 76 deposited at Marshall University,
Huntington,West Virginia.(Cabell County)

William F. Dusenberry was born in New York state and
migrated to Cabell County around 1850 when his father
(Wm.C.Dusenberry) purchased a farm and mill site from
Sampson Saunders. This mill site was first built upon by
Joel Estes about 1825. Estes sold the site to Saunders and
then Saunders sold to Dusenberry. This mill site was known
by all three names as well as Bloomingdale,Ashland and Love.
Sampson Saunders was one of the wealthest men in western
Virginia and developed the mill. It was an important mill
before Dusenberry purchased the site and had a saw mill, and
carding machine as well as a grain mill.

These diaries are an interesting look at the life in
Cabell County, Virginia/West Virginia. We have several
separated years, thus we have a record of three different
periods in the life of William F. Dusenberry.

In 1855,Wm.F.Dusenberry was the son of a well-to-do
businessman and land owner and he acted as representative
of his ill father as well as pursuing the profession of
dentist. Wm.F. talks about his duties,social and business
activies and all the people that lived in the area. The two
years 1855-56 are carefree and full of the activities of a
well-to-do(idle ?) young man and his family.

The 1862 section consists of only one week of material,
but the reader is struck by the fear of the writer and the
hardships he has already faced and his uncertain future.

The section from 1869-70-71 is written by a much more
experienced person who has many more responsiblities. Wm.F.
is so busy that he has little time to record social or
neighberhood actives, but he makes many comments about his
busy and the river.

These combined diaries give the reader an insite into
life in Cabell County in the 1850's that is not available
elsewhere. This author hopes the missing volumes will come
to light someday, because the county comes to life within
the pages of these diaries.

The Dusenberry Diaries are incomplete and nothing is
known about the materials that are missing...As recently
as 1991 a portion of this diaries came to light in a Huntington
book shop.

FRED B. LAMBERT

Lambert was a local historian, genealogist and collector
who lived in Cabell County, dying about 1960. Mr.Lambert did
many personal interviews and collected a mass of genealogical
which his family has deposited in Special Collections of the
Morrow Library at Marshall University in Huntington, WV.Among
the naterials of this collection at several ledgers into which
Lambert copied these Dusenberry Diaries. Nothing is know of the
originals or even if they exist.

DUSENBERRY FARM

The Dusenberry farm was located at the first falls of the
Guyandotte River at the present site of Martha. The Doolittle
Mill must have been quiet similar. Thw appendix cares a news-
paper ad for the Doolittle Mill from the 1853 Guyandotte Herald.

Ad from the Guyandotte Herald

Iwish to sell my land and mill on Mud River in the County of
Cabell and the state of Va. 6 miles from the Court House and
one mile from the Covington and Ohio Railroad. The tract of
land contains 750 acres and 67 poles, 150 acres cleared and in
cultivation, the balance timbered land. The improvements on the
farm consist of a two story hewed log house, frame kitchen and
a frame barn 40 by 60 ft., two small frame and log buildings
for the use of tentants, apple orchards and about 100 peach trees
all of which will be bearing fruit the present season. The mill
is a three story frame building 40 feet square and a basement
of stone. The mill runs three pair (4 feet stones 2 pair of which
are burrs of the best quailty). All the shatfs heads for running
the machinery are cast iron. The saw mill is 22 by 60 feet long,
and can cut 6,000 feet of lumber in 24 hours. There is also a
building 24 by 40 feet long, one and a half stories high and
used for a carding machine and cabinet shop, in the cabinet shop
is a good turning lathe run by water. There is an immense quatity
of iron ore on the land, the vein of ore is supposed to be 20 feet
thick, and said by judges of ore to be a quailty that will justify
working. Person wishing to purchase such property are invited to
call and see it, or by addressing me (post paid) at Cabell Court
House   ,Va., they may obtain any information they desire.

                                      Ambrose L.Doolittle

Dusenberry Diary
1855

Bloomingdale,Cabell Co.Va.
January 1,1855

I am residing here on my Father's
place taking charge of the store and
grist mill and overseeing the tenants
and other matters on the farm.
    The Saw Mill is being run by Miller
& Moore,their lease not expiring until
the 18th of May next. I am keeping
house in the one I built behind the
store.
    My family consists of three
children, Susan,Caleb and Sarah, my
neice Anna Marsh, my servant Margery
myself and my wife. My brother Charles
carries on the watch repairing and
jewelry business here. (signed)
William F.Dusenberry (dentist)

Monday Jan.1,1855

    Bill Saumby came up from town early
this morning to put some more plank on
the mill flumes.(Charley still going
with Miss Blake) Steamer Adrian passed
through the Locke. The saw mill running
day and night.Ben and Jim Cowens,
H.Smith,and C.Shipe are the sawyers.
Mrs.Jones here.

Thuesday,Jan.2,1855

    Charley & I went out hunting. We got
10 squirrels. Father not very well
Charley & Robert were taking a French
lesson. Old Squire Thornburg (FL-Sol.
Thornburg d.dec.30,1854) who died last
Saturday as were also the son and
brother-in-law of Joe Stanley who were
drowned last Sunday(dec.31,1854) They
found the bodies about the same place
where they went down. Felix Duffin
bought six barrels of flour at-------.
Jones, who has lived for three years in
the house by the bridge,commenced moving
to Barboursville today.
x

#=1850 household number

1850 Cabell Census
#396 father Wm.c 57y
      Susan   49y
      Robert   12y
      Samuel   8y
#397 Wm.F.Dusenberry 23y
      Cynthia   24y
      Susan   1y
buried Spring Hill-Htgn

Family born NY
Father bought Sanders Mill
@1849-Sampson Sanders

Wm.F. 1816-1903
Cynthia L.1824-1886
Caleb C. 1853-1929
Wm.C.II   1860-1935
Charles O.1828-1897

#331 Cowens
#357 HarveySmith

bur.Thornburg Cem
#714   17 jun 1791-30 dec 1854

#417 Stanley 2 sons
93 Hamilton Mays m Mary
      Stanley 1841 CCM

Wednesday, Jan.3, 1855

I was all day making a road to the ice house. Mrs.Monroe stopped in here a while this morning. The steamer Major Adriane went down this afternoon. Mr.Roffe sent 100 bu.of wheat to the mill today. Trade awful dull. Ben and C.Shipe sawing from noon till midnight and Jim Cowens and H.Smith the other twelve hours.There was a large ring around the moon which indicates a storm.

seamtress

#395 Martha merchant-owned blacksmith shop slave owner

Thursday Jan.4, 1855

I went down to McCullough's and bought me 100 segars for $.75. In the afternoon I finished making Cynthia a Leach Tub and Charley made one for mother. Albert Moore was up here this morning. Charley and Robert took a French lesson. Bill Fielder brought me a Sunday paper. Orrin Moore and Mr.Fowler went on the steamboat to the Falls the other day and made Mr.Webb a bid to repair the Falls dam for $150.00. He decline giving it. I sent Mr.Graham an order on Felix Duffin for $51.(for a barrel of flour)?

#393 Patrick McCullough Martha Merchant

tub to make soap

operated ferry at Martha

Friday Jan.5, 1855

Father worse today.I stopped at Miller and Thornburg's store and bought 300 segars,etc.& some linen for Charley & took it to Mrs.Monroe's to make a shirt for him,then to Wils.Moore's who paid me $5.00 on account of twelve bushels of meal I let him have to sell at 5%. Then went down to where Miller & Moore is building their mill.
The Steamboat Major Adrian passed through the locke(about dark) with a coal boat in tow. She left a box of gargling oil sent us from Pittsburg to sell on commission. I went to the mill with Bill Fielder and got him a little meal. Miller & Moore had several hands loading lumber in a boat to take down to their mill.Bill Saumby was amoung them.

(Barboursville)

handy man prone to accidents went to Canda to marry.

Friday Jan. 5,1855

I went to town to the blacksmith
shop to get a piece for the buggy. I
went over on the other side of the river
about Childer's house to look at some
timber that John Hensley had to sell.(He
asked too much.) We stopped in to see
Sam Childers who has been sick all
winter the rheumatism.

#683 John Hensley

#404 Sam Childers

Saturday Jan.6,1855

Miller & Moore with several hands
loading lumber in a boat.(for their
Mill)

Sunday Jan.7,1855

The Steamer Major Adrian went down
this morning. There was prayer meeting
in the school house this morning. Bowman
went to Guyandotte. Charley went to see
Martha Blake. Sam Johnson passed down I
wrote a letter to William Horsley,248
Front St. Cincinnati,inquiring what he
could get me a small steamboat for to
run up the Guyandotte river.

#389 Martha Blake 13y
d/o Sarah(Martha marries
another man)

Monday Jan,8.1855

Soon after breakfast ,Charley and I
raised the flag in honor of the victory
of the Battle of New Orleans. Sent two
letters to the post office by Conwelzie
Simmons.

#785 lived south of Martha
bur.Davidson Cem.

Tuesday Jan.9,1855

Got the Gyandotte Herald. I sold
Dick Lunsford the first bottle of
gargling oil.The steamer Major Adrian
went up just after noon.

#415 Lunsford

Wednesday Jan.10,1855

I took a dose of caster oil for my
clotters. Charley Morris came over to
take a fox hunt with his hounds. As they
came home they met Roffe's nigger Ben
who had a pheasant that he knocked out
of a tree and killed with a stone. I
took some of Doct.Rogers syrup for
stomach ache & pains in my chest.
Steamer Major Adrian went down this

constipation

afternoon. Charley & Robert took a
French lesson.

Thursday Jan.11,1855

Saw mill ran well all the afternoon.
(They brought the casting today for it.)

Friday Jan.12,1855

A boat load of wheat came to the
mill for Roffe. Tom Hensley was here
awhile. Came to hire the blacksmith shop
and house. They could not agree on the
rent. Roffe asked him $50 for the two.
The steamer Major Adrian was up about
noon. Albert Moore and Fowler went up on
her. Roffe came in and said Father
wanted me to come down there, that
mother's girl Caroline had gone off. She
left a couple of notes one for mother
and the other for Lee Bowman, in which
she stated she was going to drown
herself. Mother was much worried.
Charley,Robert and I started out to hunt
for her,none of us believing she had the
least idea of drowning herself. After
hunting at Bowman's, Roffes and along
the river bank,we found her at Mrs.
Butchers in bed. We left her there.
(Father and Mother very much relieved.)

Caroline Slocum(from out
of area ?) servant

Saturday Jan.13,1855

Just as we were about to take our
breakfast,the Frenchman Mr.Denot came
with his wife for me to take out a tooth
for her.(It crushed & I put something in
it to ease the pain & they left.)Graham
came up and took dinner with Charley.
Caroline still at Mrs.Butchers. She sent
Jim up for mother to send her a clean
frock and apron. They sent them and also
told him to find another place for her
to live.There was a meeting in the
school house this afternoon. Not many
there.

Alex Donnot/Denot/Donnate
Frenchman-rented house
taught brothers French

Sunday Jan.14,1855

There was preaching in the school
house this morning. Bill Saumby came up
here about ten o'clock(with our mail).
Anna,Margery and Susie went to church.

The steamer Major Adrian went down just
at noon. Soon after dinner old Ralph
Smith's and Sam Childer's daughters came
here and Anna and Margery went out with
them. Jim Butcher came home with Margery
and Ben Cowens with Anna. Charley went
to see Miss Blake, Caroline went down to
live with Mrs.Warren Roffe today. Kept
up a fire under my meat all day.

#639 Smith-west of River

Monday Jan.15,1855

Charley returned from Miss Blake
about nine o'clock. The Major Adrian
came up. We went over to the Locke to
see about some shingles & to see Webb
but he wasn't on the boat. The Frenchman
was all day at work for us pulling out
trees in front of Father's house.(FL
Mr.McDenott-Alex Donnot)Charley and
Robert took a French lesson. I was
making off Roffe's account.

Tuesday Jan.16,1855

Charley Morris came over with his
hounds for a chase and went up the
river. Pete Love and another gentleman
was along. About nine o'clock Charley
and I went up to Joe Stanley's to count
some new rails he had made and put up.
He was not at home. Then we came across
to the road.Got home about one o'clock.
Joe Stanley came here soon after. Father
able to be out doors awhile today.
Labeled the ink we bottled yesterday.(I
was most of the afternoon making and
bottling ink.) Steamer Adrian went down
just at dark.

#676-west of River-Heir
to Saunder lands thru
wife Martha Kilgore
(Saunders neice)
slave owner

Wednesday Jan.17,1855

Made out Harvey Smith's time. A boat
load of wheat was brought by Thornburg
for Roffe and hoisted into the mill with
the blocks. Ike Thompson worked for
Father in the afternoon. Caroline came
to Mother's this afternoon for her
clothes. Jim Butcher was with her.
Father sent a letter to her mother
today. I went down to Father's just
after dark and borrowed a candle.

#357 Harvey Smith
laborer in area

#398 son of John--14y

Thursday Jan.18,1855

About ten the rag wheel was brought
from town by Dave Thornburg. Harris(FL-
Green Harrison) had fixed it. Just
before night the steamer Major Adrian
went up. They brought a 1000 shingles
for us. They took up a barrel of flour
for Z.Nicely. Ike Thompson worked all
day for father. Old Mr.John Merritt was
buried in Barboursville yesterday.

#988 Thornburg-B'ville

#719 Harris-blacksmith
in Barboursville

#989 bur.Merritt Cem.
B'ville age 66y (mill)

Friday Jan.19,1855

I went with Charley Morris and Pat
Thompson for a fox hunt. Steamer Major
Adrian went down about the middle of the
afternoon. It brought two bags of wheat
to be ground to Vinson Nowell. I sent a
barrel of flour down to Blume,the
saddler,in Barboursville. Cynthia white-
washed & cleaned the kitchen. I went to
Fathers and got tallow to make candles.
Paid the Captain of the Adrian $.50 for
bringing up two bundles of shingles.

#407 Thompson

? maybe #512 Winston Noel
#1015 Blume owned livery

Saturday Jan.20,1855

The Steamer Adrian was just landing
alongside the mill. She brought up a
stove for Miller & Moore. Hugo Deitz
came up on her. He brought two letters
for us from Guyandotte P.O.(Sold him
five Barrels at $8.50 per barrel. He is
to take it down on the boat tomorrow.)
(Lewis was a member of Congress from
this district. He sent me a copy of the
President's message.)

#824 with mother
owned store Guyandotte

Sunday Jan.21,1855

Mr.Graham came up here from town
about 11 o'clock. Charley cut his hair.
Ate dinner with Father. Then went to
town to take care of Bill Saumby who cut
his foot with the adze. Mrs.Bowman
stopped a few moments this morning to
see Cynthia on her way up to the prayer
meeting in the school house. About two
o'clock the steamer Adrian went down,
After passing through the Locke she
rounded alongside the mill and took on
board five barrels of flour for Hugo
Dietz. Jerome Shelton was on board and

?possibly #973
never indentified

adze-wide flat hoe like ax

#460 blacksmith
maybe Hinchman Bend

told me to have a barrel of flour for
him ready to take up tomorrow.

Monday Jan.22,1855

I was around the store all afternoon
trying to collect accounts from persons
as they went to town to court. I had a
settlement with Briant(FL-teacher).Went
with Graham from Millers store to
McKendrees to see Bill Saumby. Found him
in bed. Took tea at McKendree's.Came
back to Millers and went up to the Lodge
room. The Lodge soon opened. I was
appointed J.D. Pro-tem. John Thornburg
and a young man by the name of Nowning
was initiated. Charley,McCullough,John
Thornburg and I walked home.A little
after eleven o'clock when Charley and I
came in.

Tuesday Jan.23,1855

Towards night the Steamer Adrian
came up. Jerome Shelton on board. (Took
up a barrel of flour-$8.50) Also took on
board two boxes to bring down the bodies
of Mike Wentz and his child. They were
going to disinter and bury them over on
Mud.

Wednesday Jan.24,1855

Peter Love came here and paid me
$4.00 on account. Robert went up to
Smith's & with Higgins shelled a barrel
of his corn. (Snow enough for sleighs if
not such awful rough roads) Asked Briant
$20 a year for the house where Jones
moved from by the bridge. Caroline at
Father's and wanted some more of her
clothes. (Mother refused) Warren Roffe's
boy brought word from Mrs.Roffe to keep
clothes of Caroline as she would not
mind Mrs.Roffe--sent her clothes up from
R's. Steamer Adrian passed down soon
after dark. Charley went to see
Miss Blake.

Thursday Jan.25,1855

(Fine sleighing if not frozen so
rough.) I agreed with Bill Fielder this
afternoon to do our ferrying for $3.00

$848 Whitfield Bryant
b SC-rented a house
#757 Robt.McKendree
innkeeper-Guy.

#714 s/o Solomon 23y

#393 McCullough
store Martha

Michael Wentz & son died
1854 on Madison Ck-summer
Moved to Merritt Cem.N
for burial Sr. 26 jul 185
            son 25 aug 1854

Most of Love family lived
Ona-except Peter near
Martha-(Extinct town)

this year, provided we did not have more
than we have had in any average year
since we came here. If we have more I am
to pay him four dollars. Sam Childers is
to decide the matter.

Friday Jan.26,1855

Roads awful rough and slippery. There
was very little doing around here until
towards night when we were all taken by
surprise by the appearance of a fine
large stern wheel steamer called the
"R.H.Linsey". She just filled the Locke
and is much the largest boat that ever
came up 'this' river. She has a fine
cabin and stateroom. Fowler, Samuels, Ike
Ong, Webb, Orren & Albert Moore and Bill
Miller came up on her. The last two left
her at the Locke and came over to the
mill. The boat passed on to the Falls.
Wheeler was also on her. Weather too
cold for the sawyers.

Large river boat

#769 Ike Ong-tailor Guy.

Saturday Jan,27,1855

Charley and the Frenchman, Mr.
Donnette, went over to Charles Morris's
and got some straw which we put in the
bottom of the ice house. (We hauled ice
from the creek. It was clear & 3 inches
thick.) Graham & Albert Moore came up
here. "About three o'clock in the afternoon the new steam boat came down. We
gave her a salute and ran up the flag.
They returned the salute by blowing
their whistle. We gave them another as
they came out of the locke which they
returned the same way. There was a good
many on board congregated on the
hurricane deck. They gave us three
cheers as they passed." Just at night
Charley Morris put Capt.Jack Peyton out
of his carriage in front of (his) store
and he started up the road home. I saw
he was very drunk and watched him until
he got some distance up the road. He
fell once but got up and went ahead
again. After sawing some wood, I thought
I would go up the road and see how he
got along. I found him lying inside the
fence just this side of the house
Stewart moved from. I left him and went
up and told Fielder, then went down and

Peyton family lived
about mouth of Tom's Ck.
possibly #410

got Charley and Bob and went out to see
what we could do with him. He was laying
in the snow and would of frozen to death
before morning. We found him asleep, his
jug full of whiskey lying near him.
Charley picked it up and hid it. We were
soon joined by Fielder, Pat Thompson and
Emberson Turley. Then we got him to John
Dick. He would not take him in so we
went up to Harvey Smith and left him
there. Then we returned home, stopped on
the way and emptied the whiskey out of
the jug and laid it about where we found
it. Moore & Graham went down on the boat
this afternoon.

Charley was 27
Bob was 17 (Wm.'s bro.)

Sunday Jan.28,1855

(Hauled 2 loads of ice, broke the
sled & lost ice & sled.) There was
prayer meeting in the school house this
morning.

Monday Jan.29,1855

Cynthia sent a letter to her sister
Jane (Nagels) Matt Butcher came here
about nine o'clock to settle with us. I
bought as sled of him for $1.00 to haul
ice. Charley and I took a yoke of cattle
and went up to Bill Peyton's after it.
(They returned about 1 o'clock.)

#705-Butcher

Thuesday Jan.30,1855

I went down to McCullough's and got
me a pair of ----- gloves to handle the
(left blank by FL)ice with. Emerson
Turley was there (at Father's) He was
trying our farm to attend on halfs.

#95 Turley to rent farm.

Wednesday Jan.31,1855

Henry Stewart came up from
Guyandotte this afternoon. He said the
Ohio River is so full ice the boats can
not run. There has none passed Guyan
either way for nearly a week. Caroline
returned this morning and begged Mother
to take her in. She has no place to go
to. Mother is going to keep her till she
hears from her folks.

Thursday Feb.1,1855

Charley returned from Miss Blake's early. I sent two letters down by Henry Stewart on the Wheeler. Graham returned to Barboursville just before night. Father able to be out. Too cold for the sawyers. The saw mill not running. Sent a letter to Wheeler in Guyandotte.

(?a boat)

#785 Joseph(minister)

Friday Feb.2,1855

Hugo Deitz came up from Gyandotte this morning in a wagon & got two barrels of flour. Mother and Ella Butcher were here to see Cynthia. Navigation on the river entirely closed by the ice.

Saturday 3 Feb. ,1855

Higgins & Donnate helped haul ice. Roffe sent a load of flour to Guyandotte. They are depending on our mill because of ice. Roffe's nigger Spencer was married this evening to one of Conwelzie Simmon's wenches. Mr.Blume came up here this morning and I lent him a book called"The Children of the Abby".

(Did a good business in ice-all year)

Sunday Feb.4,1855

Charley went to see Miss Blake about 10 o'clock and was away all day. Jim Butcher took tea with us. Wm.Fielder came in and sat awhile.

Monday Feb.5,1855

I walked to Barboursville. Went to Bill Miller's and got our mail. Then went to Blume's shop where I found Graham & Bill Saumby. Blume has not got my saddle finished. Duffin paid $51 for six barrels of flour. I went to Jones & got a pair of pants for Robert after waiting about half an hour for him to finish them.
I went over to Sam Childers and got from him the account the company has against us. Soon after tea Simmons, McCullough and John Thornburg came to the store. I went with them. They

#729 Miller's Store/ post office-Cabell Court House for 30y

#673 Wm.Jones-tailor B'ville

(Did Childers run the lock)

lectured Charley on the first degree in
masonry.

Thuesday Feb.6,1855

Albert Moore was at the mill most of
the day. Matt Butcher came down and told
us that eleven of our hogs(he had heard)
were in the woods wild. Father agreed to
give him a third or a half according to
the difficulty in getting them.

Wednesday Feb.7,1855

The Thermometer in New York City
this morning was eight degrees below
zero and at Island Point,Vermont 39
degrees below,which is within one point
of the mercury freezing. Soon after
breakfast Charley·Rover and I started
for Captain Jack Peyton's. We got there
at 9 o'clock but Mat Butcher had left.
The we went to Widow Peyton's where we
found him. Soon after we started out to
hunt the hogs. We had our rifles and
dogs and we went up the creek back of
Widow Peyton's, then got on the ridge,
then the waters of Mud River. They
caught one(hog) which brought the rest
up. We decided (after Perry Peyton came
up) to let Matthew Butcher get them the
best way he could.

Rover is the dog.

?Tom's Ck.
#414 Mary had son Perry

Thursday Feb.8, 1855

I wrote a note to Emerson Turley
stating Father didn't want to make any
futher arrangements about renting our
farm on shares. Peter Clark and Webb
stopped as they went up the river. I
sent a letter by Mr.Walton to be mailed
at Guyandottte.

#784 Lawyer Clark

Friday Feb.9,1855

Bryant paid his rent($25). Fielder
was to see (Father) him about a coal
bank on Tom's Creek. Cynthia lent
Patterson Thompson's wife Susie's cloak
this morning to cut a pattern from.

Saturday Feb.10,1855

Harvey Smith moved into the house above the mill where Cowens used to live. He moved from the place where Willis used to live. Turley was to come today to conclude the arrangements regarding his taking our farm to cultivate,but he did not come.

Sunday Feb.11,1855

There was preaching in the School House this morning. Anna went. Bill Saumby came up here, walking with a cane.(had been hurt) Just at dark Anna came home bringing Ella and America Butcher,Miss Dundas,and Miss Roberts, with Ben Cowens & Jim Butcher. Soon after Robert came with Bill Saumby and then we had a house full.-------
Guyandotte paper- the Herald

#675 dau/James Butcher
#386 Dundas

Monday Feb.12,1855

The Frenchman, (Mr.Donnet)& I went over to Charley Morris's and got some straw for our ice house. We got the rafters up,etc. Mat Butcher brought down three hogs out of five of ours he killed in the woods(kept two) Father let me have one. I brought it home on a wheel barrow. Albert Moore brought up our mail. There was four Sunday papers & the Guyandotte Herald for me. The later was about the size of a sheet of writing paper. I was all evening drawning up writings between Turley and Father.

description of paper

Wednesday Feb.14,1855

Bill left us in the afternoon to go to a party at Harshbarger's on Mud River.We let him have the Grey Horse to ride. Ben Cowens and Charley Snipe started over to the party this morning.

?#35 Jacob Harshbarger
lived near Yates Crossing

Friday February 16,1855

Just at noon the steamer R.H. Lindsey came up. She landed below the mill & took on the freight we had in the store for Col.Webb. Also two barrels of flour I sold to Capt. Jerome Shelton for

$8.50 cash each barrel. There was a
number of passengers on board. In
backing down to run in the Locke,she
came near to running into the tree at
the mouth of the creek. They intend to
lay her up above and do some repairs. I
sent two letters to Guyandotte by young
Bomgardner. Wrote D.Longworth,
Philadelphia for Father about some fruit
trees.

Saturday Feb.17,1855

There was a meeting in the School
House this morning.Mr.Rece preached.

J.C.Rece a Baptist minister
Bloomingdale Church(R 10)
began here and was moved

Sunday Feb.18,1755

There was preaching in the School
House this morning. Charley left early
to bring Martha Blake to church and here
to dinner,but they did not come. Cynthia
got all ready and waited to go with
Martha to the meeting,but they not
coming, she staid home. Mother went and
stopped here as she went home.

Monday Feb.19,1855

Higgins came here to have a
Settlement. After making off the account
I went down to Father's with him
finished Higgins, owes us fifteen
dollars thiry-four cents, for which he
is to give us a joint note with his sons
William. Soon after dinner, the Steamer
Adrian came up here and took on eighteen
barrel of Roffe's flour for Thorn in
Guyandotte and then started back. Sent a
letter to H.H. Wood containing an
account on Wm.Jones for him to Collect.
Soon after tea, Charley and I went
down to McCullough's store. Charley told
us that the reason Martha Blake did not
come over yesterday was that her sister
had gone to town with her horse and
saddle.

#762-Thorn Dusenberry
store clerk(cousin)

Tuesday feb.20,1855

Bloom sent my saddle up this
morning. I am to pay him $25 for it and
the bridle. There is a notice on the
mill door stating that Stewart's Carding

Wool carding

Machine and picker would be sold by the
sheriff the first of next week. I went
down and told Father about it. We came
to the conclusion to lay a landlord's
warrant on them for his last years rent
which is $120.

Wednesday Feb.21,1855

Sam went to town after the mail. I
sent three letters down by him. One to
the Post Master of Marietta,Ohio
inquiring about a school there,one for
Charley and the other to Thomason,NY
about a farmer who wants to come here.

Marietta College

Thursday Feb.22,1855

I went to (Barboursville) Tom
Thornburg's and got him to make out a
Landlord's warrant to be levied on
Stewart's Carding machine.------ Jones
was waiting for me and I settled with
him.
About 4 O'c. the steamer Major
(Adrian) went up. She stopped along side
the mill & we took off two bundles of
shingles for us. Webb was on board and
gave me a note from Thorn stating that
Aunt Nancy arrived at Guyandotte this
morning after being four weeks coming
from New York and wants us to send down
for her. I went over to Charley Morris &
borrowed his buggy to go after her
tomorrow. This being Washington's
birthday we have had the flag hoisted
all day.

Aunt Nancy appears

Friday Feb.23,1855

The Steamer Adrian passed down about
three o'clock without stoppingSoon after
tea Aunt Nancy had just arrived. Aunt
Nancy was on the Steamboat on the Ohio
River better than three weeks frozen in
the ice. Her trunk has been left at
Wheeling.

Saturday Feb.24,1855

H.H.Wood came up and laid the
Landlord's warrant on Stewart's Carding
Machine.Soon after I fixed myself and
rode to Barboursville on horseback,took

sheriff(not on census) ?
(deputies listed various
households)

dinner at McKendree's then I went up to
the sale of furniture- belonging to the
estate of the late John Merritt.Then I
went into Bill Merritt's house to attend
to a case we have-to be tried against
John Hensley. When it was called I laid
it over to amend the notice. I bought at
Bill Miller's a half bu. of peaches, a
sack 2 lb Maple Sugar & 50ct.worth of
commom sugar & paid for a pound of candy
at Mat Thompson's. Bill Saumby is
crippled again,having run a sliver in
his hand while at work raising Miller &
Moore's mill day before yesterday.Bob &
Charley took a French lesson.

#989 Merritt,John
#160 Wm. 37y

#684 Hensley -Martha
west of River

Sunday Feb.25,1855

There was Prayer Meeting in the
School House this morning. Margery took
Cale and was out most of the afternoon.
She came home just at dark bringing Jim
Butcher with her. Wrote a letter to
Charlotte Horsley inviting her to come
up and spend the summer with us. I wrote
a letter to the proprietor of the Sprigg
House, Wheeling directing him to forward
Aunt Nancy's trunk as soon as possible
it having got left at the Rail Road
Depot there.Jim Butcher staid here
smelling around Margery till nine
o'clock and after.

(Didn't think much of Jim.)

Monday Feb.26,1855

Many went to town to court on foot.
I met Bill Saunby coming up here about
half way between here and Town. He told
me that Charley's girl Martha Blake was
married. Mr.Salmon and her went to
Cincinnati with her sister and husband
and they were married there last Friday.
(FL feb.23, 1855) I was around Town
until night. Took tea at McKendree's.
Just at dark Charley came. He had been
at Blake's and asked Martha Blake if the
report of her marriage was true. She
informed him that it was. Major Whitney,
Sam Johnson& Wheeler from the Guyandotte
Lodge met with us. C.Simmons, John
Thronburg & Nouning were balloted for
and elected to take the second degree.
Nouning was put through. After eleven

Charley had courted her
for quite some time.

#829 Alfred Whitney
innkeeper-Gyandotte

o'clock, McCullough,Charley and I walked home. Sent $4.00 for Aunt Nancy's trunk.

Tuesday Feb.27,1855

Briant moved into the Jones house. Bob went to Blakes towards night & got what things was there belonging to Charley, among them the ring he made for her.

Sent brother to girl friends for the ring.

Wednesday Feb.28,1855

I bought 8 head of sheep for $1.00 a head from Pat Thompson. They have been in our pasture.

Thursday March 1,1855

I got some alder to make sugar tree spouts. I went and examined some trees that John Dick was cutting in the pasture. Rake Wood came here and I went with him down to see Father. The Dutch Butcher came and got my cow this afternoon.He paid me $2.00 in gold.($10.00 next wk.)

Feazel-the butcher ?

Friday March 2,1855

The Emperor of Russia(Nicholas I)died just after noon this day in the 59th year of his life,very sudden some suppose poison. He is succeed by his oldest son Alexander.

News from everywhere

Saturday March 3,1855

Charley and I went to shingling the half of the ice house roof we had to leave for want of shingles. We opened the other(shingles) and found them good for nothing so we put some boards on the roof and quit until we could get some others. Mr.Sites here and I took an impression of his upper jaw. I am to put in two front teeth for him on a plate. I was in the store awhile. Briant was there playing the fiddle with Charley.

split wood shingles

Godfrey Scites b Germany lived near Salt Rock

Sunday March 4,1855

Mr.Graham and Ben Cowens was up here awhile in the afternoon. Charley cut

their hair. Emberson Turley moved in the
house that Briant moved out of.

Monday March 5,1855

I went to Guyandotte in the Buggy.
Got there about noon. Put up the horse
at Bumgardner's. I went to the Post — *livery in Guyandotte*
Office and mailed three letters, one for
Charley to Job, the other to Peter
Cooper,N.Y. & to the Principal of the — *Translyvania U. or*
Institute at Lexington,Va. I passed — *University of Ky*
(going home) the Steamer Lindsey at the
Locke at the mouth of Mud River going
down. She came very near to smashing up
as she was going into the Locke. The
wind carried her to the side of the
river, her upper deck and chimneys
striking a tree top. I stopped at
Barboursville and got our new double
harness of Bloom, then ordered the Dutch
cabinet maker(FL-Godfrey Espy no doubt) — *(not listed 1850)*
there to make me a trundle bed, then — *bed designed to use as*
stopped at the Post Office and got two — *sled.*
Sun(N.Y. Sun-FL)papers and the
Guyandotte Hearald.

Tuesday March 6,1855

Soon after breakfast I went out to
the Frenchman's and got him to help me — *Alex Donnett*
put up my garden fence. (Later)The
Frenchman was in the store giving
Charley and Robert a lesson.

Wednesday March 7,1855

Charley and I went up to the upper
end of the farm to the place occupied by
Joe Stanley to count some rails. He was
not home, so we crossed the road. We had
our rifles,etc.

Thursday March 8,1855

Cynthia received a letter from her
sister Jane Nagles. Robert went down and
brought up Nigger Ben's boat and we — *#395 slave of C.L.Roffe*
tried to loosen the shiffs and canoe. — *Ben did everything*
(water had raised last night. I was most
of the afternoon making a metal case for
Site's teeth. Charley had used up all my
zinc to make a composition to put in the
saw gate(?) and I had to use some of

that, but after getting two cases and
putting one of them in the hot lead, I
had to give up for a bad job, the
composition being too soft, the hot lead
having melted all the teeth off the
cast. Wash Hensley came here this
morning and I tried to pull a tooth for
him.

#684 10y s/o Sam.

Friday March 9, 1855

The Frenchman worked nearly all day
on my fence.
Carler came up about noon for a
barrel of flour. The Frenchman took
dinner with me and after which I sent
him up to where Smith used to live to
help Smith take up some fruit trees.
Alexander Peyton was rafting his
logs at the mouth of the creek. They had
been laying along the bank for about a
year.

Carter ?

Logs were bound together
into rafts and waited for
the river to rise.

Sunday March 11, 1855

I couldn't read this morning till
after ten o'clock without candle light.
The river was rising and we ground five
barrels of meal.
There was preaching in the school
house this morning. A good many attended
for it was such a disagreeable day.

Monday March 12, 1855

I went (cow hunting) up with Thompson
where he used to live. Just at dark the
Steamer Adrian came up. She laid in the
Locke all evening. I think will all
night.

Tuesday March 13, 1855

Wednesday March 14, 1855

Mills being stopped makes everything
look dull around here. Turley finished
building the cross fence out by the
Frenchman's.

River to high for mills.

Thursday March 15, 1855

This Steamer Major Adrian passed
down this afternoon.

Friday March 16, 1855

The Frenchman worked today for us. Bill Fielder hired the house occupied last year by Harvey Smith. I sent a letter to Guyandotte to be mailed by Victor Letulle.

#797-Guyandotte merchant b. France

Saturday March 17, 1855

Simmons brought our mail from Town.

Cornwesley Simmons

Sunday March 18, 1855

Monday March 19, 1855

Soon after dinner a blacksmith moved in the house Fielder (Bill) moved from Saturday. His wife and children came in here and warmed while things were being unloaded. They have been working for the Rail Road men & came here from Pensylvania.

Thursday March 20, 1855

Aunt Nancy received her chest she left at Wheeling. About two o'clock the Steamer Major Adrian came up here bringing Aunt Nancy's chest and a bundle of pills for me to sell on commission, and a large box of things sent her from New York by Aunt Sally. A lot of rafts went over the dam.

Box from Aunt Sally-NY

Wednesday, March 21, 1855

Thursday, March 22, 1855

I went down to Fathers. Turley was there with a yoke of cattle plowing up Father's garden. Sarah has been quite sick with a cold. Jeff Samuels was here awhile this afternoon and stopped to see Father a few minutes.

Friday March 23, 1855

Bowman started the grist mill it ran well all day.

Saturday March 24, 1855

Charley and Robert drove to Guyandotte in the buggy to collect some money from Carter, Detz & Co. John Stanley drove my cow home this afternoon. She was found about Eight miles up Guyan. I took some brandy and sugar for my cold.

Stanley ?#485(s/o#313)?

Cow near Falls of Guy. Brankhland.

Sunday March 25, 1855

Charley lent Bill Fielder the grey horse to go after a girl for Sam Childers.

Monday March 26, 1855

Soon after breakfast. I fixed myself to go to Barboursville. Went to see Father. Matt Butcher and Joe Stanley was there. I started to town about ten o'clock. Took my dinner at Bloom's (FL-Evan W. Blume's). Court adjourned at noon and I went with the rest over to the Methodist Church where I heard Judge McComas deliver a political speech in favor of Henry A. Wise for Governor. He denounced the KnowNothing Party in unmeasured terms. There was a great many town. The Steamer Adrian passed just as I came home.

The Dutch cabinet maker sent my Trundle bed sled up here this morning & left it at Bowman's house.

#417 Stanley moved around ?

Political rally

Tuesday March 27, 1855

About ten o'clock, Sam Johnson and I rode to town. I went down to see Graham but he had gone to New York. I was down to see Father awhile towards night. He wanted me to go up home with him to look at a couple of heifers he wants to sell us. Cynthia went up to Smith's a few moments to see his sick child.

Harvey Smith's several ill

Wednesday March 28, 1855

The Steamer Adrian came down about two o'clock. She came up along side of the mill and left fifty bushels of wheat for Roffe. I paid Ben Cowen's $2.00 on Graham's account this afternoon.

Thursday March 29, 1855

I paid Espe two dollars and a half for my trundle bed. A letter came for me from Monroe's father.

Friday March 30, 1855

H.H. Woods came up here this morning and I paid him $20, part of the account of $26 due on the accourt of Grahams & Stewart. Steamer Major Adrian passed up about noon.

(missed by census-sheriff usually well known) ?

Saturday March 31, 1855

The Steamer Adrian passed down soon afternoon. Donnet was in the store with Charley & Robert (all night) giving them a French lesson.

Sunday April 1, 1855

There was a meeting the School House this morning. Not many attended. Aunt Nancy and Mother went up to Mud Church in the Buggy. Sam went along with them on horseback. Sam brought me two Sun papers and the Guyandotte Herald from the Post Office. I set a hen on thirteen eggs this afternoon.

Baptist-founded 1807

Monday April 2, 1855

I bought a dollars worth each of sugar and Molasses, and also bought some tallow of Fred Miller, then I went to Eggers and bought a pair of shoes for the baby. Charley, Donnet (the French Teacher) & John Fielder was until near night hauling manure and putting it on Father's garden. Caroline came back to Mother's this afternoon.

Tuesday April 3, 1855

Mr. Bowman came here with his boy Tom. I pulled a tooth for his boy.

#399 the miller at Martha
Benjamin-w/Sophia
s-Tom 5y

Wednesday April 4, 1855

I took my hogshead up to the blacksmith shop to have some iron hoops

cask containing 100gal. +

on it. Found the iron myself. Towards
night, Sam with two yoke of cattle &
wagon moved the Blacksmith in the house
of ours occupied last year by Stewart.
Anna,Margery and I got our chickens from
Bryant's coop and shut them up.

Cynthia lent Mrs.Bowman her saddle
this morning. She has gone up to
Doolittle's Mill to Peter White's
wedding. Ella Butcher was here to see
Cynthia.

Doolittles Mill(later
Howell's Mill) N of Ona
2nd falls Of Mud-Peter
White-miller-had lived with
Dusenberry in 1850
m-Mary Blackwood CCM

Thursday April 5,1855

The Frenchman was in the store
giving Charley and Robert a French
lesson.

Friday April 6,1855

Nearly finished painting my martin
box. Just before noon I went out in the
field and got Turley to fix a culvert in
the road below where he lives. John
Martin moved in the Bud Davis house this
afternoon.

The steamer Adrian came up as far
as Roffe's.

Saturday April 7,1855

The Steamer Adrian came up here just
as I was sitting down to breakfast. She
laid all night down by Roffe's where she
left three barrels of potatoes for
Bowman. She brought up Miller's flat
boat from Thornburgs this morning. I
sent a barrel of flour by her to
Hillbruner in Guyandotte this morning.
Miller & Moore was up here all the
forenoon. Miller told me they should
give up the saw mill at the expiration
of the year(the 18th of May next). There
was preaching in the School House this
morning held it until about three
o'clock. Mother and Aunt Nancy went.
There was a good many attended. After
dinner Donnet,Robert and I with the
cattle and wagon went down to Roffe's
and brought up Bowman's and our
Potatoes. We took a cow to Morris'. Had
a great deal of difficulty getting her
to cross the river in the boat.

#776 JACOB Hiltbruner
tinner-Guy.

(Morris had a bull)

Sunday April 8,1855

The river was too high for the grist
mill to run I was in the courthouse(at
Superior Court) awhile. Patterson W.
Thompson's suit against Father about a
boundary line was called and dismissed.
I borrowed a horse from H.H.Wood & Thorn
came home with me. When I got home this
afternoon, I found a Mr.Webster at
Father's who had come here to see about
running the carding machine. I went to
the mill and showed it to him.

Tuesday April 10,1855

I was in the Court House most of the
afternnon listening to the summing up in
the case of Jack Parsons who was
indicted for breaking open and stealing
goods from Albert Laidley's store. The
Jury had not returned with their verdict
when I left.
I brought tow pair of boots from
Allen's home with me to select a pair.
Sites was here & Charley took another
impression of his mouth. The Steamer
Adrian passed up today on her way to the
Falls.

#919 Laidley along Ohio
W of Guyandotte-merchant

#733 Robt.Allen B'ville
b.Scotland

Wednesday April 11,1855

Charley gave Sam Johnson the level
he made for him. I went to
Barboursville. The Jury found Parsons
guilty. He was sentenced to eight years
in the State Penitentiary. Bill Johnson
was tried for horse stealing.(3 yrs.)I
bought seven yds of Tow Linen,3 yds of
Flannel, 1 gallon molasses, 1/2 bu.
dried apples, & 2 pair stockings for
Margery at Miller's (Bill).The Steamer
Adrian passed down this afternoon. The
grand jury indicted me as overseer of
the road for its being out of
over. As I am not the overseer,it cannot
stand.

Thursday April 12,1855

Went to Barboursville. They were
trying a Hatfield for forgery.There was
a party of us in Latulles.(FL_Charley,
county surveyor ?) office-------. The

#797 Victor Letulle
Guy.merchant(baker)
b.France-1w tombstone
French/English

Steamer Adrian came up just before Sun down (at B'ville).Passed here a little before nine o'clock.

Friday April 13,1855

They were trying(at B'ville-FL)Fred Morrison for stealing money from J & S Miller.(John & Sig-FL)Henry Maupin gave me a letter for Caroline that was directed to his care, from her father containing ten dollars.

#745 Dr.Maupin-B'ville may have pickup letter letter instead of mail

Saturday April 14,1855

Charley & Robert fished awhile. They caught some black perch, the first caught about here this spring.About two o'clock I started to town on Jack. Got nearly to Roffe's when I met Peter Buffington(FL-sheriff ?)He came to sell Stewart's machines under a deed of trust. I returned to the mill with him. He bought it for $400.00. The Steamer Adrian went down this morning.
Bowman told me the jury had convicted Fred Morrison(1 yr)

#961 Buffington's owned much of Guyandotte-ferries

Sunday April 15,1855

Charley & I set the fish net. Henry Poteet & Bill Saunby here awhile(P.M.)
There was prayer meeting in the School House this morning. Ella Butcher,Ann Smith & Sarah Childers was here in the afternoon. I raised the net just before night, There was about a dozen fish in it. Small cats & red horses. We sent them down to Bowman.

#31 Poteet labored in 1850 at Doolittle's Mill

#404 dau./Sam Childers
#357 dau./Harvey Smith

Monday April 16,1855

Sold Allen a barrel of flour.$9.00

Tuesday April 17,1855

Caught 3 suckers in the net.I kept a big one for dinner and gave the small ones to Bryant. Col.Webb came up in the afternoon to get me to go as Clerk on the R.H.Lindsey. I promised to go on her one trip to Portsmouth & are to be at Guyan & go on her as she comes down tomorrow. Flour is selling for $10.00 at

Guyandotte. Several neighbors in store--
till 9'o'clock---------

Wednesday April 18,1855

    Went to Guyandotte.Charley & I went
to Col.Webb's house. Previous to going
to Adam,Carter & Deitz gave me an order
on him for $51, the amount they owe us.
Webb accepted it and paid us $10.00 on
it. I told Webb I could not run the
Steamer Lindsey as Clerk. He seemed
disappointed & entreated me to go down
on her this trip which I consented to
do.

Thursday April 18,1855

    Arose at day light, the boat still
laying at Portsmouth. bought 3 yds of
ribbon for Anna,s hat,one & a half for
my own,a jigering iron for Cythinia,some   small iron for collars
Potash for Robert & a couple of Jugs;
etc. I bought three fine oranges. Had to
pay eight cents apiece. I bought five
gallons of alcohol for ourselves.

Friday April 20,1855

    Soon after daylight, the wind began
to blow a gale. The river was so rough
that the wheel could not catch the water
more than half the time. We came near to
blowing over,as we came around the point
below Guyan. We arrived there about ten
q'clock & concluded to lay there until
the wind abated a little, I agree to go
on to Pomeroy as Webb had found no
clerk.(we arrived at Gallipolis-because
of wind-at dark,at Pomeroy at midnight.

Saturday April 21,1855

    (We ran all the other boats down
& got their passengers.)
    Hazelton was at the wharf boat
trying to get Lucien Wolcott to go down
as clerk.

Sunday April 22,1855

    There was a prayer meeting in the
school house this morning.

Just at noon Ben Cowens and Wallace
came up here. Towards night Lee Beckett
had a singing school in the school
house. Anna went.

Monday April 23,1855

I rode to town. This is county court
day. I went to Miller & Moore's mill &
sent Bill Saunby up to fix our grist
mill, after which I went to the Court
House.Court had adjourned. The house was
full listening to Lewis'speech(Present   Political Rally & Speeches
Rep.in Congress from this district & a
candiate for reelection.)He was followed
by Carlyle-the American candidate for
the same office,the latter is the
smartest man and the best speaker. They
continued speaking by turns until
sundown. I went to Blooms and got my
supper. McCullough and I went in to
Black Anna's & got a cup of coffee and
some things to eat. I sent two letters
today, one for Robert about a truss and
the other to a school teacher in New
York.

Tuesday April 24,1855

Webster commenced boarding today. I
went over to Charley Morris and got
enough straw to fill a tick. Webster,the   tick type of mattress
carder commenced boarding with me.

Wednesday April 25,1855

The Steamer Adrian came up as far as
the mill towards night. She brought Mr.
Webster's chests and some freight for
old Nick Messenger.(Left it and went   #458 Messenger 60y -miller
down again.)   possibly at Salt Rock

Thursday April 26,1855

Woods burning on the other side
of the river(air full of burnt leaves)
to McCullough's store. Col.Webb passed
down in his buggy soon after noon.

Friday April 27,1855

Mr.Webster caught four fine
black perch.(We had them for dinner)   good fishing

Saturday April 28,1855

Cynthia & I and the Baby started to Guyandotte in the buggy. Stopped at Widow Shelton's on the way down where I engaged a yellow gobbler. Arrived at Guyandotte about noon. Left Cynthia at Thorn's and then drove the horse to Bumgardner's & had him put up, then I went to Webb's house to get some money of him but could not. Then I went to the tinners(FL_-Jacob Hillbrunner's) & left directions for some tin leaders for Father, then to Thomas house, his infant child is lying very low with inflammation of the lungs.

Shelton's lived on Guyan River-1/2 way between B'ville & Guyandotte

leaders-drain pipe ?

pneumonia ?

Sunday April 29,1855

There was prayer meeting in the School House this morning. Charley, Robert, and I was down under the mill awhile trying to catch some fish. Charley Shipe gigged two & Smith one. Graham was at Father's. He brought me five Shanghai hen's eggs from New York. I put them with some others under a hen. Beckett had singing school in the school house in the afternoon. Ben Cowens came up with Graham. They returned to Barbourville soon after dinner. Robert starts to Marietta to school tomorrow.

no Shipe in 1850 census

Monday April 30,1855

Went to Guyandotte. Took dinner at the Union Hotel. The doctor had given up Thorn's baby, then we went to Carter's house awhile. Then in town again.

baby dying

Tuesday May 1,1855

The Steamer Adrian went up. The boat also brought flour barrels from town, after which she passed through the Locke on her way to the Falls.

Wednesday May 2,1855

We expected the boat down today, but it did not come. Took Father a revolver. There was a strange man prowling around his house night before last.

Thursday May 3,1855

The Steamer Adrian went down about
Two o'clock this morning. I had to get
up and lower three barrels of flour on
her to take to Guyandotte one for
Blankenship & two to Henry Miller at
$10.50 per Bbl. Went to Guyandotte.
Charley & I started home soon after he
landed(from Marietta). We had not gone
more than half way to Barboursville
before it was dark & we had an awful
dark and tedious drive home. Nine
o'clock we reached here. Charley bought
a small cannon & brought it with him.
Robert was much pleased with the school.

Friday May 4,1855

I wrote a letter to John Tiernan,
Haskelville,Ohio.

John Tiernan m Amanda
Buffington 2 aug 1836 CCM

Saturday May 5,1855

Not much doing on the grist mill.
The saw mill running all day. Wolcott
was up about noon.

Sunday May 6,1855

One of Charles Morris' nigger women
died last night. There was prayer
meeting in the school house this
morning. There was singing school in the
school house this afternoon. Charley
Morris'nigger woman was buried just at
dark back of his house. There was none
but niggers at the funeral.

slave death

Monday May 7,1855

I was going down to John Laidley's
below Guyandotte to buy a cow. I helped
Charley part of the afternoon make a
carriage for his cannon. Very little
grains comes in now.

#1011 lawyer lived on
Ohio about 16th ST-Htgn

Tuesday May 8, 1855

About Two o'c in the afternoon, the
Steamer Major Adrian came up and stopped
by the mill a moments, then passed
through the Locke on the way to the
Falls. Charley finished the carriage for

his cannon & just before dark we fired
it,making a big noise. Sam Childers paid
me $10.00 on account.

Wednesday May 9,1855

C.L.Roffe brought his wife home this
morning. Left Guyandotte(where he went)
little before five o'c. & started home.
Stopped at Miller & Moore's Mill & got
Ben Cowens. The Major Adrian went down
this afternoon. C.L.Roffe came home with
his wife this morning. Evening clear &
cold. Soon after dark, the most of the
young People in the neighborhood
collected by the store with all sorts of
instruments that would make noise. As
soon as fairly dark, we all went on the
hill below Roffe's and waited there some
time for a party from Barbousville. They
not coming, we came back as far as
Roffe's where at signal from Charley's
cannon,which we had brought along, we
all began a regular Caluthumpian
Serenade & between the firing of the
cannon,my drum,our two large circular
saws,and other instruments,we made an
awful noise,marching around the house
every time the cannon fired. We kept it
up until after ten o'clock,when Roffe
not showing himself or even a light in
the house,we came home. Broke the
carriage of the cannon the second time
we fired. Sent letters for mother by the
Steam boat Ohio No.2 to Cincinnati to be
mailed.

#395 lived Martha-east
side River near ford
several slaves

Thursday May 10,1855

In the afternoon, there was a May
party given by the children attending
Charley Morris' school up by Peter
Love's. Anna,Susie,and Margery went.
Jeff Samuels and Irvin Lusher passed
just at dark. They stopped by the gate a
few moments. Jeff thinks his election
certain.

lived S of Martha west side
of river probably just
S of present railroad
#720 Irvin Lusher

Friday May 11,1855

Made off an agreement with Webster &
handed it to him to read. Mother and Sam
went down to Mrs.Morrison's in the skiff
this afternoon and back.

took a boat down river

Saturday May 12,1855

Allen McGinnis' nigger girl fell
in the river yesterday and was
drowned. The funeral was taking place --
-- as we----- -----came on his house-Morse-
stopped-at Roffe's where he is boarding
(he rode down with us from B'ville.
There was a meeting in the school house
this afternoon. There is nothing talked
of now but politics and the election.

#764-Guyandotte

(uses Morse to mean Moss)

Sunday May 13,1855

-There was preaching in the school
house. Cynthia and I went. The house was
full. Roffe and his wife was there.
Mr.Reece preached.(FL John Calvin Rece.)

Monday May 14,1855

I giged a fine large perch under the
saw mill which I cleaned and we had for
dinner.

Tuesday May 15,1855

Mr.Ternan(Tiernan-FL) came with
hands and a flat boat and took away the
carding machine formerly belonging to
Stewart. After an early dinner,Harnessed
Jack to the buggy & drove to town.Went
up to the Court House & heard E.W.
McComas the Demo-cratic Candidate for
Lieutenant Governor address the people.
I soon became disgusted with his anti-
American remarks against the Know-
Nothings & left. Went to Mrs.Moore's
etc. I went to Ferrell's(FL_-F.M.and
bought a cow & calf of him.($25) Took
out a Landlord's warrant against Higgins
& gave it to H.H.Woods to serve.

(in responce to letter) ?

Jack-the horse

Wednesday May 16,1855

Moore & Miller's(FL-Albert M. &
Wm.C. Miller's) contract for the sawmill
expires tomorrow night. He(Moore) wanted
to hire it by the day at the yearly
rate, Father would only rent it at that
rate by the month and he declined.
H.H.Woods stopped here awhile. He had

#729 Miller-B'ville merchant

been serving the warrant on Higgins.
Aunt Nancy began to teach Susie.

Thursday May 17,1855

I was most of the afternoon making a
gate by my smokehouse to turn my cow in
and out of the pasture.We began to sell
corn today for one dollar a bushel.

Friday May 18,1855

Miller & Moore's contract years
lease of the saw mill expired this   Grist Mill-corn & wheat
morning and we now have it on our hands   Saw Mill
without any logs to keep it running.   Carding Machine

Saturday May 19,1855

John Fielder and Collins were with
Turley.About eight o'clock when they got
to work and were all forenoon hauling
and piling.

Sunday May 20,1855

There was preaching in the school
house this afternoon.

Monday May 21,1855

Charley & I bought a lot of seven
logs this morning for five dollars.

Tuesday May 22,1855

Towards night Roffe's Shepherd after   sheperd=person
building a pen on the bank of the river
just below the mill,brought up a lot of
young bucks and washed them.

Wednesday May 23,1855

I went to town to see Billy Miller.
He was not there. I bought three tin
pans of Wills Moore.Sent Charley's
letter to Robert to Guyan by Doct   ?Wilson Moore ?
Rickets.   #806 Girard Rickets

Thursday May 24,1855

(Election day) I remained, took
my dinner at Bloom's. I voted for
Thomas S.Flourney

J.M.H.Beale
John M.Patton
R.G.Morris Board of Public Wks.
Mr.Carlyle, Congress
Feleet Smith (Fleet-Sate Senate-FL)
H.J.Samuels

The whole Know Nothing or American
ticket. We heard enough from the
different polls in this county to know
that Jeff Samuels is elected.(Fleet
Smith came by. Thought he was elected.)

I went to settle with Billy Miller,
he was busy & sent me down to the mill
to see Moore & Graham.(Miller said he
and Moore would come up Tuesday next.
Steamer Adrian passed up on the way to
the Falls.

Saturday May 26,1855

Bill Fielder worked most of the day.
I was most of the afternoon getting out
the plate for Sites teeth plate. Toward
night, the Steamer Adrian passed down.
She came up along side the mill & took
on some flour. We sent three Barrels to
H.H.Miller & four Bushels to Thorn.   #797 Henry H.Miller

Sunday May 27,1855

There was prayer meeting in the
school house this morning and singing
school in the afternoon. Mrs.Howell and   #433-?Mrs.Armstead Howell
her daughter stopped in to see Cynthia   1850 he was miller at (Roach)
this afternoon. McCullough returned from   later bought mill at Ona
Cincinnati this morning.

Monday May 28,1855

About eleven o'clock, I drove to
Barboursville. This was the full
magistrates court when license is
granted. I took dinner at Bloom's After
awhile I went to the Court House. A vote
was taken on the granting of Liquor
License and decided in favor of by nine
to eleven & every person that asked was
granted. I had Turley put in as overseer
of the road instead of father. I went to
Barboursville to attend Lodge Election
(Annual).
  Tom Thornburg-Master
  A.Moore, Sen.Warden
  McCullough Jun."

        Vertigans S.D.
        Wm.F.Dusenberry J.D.
        Bloom,treas.
        Wood, Sect.
        John Thornburg,Tyler.
Sites here this morning and tried
in his plate.

        Tuesday May 29,1855

    Miller & Moore did not come to
settle with Father. Charley & Sam went
up in the pasture above Turley's &
marked some young cattle, then turned
them in the woods.

        Wednesday May 30,1855

    Margery went up to Mrs. Smiths & did
not return tonight. We waited for her
until eleven o'c. when we retired with
the impression that she had left us. All
pretty smart.(FL-A very common
expression of his)

        Thursday May 31 1855

    Margery came here about Ten o'c. &
told us she had quit work for Cynthia.
She could give no reason only the
neighbors had told her something. She
took some of her things away. She owes
me seven dollars & Cynthia is not go ing
to let her have the hat & dress she sold
to her.
    I was down to see father a few
moments after dinner. Alex. Samuels,his   #727 John Samuels
sisters, the misses Miller & Holderby   dau.Mary & America
was there. Just as we were taking Tea,   #720 Wm.C.Miller
Margery came and got the balance of her   #765 Robert Holderby
things. She is much put out because   dau.Susan & Elizabeth
Cynthia would not let her have the hat
and dress. She is staying at Smith's. He
came with her as far as the gate. I was
at him for telling a lie to her last
night. He did not deny it. Father sent   Flirting with Margery
him notice to quit the house by Saturday   cost him a house.
He sent it by Sam this morning.

Friday Jun 1, 1855

Father received a letter from a
School Teacher in New York who wants to
come out here.

Saturday June 2, 1855

Smith moved this afternoon; gone
on to Roffe's place in the house where
John Martin moved from. Margery went
with him. One of Webb's Coal Barges
passed up through the Locke, this
afternoon.

Appears to have been several
rental houses at Martha.

Sunday June 3, 1855

There was a prayer meeting in the
School House this morning and singing
school in the afternoon. I wrote a
letter to the gentleman in New York by
the name of Wright, who wants to come
out here to teach school.

Monday June 4, 1855

Tuesday June 5, 1855

Soon after dinner, the steamer
Major Adrian passed up. She brought us
a Barrel of sugar & Charley's seine
back (he had sent it down to sell).

Wednesday June 6, 1855

Just as I returned, the Steamer
Adrian came down. Charley hailed her
and she came along side the mill & took
on a barrel of sugar Thorn sent up
yesterday. Sent it back on account of
its being too black and wet.

Sounds like molasses.

Thursday June 7, 1855

Came upstairs (at night) and
hunted fleas.

Several references to fleas.
Appears dog had pups in house

Friday June 8, 1855

Mrs. C.L. Roffe was to see Cynthia
this afternoon. Father bought Brian's
cow this morning. Charley went up early
to see Higgin's cow milked but he
declined milking her. Father bought

Higgins cow for $16, Briant bought Bill
Fielder's $20. Margery came here this
afternoon and Cynthia let her have the
hat and dress.

Sunday June 10, 1855

There was preaching in the school
House this morning and singing school
this afternoon. Mrs.Jones came here
this afternoon and Anna went after her.
After catching forty fleas, we retired
at 11 o'clock.

Monday June 11, 1855

I was most of the afternoon
settling with Cowens & Fielder for the
field of corn our cattle destroyed.
Mills brought me two Sun papers
(FL-N.Y.Sun).Read my papers a few
moments but soon had to go to catching   40 fleas on night,50 the next.
fleas. Cynthia and I caught over fifty.

Tuesday June 12,1855

After dinner, I helped Charley
draw down some gold wire. Dick Lunsford
brought a bundle of Plaster of Paris
from Guyandotte that Robert had sent   #434 same house as Armstead
me. I gave one of the Pups to Arch   Howell(miller) and James
Peyton this morning. I have just one   Gillenwaters(Rev.War)
left ant that is running around and
yelping like the devil. It is lonesome.

Wednesday June 13 1855

Charley drove Louisa (Mrs.Thorn)
Dusenberry to her mother's (Mrs.Martin
Moore Sr.)in Barboursville. No grain   #81 Mary & Martin Moore
coming in.(FL-for the grist mill.)

Thursday June 14,1855

Sam Childers came over and wanted
to hire the mill for a few days. I went
with him to see Father about it.
H.H.Woods came up here towards   Sheriff.
night and served a Landlord's warrant
on the Frenchman. Webster paid me my   (Donnet-French lesson must
bill for boarding.($17.50)   not have been enough for rent.)

Friday June 15,1855

Col.Moore & his brother passed
here going up the Guyandotte River.
Sam Childers commenced running the
saw mill on shares. He finds one hand
and gives us half the Lumber. We hired
Jim Cowens at a $1.00 a day and board
him. Sold a bushel of Meal for $1.00,
the first cash we taken in for some
time. Caught fleas as usual.

Saturday June 16,1855

The Steamer Adrian passed up just
after dinner. Morris' nigger Pete came
here and helped us take out about ten
pounds (Of honey), then I went to the
store and wrote a letter for Nigger
Pete to his aunt.

Pete did many things in the
neighborhood & They sent him on
trips.Dusenberry wrote letter
to aunt.

Sunday June 17,1855

There was preaching in the School
House this morning. There was meeting
again in the afternoon. Bill and
Charley went. It came out as a shower
commenced. A Great many had to stop at
Mother's. Bill Saunby took tea with me.
Rain continuing, he concluded to stay
with Charley all night. The Steamer
passed up just at dark.

Mother's house closer to church

Monday June 18,1855

Charley & Sam drove to Guyandotte
in the buggy to see the floating museum
that was there. Just after dinner, a
couple of swarms of bees left Charley
Morris's. One of them came straight
over the river and passed through our
yard. We tried to get them to settle by
making a noise on tin pans, but they
went on over the hill. I followed, but
lost sight of them. There was a great
many (from Guy.) went to see the
museum. I am to give Bill Fielder $1.00
for finding and helping me hive the
bees. Father seemed so anxious, I gave
the hive to him. The Steamer Adrian
passed up about noon. They would not
bring my box up from the Wharf Boat.

37

Wednesday June 20,1855

Charley returned from Guyandotte about 6 O'clock with the box. Upon opening, we found the pineapples had rotted. Also a part of the oranges & some of the lemons. It also contained a Leghorn flat for Anna which was covered with mold and much bent. There was a nice lot of nuts, a small box of candy, one of Candy, one of Sugars, and two of prunes. One of the last was considerably damaged by the rotten pineapples-calico dresses & gingham for aprons for Susey & Cale, a nice white hat for Sarah, in a Ban box all safe. There was more than half the oranges and a third of the Lemons spoiled. The freight on the box was $2.93.

There was preaching in the School House, Charley and Aunt Nancy went. The Steamer Adrian passed down from the Falls about the middle of the afternoon

Type of popular flat hat made of straw.

Thursday June 21, 1855

Old Billy Thompson died this evening.

#406 -1850 age 66yr probably buried above bridge in new houseing development Cem.S28B-Thompson child there

Friday June 22,1855

Sam and I with a yoke of cattle went around to the flag stone querry (FL-quarry) and hauled some flat stone to stand our bees hives on.

Saturday June 23,1855

Mrs.McCullough was here. I took an impression of her mouth to see if I could make a plate stay in. I went ot Barboursville. Stopped at McCullough's & he rode down with me. Father some easier today. (Health not good-FL).

Sunday June 24,1855

After dinner Charley & I put some boards on one of the Skylights to the Carding Room to keep it from leaking.

Monday June 25,1855

I served on three juries, made
$1.25 today. (took dinner at Bloome's)
Bod's case was tried for running the
buggy against one of the Johnson's
horses.($5.00 fine).

Tuesday June 26,1855

Old Mr.Gardner, Billy Miller's
father-in-law, died this morning in
Barboursville. I drove to B'ville met
Lou Handley(FL ?) by Tessen's & he and
I rode down. Father's suit with John
Hensley came on. I went to Allens and
bought a Panama hat for Charley. I
started home, brought up two small
bundles of wool for peter Buffington.
It's been carded. (Father came
downstairs today.)

#727 Joseph Gardner 76yr
same house as John Samuels
Buried B'ville Cem.1774-1855

Sheep produced the wool,that
must be carded(cleaned),then
spun,then woven before it
could be made into clothing

Thursday June 28 1855

I brought Jeff Samuels out to see
Father about a disputed account. I took
him back in the buggy.

Friday June 29,1855

Thermometer stood a 92. I
harnessed Jack to the buggy and about
Eleven o'clock started to Guyandotte.
Drove very slow down, was almost
suffocated with the heat. Had to stop a
while & seek the inviting shade oa a
Beach tree, Near Two o'clock when I got
to Guyandotte. Went to Moore &
Vandiver's & fed myself and horse.
There was a funeral at Bumgardners. One
of his daughter's,Mrs.Degra-- died of
consumption.
    I went to Henry Millers to see him
about note of Father's in favor of
A.M.Whitney.($60.00) which I thought
nearly paid in flour, but suit brought.
Miller had credited it with $30.00 &
Flower had taken it out of his hands.
    I bought a cake & bread pan of
Hiltbruners & 6 yds cotton cloth of
Blankenship. I started home. Daniel
Love had just arrived from Pittsburg.
He rode up with me as far as
Mrs.Sheltons. E.W.McComas,Lieut.Gov.
Elect was in Guyandotte.

#791 James Vandever married
Martha Stone 1849. He was
stage driver.
#923-Philip Bumgardner

#829 Alfred Whitney-innkeeper

flower=flour

#1012 Love's were on both sid
of Mud River just above Ona.
(Poore's Hill)
Shelton's lived on Guyan
halfway between B'ville and
Guyandotte

Saturday June 30,1855

I worked some at Sites teeth.

Sunday July 1,1855

Charley & I rode up to Joe
Stanley's on horseback to see about the
heifers we bought of him. He was not
home. We hunted all around Tom's Creek
but could not find her. Graham and Ben
Cowens took dinner at Fathers. Prayer
meeting this morning and Singing School
in the School House this afternoon.

Monday July 2,1855

Steamer Adrian passed up in the
afternoon. Pat Thompson came here &
with Charley, we tried to drive the
Bees out of my old into my new hive.
The worms have nearly destroyed them.
Ground the first turn of new wheat for
Hez.Swann.

#314 Hezekiah m.a Hatfield

Tuesday July 3,1855

Ike Ong came up here from
Guyandotte to borrow Charley's cannon
to fire there tomorrow, but he would
not let him have it. He offered a
Dollar & a half for tis use. The
steamer Adrian passed down just at
night.

#769 Ike was a tailor

Wednesday July 4,1855

Cynthia spoiled the ice cream by
putting in too much oil of lemon.
Charley fired a salute of 32 guns.
Toward night Cynthia went over to
Mrs.McDaniels. AN awful dull Fourth.
They had an oration by Capt.E.W.
McComas & a dinner at Guyandotte.
I,McCullough,John Thornburg & Daniels
fired off a few fire works at the
store.

Thursday July 5,1855

The steamer Adrian passed up.

Friday July 6,1855

Saturday July 7, 1855

I bought a hive of bees of John Hensley. Bought three tin pans of Wilson Moore for ninety cents.

Sunday July 8, 1855

There was preaching in the School House, Singing School in the afternoon.

Monday July 9, 1855

Miller & Moore came up to settle, but could not for want of Graham's evidence about the time the saw mill was repairing.(FL-Graham had been working at the Grist Mill.) (Father wouldn't accept Miller's terms.)

Tuesday July 10, 1855

Father worse. Sent for Dr. McC---- who soon came & told what to give him. Charley setting up with him all night.

Possibly McCullough

Wednesday July 11, 1855

Mr.& Mrs.Roffe up to see Father.

Thursday July 12, 1855

Mr.Hillbruner, the tinner in Guyandotte, came up to see about the Leaders Father wanted made.
      I went to Bob Allens, bought a dollars worth each of Sugar & coffee. Also gave him a dollar for a gold pen Then I drove down to Mud River Bridge and up the river opposite Merritts Mill to where Mrs.Monroe resides, got her and her little girl & brought them home with me in the buggy. She staid all night. She is doing some sewing for Cynthia.

These leaders seem to be drain pipe.

Friday July 13, 1855

Mrs.Monroe's little boy came and staid the night.

Saturday July 14,1855

I wrote a letter for Caroline to
her Father.(John Alford was elected
constable over Sam Childers.)

Sunday July 15,1855

Preaching in the School House both
fore and afternoon.

Monday July 16,1855

Mrs.Monroe & children still here.

Tuesday July 17,1855

Anna, Caroline, & Mrs.Bowman went
in swimming. Bowman got the mill
started soon after dinner.

Wednesday July 18,1855

After dinner, I took Mrs.Monroe
home to B'ville in the buggy. Her
little girls and Susie rode down with
me. I stopped at Allen's and got a
dollars worth of sugar. Cynthia gave
Mrs.Monroe 1/2 Bu. of meal and 15 lbs.
of flour. Her little boy staid here all
night.

Thursday July 19,1855

Grist mill ran all day.

Friday July 20,1855

Sam and I went up opposite Peter
Love's to pick Blackberries.

Probably about 1 1/2m south
of Martha W of river

Saturday July 21,1855

I went to Eggers and bought me a
pair of patent leather boots which I am
topay $5 for them. Then I got old John
Samuels and brought him up home with me
to take Father's acknowledgement to
Trust Deed (I took him back in the
buggy in about 1/2 hour). Got a gallon
of molasses. Morse rode up with me from
Dave Thornburg's.

Is Eggers=Egners #556

#727 John was 64y and had
served as Clerk of Cabell
County about 35y.

Lambert probably could not
read hand writing.It's Moss.

Sunday July 22,1855
          I commenced writing a letter for
Cynthia to her sister Jane.
          About nine o'clock Godfrey Sites
came here and I fitted and finished his
teeth. He was much pleased with them
for which he paid me $10.00.

#433 Sites = Scites
family from Germany,Godfrey
married in 1855.

Monday July 23, 1855

          I told Jeff Samuels to bring a
suit against Miller & Moore.
          McCullough's son rode up (from
town-FL) with me from Dave Thornburgs.

Tuesday July 24,1855

          This morning about 8 o'c I went
down to Mrs.McCullough's and took
another impression of her upper Jaw,
then stopped in the store and talked
with the Doctor a while.

#393 McCullough is listed
as merchant at Martha--
also a Doctor ?

Wednesday July 25,1855

          Got some sugar of Mat Thompson for
mother & 1/2 lb. tea for her of J & S
Miller. John Thornburg & Doct
McCullough's little boy rode up with
me.

Thursday July 26,1855

Friday July 27,1855

          Turley & his hands worked on the
road. I went down and saw Father with
Alford. Bill Peyton had sued him for
some hauling we had done under a
contract we made with Dick Lunsford.
(In margin-He claimed pay by the log
contract with Lunsford was $1.25 a
load.)

Saturday July 28,1855

          We got home about 6 o'clock. While
we were gone Charley flexed the house
by the upper end of the Bridge opposite
Briant's for the buggy.

Sunday July 29,1855

(Charley, Robert & Sam on horses
hunted cattle in the woods till noon.
Didn't find them.)

Monday July 30,1855

Robert rode up to Hinchman's to   #106 site of Roach-River
try to borrow some money(Failed).   called Hinchman's Bend
Lunsford settled his account by giving
a note for $50.00.

Tuesday July 31,1855

I drove to Barboursville, and
borrowed $30 of Bloom. Got Mrs.Monroe &
little girl and drove home. Turley &
Bill Collins came down about 8 o'clock
to fix the hole below the mill. Bill
Fielder worked with them in the
afternoon. Mrs.monroe's little boy came
up here towards night.

Wednesday Aug. 1,1855

Charley started for New York this   Down the river -New Orleans
morning(via Cincinnati by Boat.)

Thursday Aug.2,1855

Picked wool until Ten o'c.

Friday Aug.3,1855

Stopped(the mill) to get Graham to
repair it.

Saturday Aug.4,1855

Sunday Aug.5,1855

Patrick Morrison's wife died last   #674 Morrison m Anna Scales 181⁹
night, also John Miller's wife. There   #731 Miller m Sarah Chapman 184⁷
was a nigger meeting in the School
House this morning. Nigger Tom preached Uncle Tom belonged to John
Morris' nigger woman's funeral sermon.   Everett #768 about 1m S of
She died last spring. Singing School in Guyandotte.
the School House. Irvin Lusher passed
here just before night and told me John   #720 Irvin Lusher
Miller's wife died last night.

Monday Aug. 6,1855

I bought 3 bu. & 40 lbs. of wheat
of John Hensley. Gave him a dollar a

Bu. in Bacon at ten cents a pound.
Anna Cynthia and picked wool until Ten
O'c. I was in the store awhile with
Daniels. We each brought a bushel of
apples of John Howell.

#433 s/o Armstead
John m Elizabeth Hatfield 1851

Tuesday Aug. 7, 1855

I was on the store stoop a while
with Sam Hensley who was pretty drunk.

Wednesday Aug. 8, 1855

Charley Morris stopped by here and
gave us an invitation to his daughter's
and Morse's (FL-Moss) wedding next
Tuesday.(Aug.14).

Dr.V.R.Moss 1827-1909
bur. B'ville cem#26

Thursday Aug. 9, 1855

About Ten o'clock, I drove to
Barboursville in the Buggy. Went to
Allen's and got some blue cloth for a
frock coat. It and the silk for the
lining cost $9.00. Then I took it to
Mather's to be made. I went to the
Post Office(at Miller's) I got a jar of
lard that Solmon Thornburgs boys(He was
dead) left at Miller's for me. I
bought a dozen & a half chickens for
$1.25 per dozen. Jones paid me $3.00,
and I paid it to Farrell, part of the
balance due on my cow.

Dusenberry ordered a fancy
coat for the wedding.

Friday Aug. 10, 1855

Lent Lee Bowman the grey horse to
ride to Guyandotte. Sent the trimmings
to Mathers by him for my coat.

#726 the tailor

Saturday Aug. 11, 1855

Sunday Aug. 12, 1855

There was preaching in the School
House this morning. Bill Saunby and
John Alford took dinner with me. They
and Anna went to singing school.
I sold half a dollars worth of
ice. A quarters worth to Widow Everett
up the turnpike, and a quarters worth
to one of the Newmans.

part of #567 listed
Alford as constable

#306 w/o Nathan Everett
at Ona
Ice in August--good house.

Monday Aug.13,1855
    I went over to Charley Morris to
get a piece of beef. He had not
killed.

    Tuesday Aug. 14, 1855

    Mary Morris & V.R. Moss was
married this afternoon. Went to
Mathers and got my new Frock Coat.   See Cabell Marriages.
Then to Millers and got a dollars worth
of sugar & coffee for which I paid. My
coat was a pretty good fit. After
dinner Cynthia and I fixed ourselves
and just before Four O'c. we went over
to Charley Morris' to see his daughter
married to Mr. Morse (FL-Moss). the
ceremony was performed by Mr. Rece soon
after we got there. Mother, Aunt
Nancy, Mrs. Boweman, Robert, Lee, and a
great many others was there. We had a
fine dinner after the ceremony. Jeff   Members of lodge ?
Samuels, McConoughey, Sam Childers &
myself waited on tables. We came home
just at Sun down. Cynthia lent her
dishes an three doz. & five eggs for   41 eggs
the wedding party.

    Wednesday Aug. 15,1855

    Sammy went to town and got the Sun
papers for me.

    Thursday Aug. 16,1855

    Mrs. Daniels stopped in to see
Cynthia. Roffe and McCullough was up
here a while.

    Friday Aug. 17,1855

    Had a settlement with Green
Harrison and Wm.Mitchell. Mrs. Monroe   #426 Mitchell part of Rolen
sent up here for some medicine. Carter   Bias household.
passed through the Locke this morning
with a coal barge.

    Saturday Aug. 18,1855

    We had a fire in the hearth in the
dining room. Simmons brought Father
and I each a letter from the Post
Office, mine from the School Teacher I
have been corresponding with in New

York. Elisha Peyton brought me three
Sun papers, the Guyandotte Herald an my
American Free Mason.

#410 s/ John

Sunday Aug. 19,1855

Not any meeting here and it was
quite lonesome.

Monday Aug.20,1855

Tuesday Aug.23,1855
(dates are wrong eith FL or WmD.)

Turley went up to his old place to
haul tanbark. I with Caley,etc. went up
to George Hatfield's to get some
peaches. After getting nearly to
Capt.Jack Peyton's Caley wanted to come
home and I had to bring him back. Staid
till after dinner. Four o'clock before
we got home.

Tanbark often used on race
tracks after tannin removed.
#310 most Hatfields lived
just north of Roach.

Wednesday Aug. 24,1855

Bowman had to go several times
down to see his little boy who is very
low with the flux. Robert, Lee Bowman,
and I went up to Doolittle's Mill after
some peaches. Bill Saunby starts home
tomorrow.(Wed in Canada).?

Flux-serious diarrhea.
#31-Doolittle's Mill later
Howell's Mill located 2nd falls
of Mud River.

Thursday Aug.25,1855

Ben & Jim Cowens helped us(at
mill) for a while.

Friday Aug. 26, 1855

Went to haul a log we sawed off
yesterday. Got as far as the hill
opposite Dides & had to cut a piece off
before the cattle would pull it. Joe
Stanley rode the Bill horse up to
Franklin's after the yoke of cattle we
bought of him. Ben(Cowens) and Graham
worked all day.(at the mill)

Franklin was near Salt Rock.

Saturday Aug 27,1855

Robert and I started up to
Turley's in the buggy to get some

plums. Sam followed on horseback. Just
as we got to Turley's gate, I saw a
young deer in the road. (It died soon
after we got home. Had been run by
dogs.) Took Graham's tools to B'ville.
Put the horse in Bloom's stable & went
around to the Lodge Room. Graham sent
Johnson Lusher up here for some ice.   #738 Lusher listed as constable
Ben Cowens was made Master Mason, after
which we had a very nice supper got up
by Graham, as a farewell treat, this   Graham was born Vt.
being the last meeting he thinks he
will be here to attend.

    Sunday Aug.18,1855

    Monday Aug.17,1855 ??

    I went to J.S.Millers, bought a jug
and two gallons of molasses. Paid
$1.20, then went to Hibbens, and saw   #735 Hibbens listed as
him about making me a wagon.   waggonmaker 27y old.
    The Steamer Adrian came up about 3
o'c. She laid below the mill & put off
four bundles of shingles sent up by
Webb for our mill roof. Also a lot of
tin leaderfor Father's house. She then
passed through the Locke.

    Tuesday Aug.28,1855

    Father sold a yoke of cattle for
$100, and another for $65.
    Bowman told Father this morning he Bowman had been miller for at
intended to leave soon, so we have to   least 5 years.
look for another Miller. Steamer Adrian
came down about 3 o'c.

    Wednesday Aug.29,1855

    I was up to the Blacksmith Shop
awhile this morning. Webb (FL-Col.
Webb) want me to take charge of the
Locke. He went on to the Falls.   Falls of Guyandotte near
                                        Branchland

    Thursday Aug. 30, 1855

    Webb came here (in Mid afternoon)
and I went over to the Locke with him
to see about putting some timber for
Keyser through. Webb soon left. I got   Possibly #627 Eli Keyser
West Childers to assist Keyser. One of listed as school teacher.
the upper gates would not open all the
way. Only put one Locke full through.

Charley returned form New York. Mat
Thompson brought his trunk and a box
sent by Uncle Cale for Cynthia as far
as Barboursville. Robert took the Jack
horse and went down to get Mat's wagon
to bring them home.

Friday August 31, 1855

I went over to the Locke soon
after breakfast & assisted Keyser put
two more lockes full through. Also put
through a canoe for Sam Hensley.
Keyser's lockage amounted to $4.00 &
Hensley's to 50 cents. Neither of them
would pay me. Soon after dinner I
returned to B'ville to bring Mr.
Samuels up to receive the last payment
for our place. He could not come. Then
I went to Allen's & bought me a linen
coat for $1.25, then to Mat Thompsons
and brought up a box of soap Charley
brought with him and Robert forgot last
night. Just before dark I went over to
the Locke to let a coal flat of Green
Harrison's through. West Childers was
not there and I could not open the
gates.

#683 Hensley had 8 ch. in 1850

Saturday Sep. 1, 1855

Soon after breakfast, seeing
Charley Morris and West Childers on the
Locke, I started over. As I got in the
middle of the river, heard Morris call
for a rope, Hurried over and found West
in the Locke holding on to a rail.
Threw one of the ropes off the Gates to
him & we got him out. He and Charley
was locking Harrison's coal Boat and it
sunk and they were letting the water
off. West being in the boat, we shut
the lower gates and let the Locke fall
again. Something had got into the upper
wickets, as it could not be shut which
was the cause of the boat sinking. Not
being able to do anyting, I came home.
Harrison came soon after & returned
immediately to have the water drawn off
below. Eleven O'c Sam Childers helped
us get the chunk out of the gate. Then
we let the water out low, as low as we
could, then came over home again.

Green Harrison was also
blacksmith at B'ville

Sunday Sept. 2, 1855

Monday Sept. 3, 1855

Soon after breakfast, Green
Harrison came up here and I went with
him over in the Locke to see if we
could do anything toward raising his
boat. Could not on account of there
being too much water. Then went home
and up as far as Bill Fielder's. He was
not home and I returned. The Carder
(FL?) paid me his rent this afternoon.

The only Fielder in 1850 is
#96 Jonathan m to Eliza Turley

Tuesday Sept. 4, 1855

I rode up and saw Richard Lunsford
then came as far as Turley's where I
found Sam. We gathered some planks and
started home, but the rain drove us
back to Turley's where I had to stay
about two hours. Sam stopped at
Higgins. Green Harrison succeeded in
raising his coal boat out of the Locke,
this morning. Very little coal had
washed out.

Wednesday Sept.5,1855

No importance.

Thursday Sept.5,1855

(Much rain. Creek very high a
torrent washed out the water gates,etc.
Billy Miller's boat with a lot of
lumber broke loose and went over the
dam. It broke in two and came down,
lumber and all together, as far as the
mouth of the creek. I ran down and
tried to catch it, but having no cable
it went up under the dam and all tore
to pieces. The lo se to Miller & Moore
is about $250.00. The dam at the mouth
of Mud commenced washing around but the
River's falling saved it, but had it
continued rising, nothing could have
prevented it going. There is no telling
yet what amount of damage was done
(River rose 6ft.). Lent Sam Childers a
large cabel-weighing 72lbs.-to put on
one Carter & Dietz' raft. I fixed
myself and went with Charles and Robert
down to Mrs.Roffe's. Charley took his

fiddle. Mrs.Roffe sung and played some
on the piano.

Friday Sept.7,1855

I rode to Barboursville, saw Billy
Miller & with him agreed to settle the
difference between him and Father by
arbitration. Towards night Capt.Elias   #746 a Lawyer in Barboursville
McComas,Liet.Gov.Elect and Lawyer
Fisher stopped to see Father. I went
down with them. They took tea there.

Saturday Sept.8,1855

(Superior Court Day) My present-
ment for not keeping the road in repair
came up. Jeff Samuels put in a plea of   maybe #728 Henry J. ?
not guilty.

Sunday Sept.9,1855

I read my papers all day. There
was preaching in the Forenoon and Four
O'clock in the afternoon. Anna went in
the morning, and Cynthia in the
afternoon. About none o'c. Anna,
Caroline and I went over to Father's
and tried to get a few peaches. Only
got four or five.

Monday Sept. 10,1855

I went to town. I took my dinner
at Bloom's. Robert came down(to down)
after dinner & brought me the money to
take up the last note on our place, but
I sent it back home by him as I can not
pay it until tomorrow. I went over to
the Locke this morning & helped Sam
Childers put a load of Tan Bark through
for Baker. Preaching in the School   maybe #347 John L. Baker
House. I went up there a few minutes,
but did not go in.

Tuesday Sept.11,1855

Made the last payment on our place
today $2029.12. I went to Allen's and
got $100.00 Father borrowed of him
yesterday.
I was around the Court House until
nearly noon, when I went with Thorn
down to old Mrs.Moore's and got our   his mother-in-law(Thorn's)

dinners. I returned to the Court House.
Waited there until Samuels and Laidley
returned from dinner. Then I paid them
the last payment.(I went back home.)
    Caley had eaten a whole box of
worm Lozenges. I waited to see if they
would hurt him. John Rece,Bryant &
Charles were in the store practicing
music.

Wednesday Sept.12,1855

    Bob harnessed Jack soon after
dinner and rode him to Barboursville &
brought up Merritts buggy for me, and
about Ten O'c. Cynthia with the baby
and I drove to Barboursville (I) left
Cynthia at old Mrs.Moore's. I took some
ice to Bill Merritt. Charley was
summoned as a witness in the Maupin
divorce case. I came up soon after he
got there. Elias McComas is Maupin's
Lawyer & Fisher & Laidley-Holderby's.
Cynthia, Louisa and old Mrs.Moore being
at Wilson Moore's, Charley and I took
dinner there. The Steamboat Adrian
passed up toward night.

Wilson a son of Mary & Martin
makes him bro-in-law to Thorn
Dusenberry

Thursday Sept.13,1855

    Jim Cowens was married tonight to
Sarah Butcher. I sent a lot of ice down
to Bob Allen, then got some out for
Bill Merritt which I took down to him
about ten o'clock.
    Maupin's suit took all day and
then they did not get through. Borrowed
a coat & umbrella of Allen and started
home after dark.

#331-1st w Hester Turley 1844

#733 Allen b Scotland.

#745 Dr.Henry B.Maupin wife
Martha(Holderby) listed as
insane.Divorce granted on the
grounds of insanity.

Friday Sept.14,1855

    After Ten o'clock when Charley and
I rode in the buggy(Merritt's) to
Barboursville, Bryan & Charley followed
on horseback. We drove around by
Bloom's and left some more. Then Bryant
left the horse he rode down in
Merritt's stable and rode with Charley
in the Buggy up to attend Walker's
Concert. Sam went up with them.
    I remained in town all day to
attend Court. The divorce case of
Maupin's was not given to the Jury

until after dinner. They were not out
long. They decided that she was insane
at the time of her marriage.(Returned
home).

The _Steamer Adrian_ passed down
this afternoon. We sent two barrels of
flour to Flowers(FL-Ezra ?)in
Guyandotte at $6.75. Harrison Peyton
brought me two bushels of peaches.
(Miserable)

#781 Ezra a lumberman ?
#432 -near Osley Gap ?

Sunday Sept.15,1855

Right after breakfast, I started
in Merritt's buggy Barboursville & took
a little ice to Bloom. Beech's case
against me was the first case tried.
The jury went out out about Ten O'c. I
took dinner at Bloom's. (Jury failed to
agree. Case laid over.)
Charley's melodean has arrived at
Guyandotte. The Judge today divorced
Doctor Maupin from his wife and gave
her her maiden name.

maybe #412 Walton Beech
also near Oswley Gap.

Sunday Sept.16,1855

I lent the skiff to one of Morris'
niggers to go down the river. Just at
night, he returned and had about a
bushel of fine peaches for which I gave
him twenty-five cents.
There was a prayer meeting in the
School House this morning. Susie rode
on horseback with Sam and Sam Bowman to
Barbourville.

Monday Sept.17,1855

Charley & Sam started early to
Barboursville to borrow Hibben's wagon
to bring his melodean from Guayndotte.
He gave $135 for it. I would have
squeezed it until it squealed before I
would have paid so much for one of
them. Bob Allen was here waiting to
have a tooth pulled. I broke it off
both times.

Every tooth he talks about
seems to be a problem.

Tuesday Sept.18,1855

(I traded Turley for a bull calf.)
Mat Butcher told me he was only common
stock and as old again as Turley

represented. I then concluded to make
Turley take him back. Robert and Lee
Bowman ran the corn stone.

Wednesday Sept.19,1855

Billy Rogers ground a turn of
wheat for himself and two others.
Fathers went up on the upper end of the
farm with Mat Butcher to show him 100
acres he wanted to show him.

#405 Wm.m Clarinda Bias

Friday Sept.21,1855

Father bought $18.00 worth fruit
trees from a gentlemen in Rochester,
New York, to be delivered to
Guyandotte.

Saturday Sept.22,1855

Just at dark Simmons came along &
with Charley and I & went right to
Bloom's. Gave him the ice, put our
horses in his stable, then went in and
saw Graham. (Been sick most of the
week)Ben Cowens,Charley and I went to
the Lodge. I was presented two
petitions,and for Sam Chiders, the
other for Daniels. John Dirton was
raised to Master's degree.

#760 John was toll collector
on James River Turnpike

Sunday Sept.23,1855

Mat Thompson sent up here and got
some ice. When I returned home (from
B'ville) I found Robert Allen and his
little girl here. (Broke it off again
till only a few roots left.)

Monday Sept.24,1855

Just at breakfast Anna cut a caper
& talked so saucy. I gave her a licking
after which she cleared out to some of
the neighbors. County Court today. I
took dinner with Robert Allen. I heard
that Anna was at Bowman's.

Anna was about 3yr old

Tuesday Sept.25,1855

Turley, John Fielder, Collins, and
Joe Stanley cut corn for us all day
back of Bowman's.

Wednesday Sept.26,1855

(I went to Guyandotte.) I went to
the steam flour mills. After going all
through, I went to Thorn's store, got a
dollar's worth each of sugar and
coffee. Brought up some coal tar for
MIller and left it at his saw mill.
The Steamer Adrian passed on her way to
the Falls about. Anna returned home
this morning. All pretty smart.

Thursday Sept.27,1855

About nine o'clock,I put the horse
before Allen's buggy, and drove to
town. Left the buggy at (Absolom)
Holderby's. Got my Bridle and Saddle
the went to MIller's and tried to get
some money from him, but could not,
then weht to Mrs. Holderby's &
extracted a tooth for Mrs. Allen. Did   Another broken tookh.
not get it all out. It was an old root,
and all crumbled. They made me take
some dinner, soon after which I rode
home on horseback. Charley & I put our
Buggy together. It works real nice. The
Steamer Adrian passed down about five
o'clock. She came in below the mill &
we sent a barrel of flour to Thorn,
price $6.50. Robert & Lee Bowman
hunting all day. they returned at night
with fourteen squirrels and four
pigeons (Wild pigeons no doubt-FL). The
latter they gave to me.

Friday Sept.28,1855

About 3 o'clock, we all went out
squirrel hunting. Lee Bowman and Robert
went to the other side of the river and
Charles & I on this side. We got three
apiece. Lee & Robert got fourteen.
Turley & his hands cut corn most of the
day on the bottom opposite Roffe's.

Sunday Sept.30,1855

Charley cut my hair this afternoon.

Monday Oct.1,1855

The Thompsons came down soon after breakfast & washed for Cynthia. Turley came down here and I went up the road with him & helped him catch some of our hogs that were in one of the cornfields. Then we came down and he made arrangements with Father to fatten our hogs. Turley takes Forty of the hogs, and fifty bu. of corn, fattens them and gives Father half the pork. He took about twenty hogs up with him.

Another of Harvey Smith's children was buried today.

Charley, Lee and Robert returned just at dark with Twenty nine squirrels and one pidgeon. Charley gave me six squirrels, three of which Anna and I took over to Mrs.Daniels. Thorn and Louisa starts to New York tomorrow morning. She came up to the store with Anna and I got a pair of shoes.

The Dusenberry's were very well "off".

"only" forty hogs ?

!850 Harvey had 2 ch.
Ann 10,Harrison 3

The family came from NY.

Tuesday October 2,1855

Thorn, his wife and Caroline Slocum went to New York today. Rode to Barboursville on the mare. Went down to Miller's Mill. The Muley saw was running. It cuts finely. Can't begin to count the strokes. Returned home by noon. Father had let the saw mill to Charles R.Morris and Conwelzie Simmons for one year for Five Hundred Dollars.

Pat Thompson's youngest child died this morning with the flux. Father sent a piece of beef down to Harvey Smiths, his family all being sick and in a suffering condition.

New type of saw.

Many people ill in the neighborhood.

Wednesday Oct.3,1855

Morris & Simmons commenced running the saw mill. Jim Cowens & West Childers sawed.(Broke on of the dogs.) Had to stop the mill & sent one of the sawyers to Barboursville to get it repaired, Daniels being sick. (Father got a letter from a Miller in answer to an ad.) I told Father to ask Bowman when he wanted to leave. Bowman told him he had concluded to remain with him, so I answered the letter accordingly. Pat Thompson's child was buried this afternoon.

Blacksmith at Martha

Cemetery has been destroyed. About 1/4m S of Martha bridge Read by WPA

Thursday Oct.4,1855

We went down to (B'villv) to have
the difficulty with Miller & Moore
settled by arbitration. I went down to
Miller & Moore's Mill to get them to
come up. (It was deffered till next
Monday.) I bought a box of segars of
John Miller for $2.50, then went to
Eggers & got a pair of boots he had
been making for me. They are to be
$4.00. Met Mrs.Roffe & McCullough
riding on horseback. rode home with
them. The Steamer Adrian passed up
today.

may be   cobbler   as well

Friday Oct.5,1855

Briant moved today from the house
by the bridge. I went over in the field
by Bowman's & gathered some beans, then
came up to the mill and staid while
Bowman went to his dinner.(FL-Evidently
Bowman lived on or near where John Love
used to live.) The Steamer Adrian went
down about the middle of the afternoon.

Saturday Oct.6,1855

Lent Sam Childers our ox yoke
pattern. Both mills running all day.

Sunday Oct 7,1855

I went over in the field next to
the Frenchman & dug a few potatoes.
(Found two pumkins in the corn field.
One weighed 56lbs, the other 49-.)

Monday Oct.8,1855

Sam Childers told me the court had
appointed me with him & Charles
K.Morris appraisers of the property of
William L.Thompson. I went down to the
blacksmith shop where William Merritt
was awaiting. He swore us and we went
up and soon got through. I commenced
getting out a frame for my wood shed.

Tuesday Oct.9,1855

Robert, Sam, & I with the wagon and a yoke of cattle hauled two loads of pumkins off the bottom or Meadow. One load, we put in my smoke house, the other we left at Fathers. A. Holderby sent up this morning and got a barrel of flour $7.00 & 2 bu. corn meal 80 cents per bushel.

If there were 50 pumkins a load. Thats 250 at 500 lbs. WOW

Dusenberry's Mill was about 4 miles-Howell's Mill about 8 miles.

Wednesday Oct.10,1855

Charley, Sam & I hauled two more loads of pumkins to Fathers, and one up here.

Thursday Oct.11,1855

Turley hauled a load of pumkins for himself. He finished cutting the corn this morning & says we have 1400 shocks of fodder & about 3000 bu. of corn. Sold a barrel of flour just at night to Calvary Swann for $7.00.

#420 near Owlsey Cap

Friday Oct.12,1855

About the middle of the afternoon the Steamer Adrian passed up. She landed above the dam having ten barrels for us. Only took off five. Lent three to Sam Childers to get apples from Rial Childers. He sent them up on the boat with two for me.
The Frenchman having his corn all gathered & a going to move in a day or two.

Rial=Royal #85 ?

Saturday Oct.13,1855

We(Charley,I and Lee Bowman) started in the buggy to Barboursville, Bowman on Horseback). We went down to have the difficulty between Miller & Moore arbitrated. I had run about town two or three hours to find Jeff Samuels. Found him about half a mile above town playing cards with Fred Miller and Jesse Dodson. After going up there twice, I brought him to the Court House with me in the Buggy where he handed me an account against Miller & Moore, then I went to Miller's store. He refused to have the difficulity arbitrated fairly. He said he and Moore

#773 Dodson was a boatman

intended to Swear wich I objected to
and gave up the settlement with a suit.
     Got a pair of boots of Johs
(Thos.?)Hatfield for Bob. Charley got
his & Bobs coats --and a vest---?(FL)
Procter has been making for me. There
was preaching in the school house in
the afternoon.

#753 George Proctor=clothie

Sunday Oct. 14,1855

     Just as I was going to take my
breakfast, The Steamer Adrian came
down. She came in below the mill and
put two barrels of flour on board, one
for Jacob Hillbruner, Guyandotte & the
other for Thos.Thornburg in
Barboursville. There was preaching in
the School House this morning. Sam
Johnson was here and got the plans
Father borrowed of him. I sold five
barrels of flour to Mat Thompson at
$6.75 a barrel. Turley took two yoke of
our cattle and wagon up to haul tanbark
with this afternoon.

#914 Sam m Eliza Kilgore

Monday October 15,1855

     Dave Thornburg hauled the five
barrels of flour to Mat Thompson, I
sold him yesterday. Just at night I
went down to Bowman's and borrowed a
candle.

Borrowed a candle ?

Tueday Oct.16,1855

     About Ten O'c I drove to
Barboursville in the Buggy, Miller
having appointed today to take a
deposition of Graham, He told me he
would not be ready until after dinner.
Then I went home with Jeff Samuels and
Took dinner, after which we returned to
Miller's store.(Miller decided not to
take Graham's testimony after talking
to John Laidley.)
     Charley Shipe and Ella Butcher
passed me in a buggy going to
Guyandotte to get married. Then I drove
to Proctor's and got some things for
Charley.
     I met Hillbruner from Guyandotte
just by Roffe's as I went down this
morning. He rode with me to

See Cabell marriages

Barboursville. Feazle came up toward
night. I bought 8 1/2lbs. of Tallow and
11 pounds of beef of him.

#Feasle,Everett a
lumberman in 1850

Wednesday Oct.17,1855

The mill quite crowded with wheat.
The Panorama of New York City was
exhibited in Barboursvill this
afternoon. A great many went down to
see it. I felt bad. I took a dose of
pills.

Thursday Oct.18,1855

Mrs.Moore's nigger girl Juda(FL-
colored girl) came up here. I have
hired her for a year for $40 and her
clothes. (I wrote Mr.J.S.) Gisiner,
Brownsburg, Rockbridge Co.VA. an
advertisement foa a miller in the
Staunton paper.

Mrs. Martin Moore had
12 slaves in 1850

Friday Oct.19,1855

James Morrison brought me three
barrels of apples for which I am to pay
him $1.50 per barrel. I bought a lot of
wheat of Hezekiah Swann for $1.00 per
Bu. delivered on the river bank. Ben
Cowens came up to bid us farewell in
the afternoon. He and Graham intends
leaving for home tomorrow morning.

#681 near Salt Rock

Saturday Oct.20,1855

After we got the mills running, I
went over and shut the Locke.

Sunday Oct.21,1855

Judy went down to John Everett's
to hear Uncle Tom preach a funeral
sermon. She rode the mare and was gone
most of the day. Singing School in the
School House this afternoon.

Everett's was just above
Guyandotte (1m) and on
Guyan River.

Monday Oct.22,1855

I fixed myself and rode to
Barboursville, County Court today.
Doct.McCullough rode down in the buggy
with me. There was considerable
excitement most of the afternoon. There

was eight or nine niggers sold. Some
belonging to the Hanley estate, the
others to Simmons heirs. The yellow
girl Eliza was bought by George
Gallaher for $1615.

#658 George had 1 slave 18

Tuesday Oct.23,1855

I got Cowens & Higgins to help us
put braces outside of the upper end of
the grist mill flume. The mill is full
of grain.

Tuesday(Wednesday) Oct.24,1855

Charley & I was in the grist mill
all day. We ran two stones on corn all
the morning. Royal Childers brought me
down a Bll. of apples. (Had trouble
with mill).The mill is full of grain &
people getting very impatient.
The Steamer Adrian came up in the
afternoon. She got on the bar just
below the Locke & had to get Childer's
lighter to take her cargo out. Before
she got off after she passed through
the Locke, she came on by the saw mill
and took eight barrels for me up to
Leven Swann's for apples. Sawmill not
running. The water in the pond not high
enough.
Roffe's Ben hauled my flour
barrels of apples from McCullough's. I
gave him a bit. Two of the barrels I
let Father have.

Tursday Oct.25,1855

Royal Childers brought me down a
barrel of apples this morning. I paid
him $1.50 for them. The Steamboat
passed down in the forenoon.
The Agriucultural fare was in
Barboursville today. Charley Morris and
others took considerable stock down.
Father has been sick in bed all
day. Doct McCullough was there. He
thinks he has an attack of intestinal
Feaver. I soon returned home & had to
go to the mill & let some fellows who
staid in town to get drunk have their
meal. There is an eclipse of the Moon
about midnight.

Friday Oct.26,1855

The Burr(we only ran one)ran
finely. Morris & Simmons started the
saw mill. The water rose considerable
in the pond last night. Considerable
grain came into the mill today.
Childers & Burl Hensley commenced
weatherboarding the front of the grist
mill. The mill crowded with grain. We
had to run two stones on grain.

2 Hensleys named Bird

Turley came home this afternoon
with our cattle and wagon. He brought
eight barrels of apples from Leven
Swann's for us.

There was a called meeting and Sam
Childers and Daniels was initiated.

Sunday Oct.28,1855

I ground a turn of corn for a man
who lives about twenty miles from here.
Charley gave me about three pints of
his strawberry wine. Soon after dinner,
Pat Thompson came along and I went with
him up to Turley's. Sooon returned home
and with Anna went up to the Thompson
place to get some persimmons.(Not ripe)

Monday Oct.29,1855

There was considerable excitement
around here this morning accasioned by
all of Roffe's niggers, with a good
many others starting to the Ohio River
Saturday night with the intention of
running off. It appears Ike, his wife
and children) with Ben borrowed Pat
Thompson's Buggy to go to Everett's on
a visit. They intented to meet with a
lot of other niggers about three miles
below Guyandotte and there cross the
Ohio. But they all failed getting
together Saturday night, and yesterday,
some of them discovered Wilson Moore
watching them so they all concluded to
return home.

About mouth of Symmes Creek

Turley was all day hauling wood.
He hauled a half cord for Father,
Bowman, Charley, Daniels, & myself.

Sam Childers and Hensley still wetherboarding the mill. Sent two barrels of Flour to Barboursville this morning, one to Bloom, the other to Allen at $8.00 a Barrel.

Susie commenced to school over the river today, Sam commenced yesterday.

Susie was 6y
Sam was 13

Wednesday Oct.31,1855

As soon as Bowman came up to the mill, Charley an I helped him take up the corn stone. We found the collar on the spindle so much worn that there would have to be a new one made. Daniels tried to weld a piece on it but it proved to be cast & he could do nothing with it, so we concluded to send it to Harrison in Barboursville & get him to make one. We ran one of the Burrs on corn today.

Webb was here this morning with Mr.McFarland & another man of the New York Co. Soon after dinner Bill Fielder stared to town with the Corn Mill spindle in the wagon with two yoke of cattle.(I followed)

The people who built the Guyan River dams ?

As soon as Harrison saw the collar, he said he had no iron to make one. Then I told Fielder to take it back home. He went to Null' and got three flour barrels.

There are 4 Hull's.

The sawyers took the saw to Miller's Mill to gumm it.

Susie went to school today.

Thursday Nov.1,1855

The mill much crowded with corn. Charley was all morning making a platform for the collar of the corn mill spindle. He got it finished by noon. As soon as I got my dinner, I fixed myself & started in the buggy to Guyandotte on my way to Ironton with the pattern & the spindle to get a collar cast.(Ohio River so low no boats running) I then crossed Guyandotte River & drove down to Sam Johnston's where I remainded all night.

On turnpike about 1/2 way to Big Sandy from Guyandotte. Area called Johnson Hollow today.

I started from Sam Johnstons,
about nine o'clock, Crossed the Sandy
River in a horse boat. Had an awful
time. The rivers are very low and the
banks vey mirey. Drove to Ashland,
Kentucky where I crossed the Ohio River
to Ohio. Arrived at Ironton about 3
o'clock. The roads were awful muddy. I
drove right up to one of the foundries
& left the spindle and pattern, then to
a Hotel & had my horse put up and got
my dinner, after which I went back to
the foundry where I remained until
nearly dark. Saw them cast a large
Cylinder. Returned to the Hotel. I was
in the sitting room of the Hotel by the
stove until nearly ten o'clock.

Saturday Nov.3,1855

I went to the foundry,etc.(Not
done.) I ordered my horse, paid my
tavern bill which was $1.75 & went back   Total cost $6.75
to the foundry. (Their bill $5.) A
quarter after ten, I started home
(crossed at Ashland) then drove up to
the mouth of Big Sandy where I stopped
at a Hotel and had myself and horse
fed. Had a bad time getting up the bank
after crossing Sandy. Broke the single
tree of the Buggy, but managed to get
home with it. Stopped at Sam Johnston's
a minute then came up the turnpike to
Barboursville, Where I crossed the
Guyandotte River. Stopped in
Barboursville-got some coffee and tea.

Sunday Nov.4,1855

(One of our steers got [out]). Mat
Butcher learned he was at Bill Turner's   #137 near Madison Creek
(who refushed to give him up until we
proved him.)

Monday Nov.5,1855

I, Turley, & Fielder started for
the Falls of the Guyandotte. We crossed
the river here and went up the other
side. When opposite Jim Morris, we   #424 near Roach
waited about two hours for Mathew
Butcher, he not coming, we went on.
Found the ox at Turner's.(He was ours.)
Had a great deal of trouble driving

him. Got down as far as Leven Swann's
(FL-They got this ox of Franklin) when
we turned him in a lot and Mrs.Swann
prepared us a first rate dinner.
(Rested about an hour & got home about
dark.)
    Pat Thompson commenced moving on
the Turnpike above Barboursville.

Tuesday Nov.6,1855

    Went to Barboursville. Hunted up
Jeff Samuels. Paid him $25.00.
    A raft of Adam,Carter & Dietz got
on the dam today & some of the logs
came over, the rest remained on at
dark.

        Wednesday Nov. 7,1855

    Sam Childers succeeded in getting
a part of Carter & Dietz's raft off the
dam.

        Tuesday Nov.8,1855

    Charley Morris came home just at
night with a new two horse wagon.

        Friday Nov.9,1855

    Butcher was here in the afternoon
I tried to make a trade with him for
his pacing colt. Made off Roffe's mill
account.

        Saturday Nov.10,1855

    There was a meeting in the School
House this afternoon. I settled up with
the Carder this morning, and paid James
Morrison $4.50 on account of apples &
oats I bought of him. Owe him a balance
of $7.00.

        Sunday Nov.11,1855

    I fixed myself and went to church
with Anna, Susie and Caley. Mr.Rece
preached. A vote was taken, and they
decided to hold a Protracted meeting
here all week. After dinner I took a
walk up as far as Turley's. So warm I
went without my coat. Turley came down

#90 about Madison Ck.

Reason Cemetery abandoned

with me just as church was going in &
the children went.

Monday Nov. 12, 1855

There was a meeting here this
morning .(Several of us went to
Guyandotte.)

Tuesday Nov. 13, 1855

I went to Barboursville to get some
money from Feazel for a cow he bought
of Father. Did not see him.
I bought 29 1/2 yds. Domestic of
Allen to make sacks of. Also seven yds.
calico of Tom Thornburg for a dress for
Anna.
There was meeting twice today.
Cynthia went in the afternoon.
The Steamer Adrian passed up
through the Locke about 8 o'clock. She
landed above the dam. I sent 8 barrels
to Leven Swann's for apples.

(FL-For remainder of this book look in
back of book for 1854.)
Book not found to date.

EVENTS

BLACKS/SLAVES

THE DUSENBERRY MILL
reproduced from painting in possession
of Mrs. O. E. Bird, Guyandotte, WV

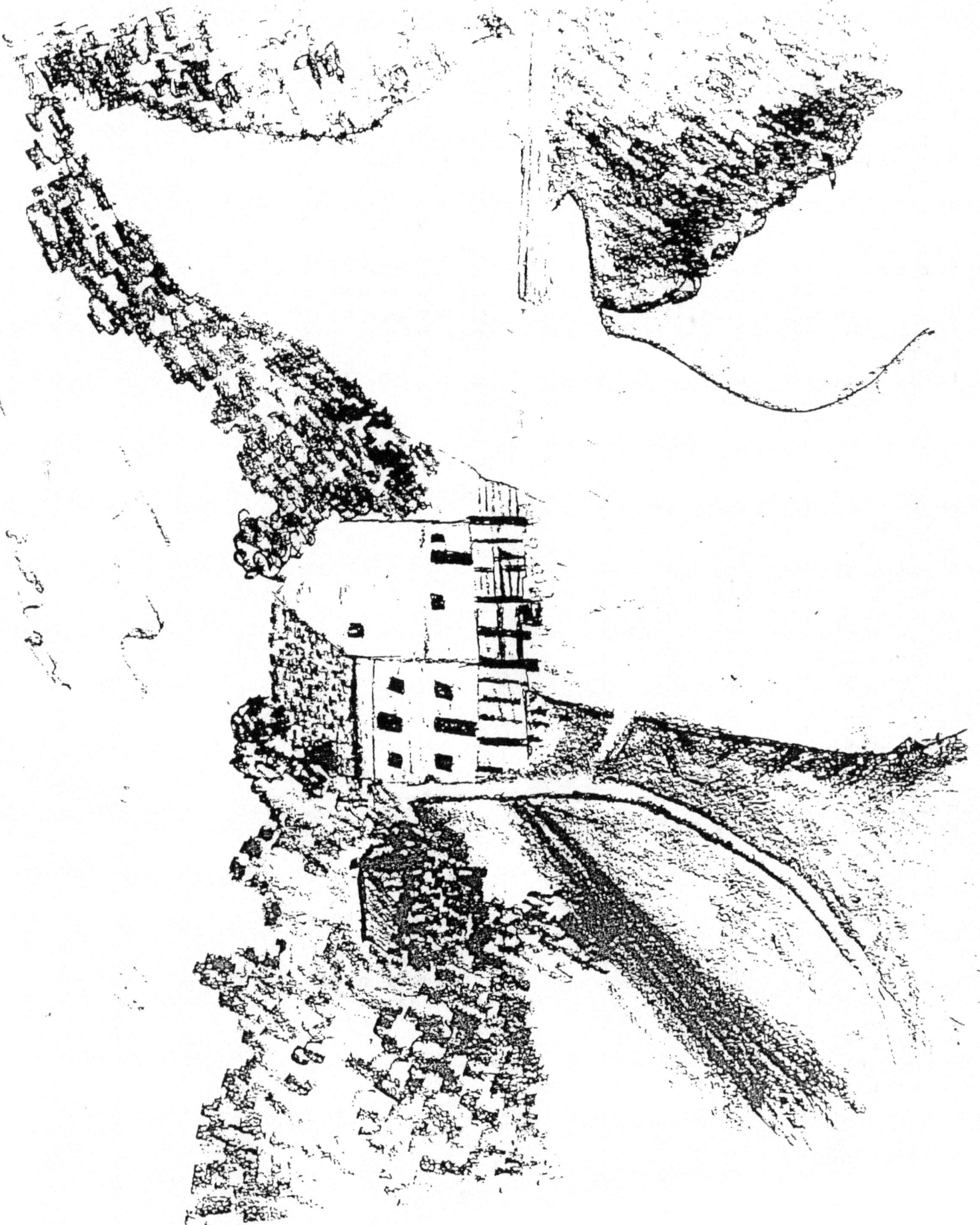

THE DUSENBERRY MILL
reproduced from painting in possession
of Mrs. O. E. Bird, Guyandotte, WV

RIVER BOATS

IN

THE DUSENBERRY DIARY   Events-chronological

(Photography Boat)
America
Annie Laurie
Arlington   Panorama
Charley Bowen   Fancifuls-The Raging Tadds
Charmer   Ball at Merritts
Dexter   Corn shucking
Edenburg   Singing school
Fayette   Exhibiton at Academy
Fleetwood   Agricultural fair
Florence   Circus
Golden Eagle   Political meeting
Henderson   Wedding sheveree
Hudson   Small pox
Hunter(Guy)   Methodist Conference
J.C.Crossley   Party by invitaton
James Fisk Jr.   Exhibition at Academy
Kenton   Shooting Match
Major Adrian (55-56-Guy)   Lodge Parade
Major Weimer   dance
May Anderson   serenade
Mountain Boy(K)   Guyandotte Baseball Club
Ohio #4   Barboursville Brass Band
Piketon   Rebel Church Festival
R.C.Gray   Temperance Lodge
R.H.Lindsey(55-56)   Dance Party on River Boat
R.R.Hudson   Sunday School Festival
Reindeer   Singing School at Baptist Ch
Sam Irwin   Circus
St.Charles   Dan Rice Circus
Tigress   Circus
Victor #3
Victor #4
Webster
Willis Hay
Yanthe

        The people of the period were busy in
both business and social life. The events in
the 1855-56 period deals mostly with farm
life. Once he moves to Guyandotte,Dusenberry
and family attend many social events.

Measures in common use in the 1850's

LIQUID Measure

```
        4 gill = pint
        2 pint = quart
       4 quart = gallon
31 1/2 gallon = barrel bbl
        2 bbl = hogshead
```

Barrels were the common packing container.
All farm goods were shipped in barrels made
of wooden(oak) staves and bound by a hoop
(hoop pole).

DRY Measure

```
         14 pound = stone
     100 lb butter = firkin
100 lb grain or flour = cental
    100 lb dry fish = quintal
     100 lb nails = keg
      196 lb flour = barrel
       200 lb meat = barrel
       280 lb salt = barrel
```

Salt was produced at Salt Rock and in the
Kanawha Valley. Hogs were butcher,packed in
barrels and sent to the Kanawha Salt Works.

Each Mill ground flour and meal usually keeping
a portion for the meal. All flour was shipped in
barrels. Getting the wood and hoops for barrels
was a common job of the carpenter. One road in
Cabell County is known as Hoop Pole Road.

There are several interesting articles about the
local mills published in the Huntington newspapers
in the 1920's. Plus there is a section in "Cabell
County Annals" and the Fred B.Lambert "manuscript
collection."

DUSENBERRY DIARY

1856

Bloomingdale, Cabell County, VA.

Tuesday Jan.1,1856

Judy went to Barboursville this morning and I had to milk.

Judy hired for one year $40

Wednesday Jan.2,1856

We hauled seven loads of ice Today. Roffe hauled a load of straw for us towards night. He promised to help us haul ice day after tomorrow.
I pulled two teeth this morning- one for Tom Ward (Jr.) and the other for Nigger Pete.

#395 Roffe

#703 Ward
dentist for black and white

Thursday Jan.3,1856

Morris' paid $125, a quarter of the rent on the saw mill.(With Charley, Jim Cowens, Bill Fielder, I began hauling ice from the creek above the ice house.) A fellow by the name of Charley Johnson came here and I pulled a tooth for him.
John Dodd hauled four loads before, and four after dinner. I sent a letter for Uncle Cale and for Anna to Mrs. Weinner, her grandmother.

sawmill rent $500yr.
#331 Cowens

#711 Dodd

Anna's grandmother

Friday Jan.4,1856

I think the coldest weather I ever felt in this county.(3 degrees below zero) Cowens(Jim),(Charley) Johnson, Dodd, Bill Fielder and myself hauled nine loads of ice. About nine o'clock,Dolen brought my papers from Barboursville.

cold weather

hauled ice for ice house

#698 Dolen (Logan mail ?)

Saturday Jan.5,1856

Father let Bill Fielder have a note
on Jim Butcher for $19.09 with $6.19
interest. He went up to Jenkins and
bought a sow and pigs with it.

#705 Butcher family
traded IOU's

Monday Jan.7,1856

(Roffe & our hands hauled 14 loads
of ice) The ice is beautiful-nine inches
thick. Father took the Jim Butcher note
back from Jenkins today & brought the
sow Fielder got for the note. He is
going to pay him $12 in meal.

thick ice enough to last yr

Barter-meal for spw

Tuesday Jan.8,1856

I raised the flag early in respect
to the Battle of New Orleans.
(We hauled ice again)(cattle coming out
at the opening we made in the fence the
other side the bridge to haul ice) My
young turkeys all froze to death last
night.

more ice

turkeys froze

Wednesday Jan.9,1856

Thermometer 10 degrees below zero.
The river frozen over just above the
ferry and below the mouth of the creek.
Too cold for us to haul ice. I commenced
writing a letter to Uncle Francis.

Thursday Jan.10,1856

Thermometer thirteen degrees below
zero. Helped Charley in the afternoon
get the stove from the School House and
put it up in the store in the place of
the Franklin. In the afternoon we skated
awhile both above and below the dam.

replaced Franklin stove

Friday Jan,11.1856

Nine degrees below zero. The
machine wheel frozen tight so we could
not grind. the thermometer 20 degrees
above zero(in the evening).

cold and ice effected mill

Saturday Jan.12,1856

Soon after breakfast,Charley,Jim
Cowens & I commenced fixing shafts to

the sleigh. I took the horse to the
Blacksmith shop and got him sharpe shod. Spiked horse shoes for ice
We fixed a temparary pair of hickory
shatfs on the sleigh. Soon after
dinner,Jim Cowens and I drove to
Barboursville. Our sleigh and bells
kicked up considerable excitement. I got
a pair of shoes for Judy. Then went to   bought shoes for servant
Hibbon's shop and got a pair of bent   #735 Hibbens
hickory for a shaft. Then we drove back
home. Then Charley and Cynthia took a
ride. After they returned,Robert ,Anna,
Susie, and Sam took one.

Sunday Jan.13,1856

No one stirring except a few who
went down to the Preaching at Bowman's.

Monday Jan.14,1856

About 10 o'clock, Bill Fielder,   more ice
Charley, John Dodd & I commenced getting
in the balance of the ice.

Tuesday Jan.15,1856

Cynthia and I started to Guyandotte
in the sleigh about Eleven O'c. We got
there at at after twelve o'clock. Went
right to Thorn's house. We took dinner   Thorn -step-Uncle
there. I put the horse up at Moore &
Vandiver's. Bought a lot of groceries at
Thorn's.Then went to Rodger's and bought
a clothes basket for Cynthia also a can
of oysters for which I paid $1.50.
We started home about Three o'clock. got
here just at dark. As we went down, in   Road to Martha followed river
passing Turner's ferry there was four
mules in the ice. There was drove of
them crossed on the ice and eight of
them broke in. They got them all out. My
cold is getting worse. Never was such
fine sleighing.

Wednesday Jan.16,1856

Soon after Breakfast Charley and I
harnessed the horse to the sleigh and
drove down below Roffe's stable.
Charley,Jim Cowens,John Dodd and I piled
a lot of ice at the mouth of the creek. still more ice
Some of it was foot thick. Towards night
Charley & I commenced making a new

string of sleigh bells. Had Fathers,
Roffe's & my dinner bell with another
small bell.

Thursday Jan.17,1856

Soon after breakfast, Charley and I
finished the sleigh and bells & about
Ten o'clock,we started to Guyandotte.   Sleigh ride to show off !
Arrived there before Twelve O'c. took
dinner at Thorn's. Left there after 3
o'clock. Lost the hammers out of three
of the bells. We put on the new string
also lost the bell we borrowed of Roffe.
Went back about 300 yards and found it.
Got home before sundown. Turley hauled
me day before yesterday-what he called
five chord of wood. I had him to chord   a chord =4'X4'x8' of wood
it today. He corded it awful loose and
made it hold out. John Dodd sawed wood
for me little over half a day.

Friday Jan.18,1856

(Finished filling the ice house-4
loads) Just before we finished, Bob
Allen came up here with his horse, and   loaned sleigh
we lent him the sleigh,harness and bells
to take a ride to Guyandotte in. I was
in the store until nine o'clock with
McCullough, Sam Childers, Daniels and
Charley. We had a masonic lecture.
I got six lbs. of beef of John Dick
just at night.   1850 all Dick Ch. scattered
                                           through out neighborhood

Saturday Jan.19,1856

Soon after breakfast, Jim Cowens,
Charley, and I started out for a Deer
hunt. Charley Morris came over about the
same time and started up a fox. Charley, Morris from west side of river
Jim, and I went up Tom's Creek, where we
separated. Jim not meeting us at the
place appointed, Charley and I came down
Tom's Creek to the road. Morris' hounds
and the fox passed over the ridge within
a hundred yards of us. Found Charley and Love's 1m above Martha-west si
Peter Love just below Capt. Jack's   Capt.Jack Peyton
awaiting for it. We came on home. Jim
came about two hours after and said he
saw fresh sign of five.(deer)

Sunday Jan.20,1856

I went down to Bowman's and borrowed four candles.

borrowed candles again

Monday Jan.21,1856

About Seven o'clock. I drove to Barboursville in the sleigh. Met Doct McCullough coming up in the sleigh. got Thomas(Tom) Thornburg to make me out a warrant for the cow that I advertised for an owner. Bought two lbs. of candles of Thompson.

found a cow

Tuesday Jan.22,1856

Bob took the grey horse up there (to the blacksmith FL) and had him shod.(went to B'ville)
I met Sam Johnson coming to the mill with a sled load of grain.

Daniels was blacksmith at Martha
#914 Johnson lived 4-Pole

Wednesday Jan 23,1856

Soon after dinner we fixed ourselves and drove to Barboursville in the sleigh.We there found twenty-six sleighs with ours ready to start to Guyandotte. We started with them. we trotted all the way. passed all but Vandiver and Billy Miller. Just before we got to Guyan Wills Moore and John Miller passed on a run. Vandiver,Billy Miller,Wills Moore,John Miller, & us went in Guyandotte right after one another. The rest came along a while after in a full gallop. We put our horse up at Bumgardner's. We took tea at Moore & Vandivers. All the rest let their horses run but us. About half after six o'c, Charley and I started home. The rest were ready to start. We got to Barboursville first. Drove right through without stopping.
There was a company of Fancifuls turned out while we were in Guyandotte. They called themselves the Raging Tadds. They had drummers and a fife. It was well got up. No two dressed alike. We was just forty minutes trotting from Barboursvlle to Guyandotte.

sleigh race to Guyandotte on east side/no toll

Touring entertainment

40 minute sleigh ride to B'vill

Thursday Jan.24,1856

The river still frozen solid so that it is crossed on the ice with saftey. Bowman ground some buckwheat towards night.

Old Mrs.Butcher moved in the house by the Bridge with Jim Cowens. Bill Fielder came here for Cynthia to go over and see his wife who is sick.

river solid enough to cross
ground different grains

rental house

Friday Jan.25,1856

Robert and Sam crossed the Ohio River on the ice and brought over a trunk of books for Bowman. It belonged to Lee.

Lee moved to Missouri

Saturday Jan.26,1856

Charley and I drove to Barboursville to Magistrates Court. We had a suit with old Rowland Bias, but he put it off.

#103 Bias

There was a sleighing party of 24 sleighs went to Guyan this morning from Barboursville. We returned home just before dark. James Wilkes paid me $5 on his account while I was in town.

#413 Wilks

Sunday Jan,27,1856

After dinner,I copied a piece of writing for Sam Childers.

wrote letters

Monday Jan.28,1856

We had a repleaing suit with Joe Stanley. He cost us. He owed a balance on the rent of nearly four dollars.

Had Charley Morris,Simmons & Turley sworn to value the stray cow we have. Turley rode up with me(from B'ville) after putting the horse away, he and I went down to Father's. They had a falling out & Turley said he would move as soon as he got the corn shucked.

Cornwesley Simmons
Emmereson Turley

Tuesday Jan.29,1856

Bill Fielder hauled some wood for John Fielder.

Wednesday Jan.30,1856

I got a pair of India rubbers for
Cynthia from Mat Thompson's.

boots for rain gear

Thursday Jan.31,1856

I went up on the hill side above
John Dides, and throwed a cord of wood
down to the road.

Friday Feb.1,1856

Turley was to see Father about
keeping the place, but Father told him
he considered he had given up the place
and had accordingly commenced
negotiations with Mat Butcher.

"hard nosed old man"

Saturday Feb.2,1856

About noon Mr.McVickers from the
Ohio River came here and I gave him my
dog Rover.(He and other dogs had been
running Roffe's and our sheep.-FL) Went
down to McCullough's store.

dog chasing sheep

Dr. had a store also
at Martha

Sunday Feb.3,1856

Judy went down to Roffe's this
afternoon.

Monday Feb.4,1856

I received documents this morning
appointing me Post master at Bloomindale
(instead of Roffe & changing the name
back from Ashland to Bloomingdale.)
Mat Butcher was to come here today
& Make an agreement about cultivating
our farm.

gives name of community
as both Ashland & Bloom--

Tuesday Feb.5,1856

Wednesday Feb.6,1856

Sworn in as post master, commenced
the duties,etc. Father and H.H.Wood went
my bond. I took back a pair of boots
Hatfield sent up to Father yesterday.
Then got a pair of shoes of Allen for
him. Got a dollars worth of coffee & a
pound of candles of Mat Thompson. Then
to J & S Miller's and got a dollars

Wood was sheriff

Father so important
merchants sent items on trial

finally bought some candles

worth of sugar for which I paid. Then
drove up the hill to the Dutch Butcher's
and got ---lbs. of beef fat to make
tallow of. Also got my pants of Proctor.
he had them to alter(came home).

    I went down to to Rolfe's and
McCullough surrendered to me the effects
of the Post Office.

also got tallow to make candle

Proctor was a tailor

Thursday Feb.7,1856

    I was in the store most of the day
fixing my desks for my Post Office.
    Bob Allen stopped here in the
morning & I lent him my white overcoat
to wear to the Falls.

rearranged store for
post office

Friday Feb.8,1856

    After dinner, Sam went down with
the mail. There was about a half dozen
letters, among them my bond adn oath as
Post master. He brought five letters and
a few papers.

Saturday Feb.9,1856

    Higgins cut wood for me all day.

had to have money, everyone
worked for them

Sunday Feb.10,1856

    I wrote a letter for Mother to
J.Spencer Jones about Godey's lady's
Book, also one to the Editor of the
American Free Mason.

Monday Feb.11,1856

    Rec'd a letter from Uncle Francis
Moore. Robert took the mail down about
nine O'c. there was quite a number of
letters. He returned just as a squall
came up with quite a large mail of
Letters & quite a large mail of letters
& quite a number of papers.

Uncle Francis Moore

Tuesday Feb.12,1856

    (I) Had my mail made up(four
letter) & waited for the Logan mail to
come down, but it not coming, I came in
the house.

4 letters was average

Wednesday Feb.13,1856

The Logan mail came down about Ten
O'clock, the carrier was on foot. His
horse fell yesterday and left him about
five miles above here. He returned from
Town about Two O'c. There was not much
mail for me. The store was full most of
the time. Among the rest in the forenoon
was Shannon one of the editors of the
Guyandotte Hearld.

Logan mail carrier had to
walk about 5m with he fell
from horse

editor of Guyan- Herald

Thursday Feb.14,1856

I went to Barboursville in my
sleigh. I tried every place to buy some
sugar, but could get none,but a little I
begged of Mat Thompson.
    There is to be a ball at the Bill
Merritt's tonight. He wanted me to come
down but I told him I could not.(came
home)
    Found J.C.Wheeler here, He is going
to stay all night.

no sugar in B'ville

fancy ball at Bill Merritt's
Merritt #106 s/o #40

Wheeler first editor of GH

Friday Feb.15,1856

Saturday Feb,16,1856

The river has been slowly rising
all day.All the mills(corn & wheat) ran
all night.

Sunday Feb.17,1856

I am afraid the mills can not run
tomorrow.(River too high)

river in flood

Monday Feb.18,1856

Matthew Butcher and Father made
their arragements for Butcher to take
the farm next year.

Butcher leased farm

Tuesday Feb.19,1856

The Logan mail did not come down.

Wednesday Feb.20,1856

The Logan mail came up about Nine
O'c. He went down last night without
stopping.

Morris' hounds ran a deer in last night. It got fast in the ice on the river below Roffe's and his niggers got it out and killed it.

deer frozen in river

We received a letter this morning from Uncle Cale written by Eliza Ann Slagg.

Uncle Cale

Thursday Feb.23,1856

Friday Feb.22,1856

This being the birthday of Washington the first thing I did this morning was to raise my flag. Sent a letter to Uncle Cale containing $5.00.

sent money to uncle

Saturday Feb.23,1856

Sunday Feb.24,1856

Monday Feb.25,1856

I was summoned on a jury. Tried two cases between Hanley's heirs,Parrish and others.

Tuesday Feb.26,1856

The Logan mail came down just at night. I sent two letters in it. Bought a work stand of the Dutch cabinet maker in Town(FL Godfrey Espy). Gave him $2.50 in middlings for it.

traded hog feed(middlings) for a work stand

Wednesday Feb.27,1856

The Logan mail came up about nine O'c. There was not much for me. Received nine dollars worth of stamps from the Post office department. I went out on the hill by Roffe's line fence, and measured some wood that John Dodd had been cutting. There was six & 3/4 cords.

maybe 1,000 stamps ?

Thursday Feb.28,1856

Mat Butcher came here towards night and Father hired him the Higgins house at $12 for this year.

rented another house

After Breakfast, Robert and I went
up the road to hunt the horses. Found
them in Higgin's field.
Bill Fielder commenced to grubbing   removing stumps for $2.50a
a piece of land for us at $2.50 an acre
on the hillside below where he lived
last summer. Dave Stanley moved in the
same house this afternoon.

Saturday March 1,1856

I received $8.00 worth of stamped
envelopes, also a notice of acceptance
from P.O.Department of Charley as mail   got Charley job as mail carrie
contractor.

Sunday March 2,1856

Monday March 4,1856

Tuesday March 4,1856

The Logan mail came down towards
night.

Wednesday March 5,1856

The Logan mail came up early. There
was considerable mail for me among the
rest the report of the Patent office and
some seeds sent by Carlisle M.C. Sam and   M.C. mean mail carrier ??
Aunt Nancy went down to Guyandotte on
horseback. Jeff Butcher hauled two loads
of corn in his wagon.

Thursday March 6,1856

Friday March 7,1856

Saturday March 8,1856

Bill(Fielder) started to town with   sent beef hide to tannery
the beef hide.(We killed and ox.)   in B'ville

Sunday March 9,1856

Anna,Susie,and Caley, went to
preaching down at Bowman's this morning.

Monday March 10,1856

Tuesday March 11,1856

March 11,1856

Judy had gone to Roffe's for a
quilting.

quilting bee(slaves ?)

Wednesday March 12,1856

I pulled a tooth for one of the
Mr.Crumps.

#929 or #956

Thursday March 13,1856

I took the shot gun and went in the
pasture to shoot some pigeons. Was there
some time but only shot one.

passenger pidgeons ??

Soon after the Steamer Adrian came
up with a flat boat in tow. Robert & I
went over in the corn field to shoot
some pidgeons. He shot two and I six.
John Dick paid Father $5.00.
Charley was out in the afternoon trying
to shoot some pidgeons. He only shot
one. Bill Fielder had the wagon and
cattle all day moving Mat Butcher down
to the house Turley moved from yesterday

Saturday March 15,1856

Rode to Barboursville. took tea at
Bloom's Went to Lodge. John Thornburg, &
Geo.W.Cox initiated. We adjourned hall
after nine O'c. & went to Methodist
meeting. The Steamer Adrian passed down
this evening. She stopped at the mill
and took on some flour and meal for
Wheeler.

Cox #54

Sunday March 16,1856

The old Revolutioner Gillenwaters
died at Howell's this morning.

Gillenwaters death   98
1850 #434 next to Howell
near Roach

Monday March 17,1856

Charley and I went out to the
cornfield to shoot some pigeons. I sent
a letter to Uncle Cale with $5.00.
Father sent an ad to the Kanawha
Repulican for a carder.

Uncle Cale $5 more

Tuesday March 18,1856

The Logan mail went down just at
night.

Wednesday March 19,1856

The Logan mail carrier brought up
my mail. Bill Fielder moved in the house
he lived in last summer.

Thursday March 20,1856

H.H.Wood was up here and offered
$75 for the Bill horse.

Friday March 21,1856

Mat Butcher had a corn shucking.
He had quite a number of hands. He got
the corn nearly all shucked.

neighbors gathered to
help shuck corn-social-

Saturday March 22,1856

Mat Butcher had three yoke cattle
all day until three o'clock hauling
wood. We had a suit with old Roland
Bias, but he put it off again. Juda went
to attend Church. Bill Fielder sent Dave
Stanley to feed the cattle, he having
gone to the Falls of Guyan.

Sunday March 23,1856

About four o'clock, Father sent for
me. I went and found Lawyer English. I
remained there until nearly night.
English staid to tea there and will
remain all night. Juda returned just as
we were having tea.

Thomas Dunn English
"a real dude"-poet etc.

Monday March 24,1856

Mr.English came up to the store
and took down our evidence in our
different suits in the Superior Court.
John Fielder and Rains hauled seven
loads (of corn) for us in our wagon.

Tuesday March 25,1856

The Logan mail went down just at
dawn.

Wednesday March 26,1856

The Logan Mail passed up this
morning. Mr.English came here and I went

down to Father's with him. He took
dinner there & Alex Samuels took dinner
with me.The Steamer Adrian passed up.
 A fellow by the name of Mays moved
in the place at the mouth of Tom's Creek
today.

Mays-mouth Tom's Ck

Thursday March 27,1856

 John Thornburg came up here for
Charley and Bryan(Bryne-FL) to go down
to an exhibition at the academy on the
Ohio River tonight. Steamer Adrian
passed down just before night.(I sent
for the Life of John Bunyan) I went down
to Roffe's and brought up a hive of bees
that Father had bought of Nigger Ben.

Marshall Academy

honey for sweets

Saturday March 29,1856

 Mat Butcher shelled a wagon load of
corn on our shelling machine. Judy went
over to Morris's to meeting and did not
return when we retired little after Ten
O'clock.

hand cranked corn sheller

Negro meeting at Morris'

Sunday March 30,1856

 About 3 o'clock, Caley & I took a
walk up to Mat Butcher's. Cynthia and
the children were down to Mrs.Cowen's.

Monday March 31,1856

 Robert,Anna,and Caley started to
Barboursville with the mail. He also
took Cynthia's carpet rags to have wove.

saved rags to make rug

Tuesday April 1,1856

 Mays worked for us. The Steamer
Adrain about one o'clock. The Logan mail
passed down just at night. There is a
gentleman at Father's from Cincinnati to
see about lumber. The Logan mail went up
this morning. I and Mays ran my garden
fence up to the old Blacksmith shop. Let
Dr. McCullough have two yoke of cattle
this morning to haul hoop poles. The
Steamer Adrian passed up just at night.

says"old blacksmith's"

used to make barrel hoops

Thursday April 3,1856

The Steamer Adrian passed down just at night. I sent a barrel of Flour down on her to Thorn.

barrels used to transport about everything

Aunt Nancy, Miss Youle, & Miss Ball came here in the afternoon to see Cynthia. They all staid for tea.

Friday April 4,1856

Harvey Smith went down to Roffe's and got a hive of bees for Father.

another hive of bees

Anna received a letter from Caroline Slocum.

former servant

Saturday April 5,1856

Mother brought up for me(From Guyan) a thousand segars that I engaged from a man in Wheeling.

Mother went to town wife never did

Sunday April 6,1856

After dinner Charley,Robert,Anna, Susey,Caley & I took a walk up as far as the old School House.

Monday April 7,1856

While I was gone(up the road to this side of Bill Fielders) Sarah got down to Mrs.Cowens. Her youngest boy playing with a hatchet(cut 1/2 inch of the middle finger of Sarah's left hand.

daughter had an accident

Tuesday April 8,1856

Doctor English(FL_Thos.E.Dunn) stopped here on his way to Superior Court which commenced today.

An honorary title ??

Wednesday April 9,1856

Thursday April 10,1856

(Went to B'ville-Took dinner at Bloom's. Charley started in the Buggy to Guyandotte(Sam Johnson also)Just as they left Conwelzie & Bill Simmons came in Town with Charley Morris's Nigger who ran off last Sunday. He had offered a reward of a hundred dollars & he was caught in Ohio & put in Greenup jail in

runaway slave caught big reward

Ky. Joe Nagle's daughter Susan died today in New York.

Cynthia sister m Nagle

Friday April 11,1856

We had the first mess of fish this season for supper.

fresh fish

Saturday April 12,1856

The case of Walden Beach against Father was called and laid over.

Sunday April 13,1856

Metting at Bowman's this morning. After dinner, I went over and put a Locke on the house John Dick moved from last week. Cynthia went up to Mrs. Daniels on a few minutes. The Steamer Adrian passed up about nine o'clock.

another rental house

Monday April 14,1856

Set a turkey on 25 hen eggs. (Verdict against Walden Beach for $28.00) The Steamboat came down and left a lot of wheat for Thornburg in Miller's boat above the mill.
I got eight yards of Calico from Miller for Judy a dress.

dress material for servant

Tuesday April 15,1856

I rode to Town was around the Court House until near noon when I received a message from Louisa Dusenberry to come to her mothers. I went there. Found her in a lot of trouble. Yesterday, she and Thorn attempted to lick their nigger & she licked them. Thorn got ready immediately to start with her to Louisville to sell her and Louisa came up here . This morning she heard he had not got off yet & wanted me to go down and persuade him not to sell her,but it was too late.

Mother(Mrs.Martin Moore)

whip slave but failed sell her

wanted Wm. to interfer

Wednesday April 16,1856

I rode to Barboursville, Stewart's suit against us was laid over. I went to Mrs.Moore's a while and saw Thorn's wife. Then to Merritt's Tavern and saw

another law suit

English. Took dinner with him. Took tea
at Father's. Lawyer English also took
tea there.(He staid all night at
Father's.)

Thursday April 17,1856

Mr.English was here till about Ten
when he left for Logan. Judy went down
to help Thorn. He returned from Sandy
yesterday having sold his she nigger
Martha to old Fred Moore for $750, But I
persuaded him to try to back out when he
came after her   on account of Louisa
being so much opposed to parting with
her. They took Judy with them to help a
week until they got some help.

Lawyer to Logan

Thorn sold slave

Friday April 18,1856

Mat Butcher was running a fence
through the pasture by the house John
Dick moved from.

Saturday April 19,1856

Peter Love's nigger boy was drowned
this morning. He was fishing and is
supposed to have fallen in. No one saw
him. His hat lay by the shore and his
body was found close by. Peter gave $115
($715 I think-FL)for him last fall.
    Went to lodge. There was quite a
number present. Passed John W.Thornburg.
McCullough, Sam Childers,Simmons and I
rode home together.

slave drowned

attended lodge

Sunday April 20,1856

Monday April 21,1856

McCullough's boat load of hoop
poles passed down the river toward
night. Mat Butcher & Raines hauled me a
load of manure.

Tuesday April 22,1856

Wednesday April 23,1856

Thursday April 24,1856

George Hatfield brought me some
onion sets this morning.

#311 Hatfield

18

Friday April 25, 1856

Siders was here all day with his stud horse.

Usually one stud in area / Women kept in the house

Saturday April 26, 1856

Took tea with Bob Allen, after which we went to Lodge. had a called meeting to make arrangements for our celebration on St.John's Day(24th June) (Motion to postpone it provided Grand Master consented).David Harshbarger offered me $50 to let our carding machine stand idle this season.

offer   leave machine idle / carding machine cleaned woo

Sunday April 27, 1856

John Fielder moved this morning. John Fielder moved out of the old School House, this morning.

"old school house"

Monday April 28, 1856

Leven Swann took dinner with me. The Steamer Adrian passed up this afternoon.

leaved near Smith Ck

Tuesday April 29, 1856

Charley was all forenoon working in the saw mill for Morris. The Steamer Adrian went down just at night.(Also the Logan mail just at night.)

Charley ran sawmill for Morris

Wednesday April 30, 1856

Webster the carder came back here this afternoon.

Webster had moved

Thursday May 1, 1856

Sam went down after the mail about none o'clock. Susie rode down on the horse with him. They went to a Sunday School Concert and did not return home until the middle of the afternoon.

concert at Sunday School

Friday May 2, 1856

I gigged a fine large Black Perch under the saw mill this morning. The first fish I have caught this season.

gig-type of fish spear

Simmons returned from Portsmouth where
he went to get the crank wrist turned,
they had cast last fall.

foundry at Portsmouth

Saturday May 4,1856

Sunday May 5,1856

I took a walk to the upper end of
the farm.

Monday May 5,1856

Miss Youle commenced School again
this morning. Sam attended this morning
and Susie all day.

teacher

Tuesday May 6,1856

Judy came home with Thorn. After
dinner, he borrowed the grey horse & my
saddle and bridle and started to Logan
to buy a nigger. The mill has been
pretty thronged with grain for the last
two days. Just before dark, the Steamer
Adrian passed up. She brought three kegs
of nails for us. I took them off in the
skiff.

Thorn to Logan to buy slave

Wednesday may 7,1856

The Logan mail went up this
morning. Cynthia went over to
Mrs.Love's. She came home to tea.

Love lived east of river

Thursday May 8, 1856

Clark from Guyan came up here just
before noon to get the refusal of the
saw mill when Morris & Simmons' time
expires. he took dinner at Father's and
left soon after.
The Steamer Adrian passed down. She
stopped and took Webster,the carder's
trunks on board. He left soon after.

Friday May 9,1856

Thorn returned from Logan just
before noon. He did not buy any nigger.

Saturday May 10,1856

River so high(raised 3ft last
night) that the mills all stopped. I
went to Mrs. Merritts and got Cynthia's
carpet. McCullough returned from
Cincinnati.

flood

carpet made by hand

Sunday May 11,1856

There was a meeting in the School
House this morning.

Monday May 12,1856

Siders was here all day with his
stud horse, Russian Dunn.

name of horse-stud

Tuesday May 13,1856

Bob Allen was at the Blacksmith
Shop. He came down with me to the store.
He the went over to the Locke and put
timber through till night.

Wednesday May 14,1856

The Logan mail went up this
morning. The Steam Adrian passed up just
at night with a flat boat in tow.

Thursday May 15,1856

Friday May 16,1856

In the afternoon, Sam Johnson came
up here with some hands to take up the
remains of his first wife who was buried
in our grave yard.

mentions graveyard
reported two in area
both disappeared

Saturday May 17,1856

Sunday May 18,1856

There was a Sunday School here this
morning,but the leaders failed to
attend.

Monday May 19,1856

I went up in my garden to work
awhile, but was soon called to fill some
teeth for Godfrey Scites' wife. He paid

#443 from Salt Rock

me $2.50(Went to B'ville).We was around
Town until just at night when Vertigan
came with the box from New York.(FL-
Edward Vertigan was a school teacher in
B'ville. A brother of his also lived
there.Was this when he first came to
B'ville ? Or did he just bring a box to
B'ville ?)

teacher
box of fruit,etc. from NY

Tuesday May 20,1856

Wolcott(Augustus-FL) and John W.
Hite were up here this morning.(From
Guyandotte-FL) West Smith paid me $.50
for pulling a tooth some time ago.
Charley & I planted some potatoes I
received from New York in the box.
(Oranges & lemons were rotten.)

Wolcott #795
Hite #793
Smith #679

Wednesday May 21,1856

The Logan mail came up early-about
eight o'clock.

Thursday May 22,1856

This is election day. A great many
went down. Made a zinc cast for
McCullough, I voted for W.B.Moore for
sheriff, Isaac Ong for Assessor,
Thornburg(FL-Thomas),Merritt, Sam
A.Childers, and Poage for Magistrates
and (Evan-FL)Bloom for overseer of the
poor. Simmons, H.H.Wood, and myself went
to see the tavern keepers but came to no
agreement. (Lodge St.John's
entertainment). There was a great deal
of fighting in town today notwith-
standing the grog shops were all closed.
I saw a fight between Morris Newman and
Rains & was called before a Magistrate
to give evidence.

#671 Newman
Reins #411 ??

Friday May 23,1856

Col.Webb(of Guyandotte) took dinner
with me. I could not get any reliable
returns from the election.
The Steamer Major Adrian passed up
this morning. Fished a while towards
night. Charley caught a fine salmon two
feet long.

Saturday May 24, 1856

Went to Court. Bill Merritt(a magistrate) was setting our case with Roland Bias. He tried to put it off. (Had done so 3-4 times.)

W.B.Moore was elected sheriff by only 8-7 majority.(John)Laidley, Attorney, Thomas Thornburg,William Merritt, Sam A.Childers & Whitten-magistrates.

#739 Whitten

Sunday May 25, 1856

Mrs.Cox came up to see Cynthia a while in the forenoon. The children all went to Sunday School up in the School House.

Monday May 26, 1856

County Court today. All the magistrates on the bench. Went to Bloom's and then to the Lodge. Sam Johnson,John Everett,Beekman and Peters was there for Guyandotte. They killed my resolution to have a celebration on 24th of June. Initiated Charley Everett. After the Lodge ajourned we took a couple of side degrees.

#174 Beecham + Beekman ??

#306 Everett

Tuesday May 27, 1856

The Steamer Adrian passed down about the middle of the afternoon. She left some wheat to be ground for Blankenship(FL-E.W.) Logan mail went up this morning.

Wednesday May 28 1856

Thursday May 29, 1856

There was a letter for Charley from John Laidley stating he had some notes of John Garrison's endorsed by Charley and wanted him to make arragements to pay them. They amount to nearly $500.

Father was out sailing with Charley & Robert(In their shiff).

brothers took boat

Friday May 30, 1856

(Went to see John Laidley about the notes. Took Jeff Samuels) He inquired particulars and expressed the idea they could not make Charley pay them.

The Steamer Adrian Passed up this morning.

lawyer #1011

Saturday May 31, 1856

Borrowed Mrs. Bowman's spinning wheel for Judy to spin some yarn in the afternoon. I went over to the house where the Frenchman used to live. The Steamer Adrian passed down just at night.

each house spun yarn

(Donnet) see '55

Sunday June 1, 1856

There was Sunday School in the forenoon. Anna and Susie went. Judy went to town to church. She came home just before dark.

Monday June 2, 1856

Tuesday June 3, 1856

The Steamer Adrian came up about one o'clock. She left 6000 shingles for us. Just at dark Charley and I set the (fish) net. The Logan mail went down about the middle of the afternoon.

Wednesday June 4, 1856

About nine O'c, Bill Fielder and I went around in the first hollow with Dick Lunsford and looked at a bed of iron ore. The Steamer Adrian came down about the middle of the afternoon, and is going to lay in the Locke until morning to take Passengers to the show at Guyandotte tomorrow. Roffe's hands washed a lot of sheep below the mill just at night.

#415 Lunsford

washed sheep for agricultural show B'ville

Thursday June 5, 1856

The steamer Adrian left early with quite a number of Passengers going down to Guyan to see the show. Roffe washed his sheep here, and Charley Morris washed his on the other side of the

river.(A show at Guyandotte tonight.
Robert,Anna, and Sam went.

Friday June 6,1856

Siders here all day with his horse.
The Steamer Adrian came up about noon.

Sunday June 8,1856

Preaching on the School House this
morning. Also Sunday School. Cynthia,
Susie, Anna and Caley went.

Monday June 9,1856

Tuesday June 10,1856

The Logan mail came down about four
O'clock.

Wednesday June 11,1856

(Two men-Wells & Heck came here in
a buggy with a model of a circular saw
for sawing Fellour(?-FL). They asked
$500 for the county rights & a machine
but come down to take $300- and give
$150 for the grey horse, balance in two
years). Clark(of Guyandotte) had a
contract for the mill next year so we
agreed to see him. We went to Guyandotte
I put up at Bumgardners, They at Union
Hotel. Clark was working on R.R. back of
Ashland. We waited till near Ten o'clock
& then took boat to Ashland-The Steamer
Aurilla Wood. Arrived at midnight,put up
at the Broadway House.

Union Hotel

Broadway House at Ashland

Thursady June 12,1856

(Found Clark about 3mi. out of
Ashland. Also saw Monroe at work in a
Blacksmith Shop. His wife looks bad.
They live at Ashland.

Friday June 13,1856

My expense to Ashland & back was
$4.25.(Father & Heck traded. He started
to Guyan with the horse.)

fare to Ashland $4.25

Saturday June 14,1856

Went to Lodge, John Thornburg was
raised. McCullough was elected Master,
Bloom,S.W. & I.J.W.,Charley S.D.,
Daniels, J.D., Fetter,Treasurer,Wood,S.   lodge
Egger,Tyler.George William & Green
Harrison petitions were handed in.

Sunday June 15,1856

There was Sunday School in the
School House. The children went all but
Sarah. I wrote a Letter for Father to
Aunt Lucy.

Monday June 16,1856

Wrote a letter to Aunt Lucy and   Aunt Lucy & Uncle JOhn
Uncle John. Charley,Sam and I hauled our
shingles from above the Blacksmith shop
with the cattle and wagon & put them
inthe Grist Mill. Vertigans came up here
and made a trade for Charley Morris's
big Spring wagon.

Tuesday June 17,1856

Just at noon, the Steamer Adrian
camp up. She brought the saw we bought
of Heck & Wells.(They are to send the
other saw.)

Wednesday June 18,1856

The Logan mail passed up about
Eight O'c.(I started in the buggy to the
Falls. Had dinner there at Blankenship's   Falls near Branchland
after which I went with him to his
store. I am to send him 20bu. meal at
$.40 a bu. by boat Friday, he paying the
freight. I stopped at Jerome Shelton's   6m above Martha
(FL-now West Hamlin) got 4 Shangheigh
hens of his wife. The Steamer Adrian
passed down about noon.

Thursday June 19,1856

We heard today that a man by the   accidental death-saw mill
name of Ward was sawed up in the
Buffington Mill. His head was sawed in
two killing him instantly. Father quite
poorly.(FL-He has been in poor health a
long time.) Just before noon, the
Steamer Adrian came up, and we put 20bu.

of meal on her for Blankenship at the
Falls. She had quite a number of
passengers, Jeff Samuels, Thos. Thornburg,
Docts. McCorkle & Ricketts, Nat Adams,
Wolcott & others. Roffe had a mowing
machine come up on the boat.

horse drawn mower

Saturday June 21, 1856

Rec'd a letter from Uncle Cale.
Bowman caught a fine salmon in the
flume. the Steamer Adrian came down
about three O'c. Samuels & Adams came
ashore, and I gave them some ice, then
put them on board in the shiff after she
came through the Locke.

Sunday June 22, 1856

(Had a swarm of bees. I was down at
Fathers. Heard Cynthia screaming & ran
home & found my bees swarming. Charley
came up and helped me hive them, by
throwing water among them. I got them to
settle on one of my peach trees. We cut
the limb off, and got them hived.)
There was Sunday School in the School
House this morning.

Monday June 23, 1856

I went to Barboursville to
quarterly court. I went to Bloom's and
took my dinner. After which I went to
Hibbens and partly traded for his yellow
wagon with a yoke of cattle for part
pay. I went to Bob Allen's and got 34yds
of domestic.
    Charley Shipe and three others came
here with an order from Thos. Thornburg
for to borrow Charley's seine. I asw
Charley, then let them have it.

Hibbens-wagonmaker

plain cloth-cheap

seine-fish net

Tuesday June 24, 1856

Charley Shipe and the other fellows
that borrowed Charley's seine came in
town just at night with the fish they
had caught in Mud River. they number
over 700. They gave me four or five, one
of which weighed about twenty lbs. As I
had no way to get them home, I swapped
them to Bloom for a piece of beef.

700 fish in seine
20lb

Went to Lodge. Bloom and I took the
Past Masters degree, After the Lodge
adjourned, we conferred some side
degress.(Sam Childers and I walked
home.)

Wednesday June 25,1856

About two o'clock, The Steamer
Adrian came up. She laid by the
Blacksmith shop about one hour, then she
dropped to the log way & I put on board
twenty 20bu. of meal for Blankenship.
She then started up the river.

Thursday,June 26,1856

Friday, June,27 1856.

The steamboat returned about Twelve
o clock.She was unable to the Falls(I
carried our meal back up in the mill.)

Saturday,June 28,1856

Col. Webb passed here going up
about the middle of the afternoon.I got
an order from him to Cook the Lock   Cook was lock keeper
keeper below here for him to let off
the water so that our mills could run.
About four o clock I drove down there
stopped in Barboursville,on my return   barter
and closed with Hibbins about the wagon
(Price $110,$80 for yoke of cattle, $30
in flour.

Saturday June 28,1856

(We brought the wagon home.)

Sunday June 29,1856

About ten o'clock, the niggers
began to flock here in droves .Uncle Tom   Uncle Tom belonged to
preached the funeral sermon of Love's   Everett at Guyandotte
nigger that was drowned. There was about   boy drowned 4 moth ago
twenty of them that stopped here before
and after the meeting.Judy went with
them and then some returned and took
dinner with her. After they left,
another squad came & Judy went over to
Morris's with them, and they all stopped
as they came back to drink. They have
only drunk three pails of ice water for

me today. Thorn's nigger girl and her
child was among the rest up here to
meeting.

Thorn bought slave

Monday June 30, 1856

Trade dull all day.

Tuesday July 1, 1856

The Logan mail went down about the
middle of the afternoon.

Wednesday July 2, 1856

The Logan mail came up about eight
o'clock. About three o'clock Bob & Sam
started to Seven Mile for a girl.(Didn't
get her).Mills nearly stopped by back
water so high on account of Locke below
being closed.

Thursday July 3, 1856

Father & I went up to Peter Love's
& saw Charley Morris about the mill
rent. Two quarters are due today. He was
cutting wheat with his machine.
        Col.Webb stopped here a while. We
talked plenty hard to him about the
water being backed on us. Doctor Moss
brought me $8.00 sent by Blankenship.

Webb head of Guyan- Navigation
argued about water backup

paid on milling bill

Friday July 4, 1856

Charley & Robert fired the cannon &
raised our flag early. We had fried
chicken and some new potatoes for dinner
with green apple pie.

Saturday July 5, 1856

Bloom's wagon came up here for ice.
Allen's nigger was with it. He came for
the yoke of cattle we sold him. I went
in the pasture to show them to the
nigger but could not find them.
        Just after dark, Bill Fielder came
down the road driving my red cow having
found her with a calf up one of the
hollows. She had been gone three of four
days.(FL-Hogs often ran wild in the
woods & were hunted up at killing time.)

Sunday July 6,1856

Soon after dinner, Sam started on horseback to the Seven Mile for mother's girl. About two o'clock, Cynthia went over to Charley Morris's with Mrs. Daniels to see Mrs.Uhl who is sick.(FL-Who was Mrs.Uhl?) Sam returned with the girl and maid just at dark.

7 Mile north ofB'ville toward Ohio River

Uhl=Youle ??

Monday July 7,1856

Trade awful dull.

Tuesday July 8,1856

The Steamer Adrian came up here. She brought six flour barrels for us. She will lay below the mill until morning then start back to the Guyan with passengers to the circus there tomorrow. The Logan mail went down about the middle of the afternoon.

Circus

Wednesday July 9,1856

The Steamer Adrian left here with a few passengers about 8 o'clock. Daniels & wife went down. Susie rode down with me. I left her at Mrs.Holderbee's.The Steamboat passed while we were there. A great many went to the show. The Logan mail carrier came up this morning. I paid him the amount due the Post Office Department,being $159.00.
    Had not been in bed but a few minutes when the Steamer Adrian came up and went right back. A young man working for Hiltbruner was killed by one of the circus men tonight.

Thursday July 10,1856

Trade awful dull.

Friday July 11,1856

Saturday July,1856

About noon considerable grain came to the mill. Went to Lodge. Charley Everett was raised to a F.C

Sunday July 13,1856

There was preaching in the School House. Cynthia, Anna, and Susie went. Miss Uhl(school teacher ?FL) came home with them and staid to dinner and most of the afternoon. Anna went home with her and returned before dark.

Monday July 14,1856

In extracting a tooth for Lewis Rains, two came out insetead of one.

Tuesday July 15,1856

The Logan mail carrier came down about four o'clock. Went to Guyandotte. Stopped in B'ville and got Jeff Samuels. Got down there about 8 o'clock. The Chapter met and gave me the Mark Master's degree. Jeff Samuels,Bob Allen,Jerome Shelton & Jeff's brother-in-law rode up with us.We got home about 3 o'clock.(Beautiful night.)

Wednesday July 16,1856

The Logan mail went up about nine o'clock. Webb passed here about noon. I had a jaw with him about the backwater.   jaw=talk
(He could only grind about 1/3 of what he should.)
    Mrs.Morse & Love here & spent the   Morse=Morris
afternoon with Cynthia. After tea, I set them over the river. Grist mill grinds very slow on account of the backwater.   spelling has variety

Thursday July 17,1856

Bill Fielder & Mat Butcher worked 3/4 day(Today). Rode to Barboursville on horseback. Rode to Jeff Samuels house, got an order from him to Cook(the Locke Keeper) to open the Locke at the mouth of Mud & keep it down two feet, then I went down and gave it to Cook, then came back to Town and bought 16yds of   muslin for sheets
bleached muslin at $.12 1/2 a yd. Pr.of Boots at $5.00,Broom & two yards of Ribbon of Allen. Came home about noon. I   Allen's store was Dry Goods ?
was around home all afternoon. The water below the dam had commenced falling

before I came home. The mill is crammed
full of grain. A great deal came in
today.(Bill Fielder & Mat Butcher more
than 1/2 day cutting grass in Father's
yard.)(FL-must have used a sickle)

Friday July 18,1856

Saturday July 19,1856

Soon after dinner, there was three
or four fellow came here from Mud River
to have some music with Charley. They
staid until after five o'clock.(Went to
Guyandotte.)I was around the hotels
there until after ten o'clock when I
went to the chapter and took Past
Master' degree.   lodge degree

Sunday July 20,1856
+
There was Sunday School this
morning. Judy went to Town this morning
and was gone all day.

Monday July 21,1856

I went over to Charley Morrises to
see if we could get some of money from   east of B'ville in
him.(Got none) When I got home, I found Big Bend of river
Sites & his wife here.

Tuesday July 22,1856

Jim (Cowens) and I went Down to
Dave Thornburg's & got a load of straw
to put on our ice.   east of b'ville in
I rode on horseback up to Calvary   big bend of Guyandotte 3m
Swann's,pulled 3 teeth,1each for two   #426 Swann
children & one for himself. $1.50 for three teeth
Several wagons and two canoe loads
of grain came in the mill today. The
Logan mail went down about four o'clock.
I got $1.50 for pulling the teeth for
Swann's. As I passed Mat Butcher's he
had all the old timber on fire in the
field above his house & fire had got in forest fire
the woods on this side of the house.

Wednesday July 23,1856

The Logan mail came up about eight
o'clock.(Sam went to town & got a
setting of 13 Shanghai chicken eggs that
                                         set hen eggs

Doct Peyton had left at Allen's for me.
four or five wagon loads of grain,
principally corn, came in.

Thursday July 24,1856

I pulled two teeth for Uncle Dick's   slave ??
little girl. Bill Fielder hunted part of
the forenoon for the cattle to haul me
some wood, but could not find them.
Bloom came up this morning and got
125lbs. of ice and 5bu.meal.

Friday July 25,1856

Saturday July 26,1856

I withdrew our suit against Wood,
the carpenter, and laid over the one
against Wilks.

Sunday July 27,1856

(Went to Simmons) Sam Childers,West
Childers & Peter Love's brother was
there and rode down with us. A wagon
load of corn came to the mill just after
dark.

Monday July 28,1856

I went over to Morrises and Simmons
paid me $100 on account of the quarter's
rent of the saw mill due the 2nd of
April last.Wilson Moore & Fred Miller   caught suspected murderer
went by here just before noon with the
fellow that killed Hiltbruner's
apprentice in Guyandotte some time
since. A man by the name of Blackwood   Blackwood drowned
was drowned in Mud.

Friday July 29,1856

The Logan mail went down about four
o'clock. Young William Hensley died this William Hensley died
morning.

Wednesday July 30,1856

Soon after breakfast, The Logan
mail came up. (FL tailor) Mather's cut
me a pair of thin pants.   light weight summer

Thursday July 31,1856

Charley, Jim Cowens,Rains and Mat
Butcher went up to hunt our cattle.
Several came to Mill today,who
promised to let off the water from Smith
Creek dam tonight. Ambrose Smith
borrowed a saddle to ride up there on
purpose. Mat Butcher & Rains was out
nearly all day, but did not find any
cattle. Harvey Smith and his brother was
all day digging Father's well.(Pd Jeff
Samuels the $100 Father borrowed & $4.00
interest-from 9th of this month.)

#679 Smith

#357 Harvey Smith ??

Friday August 1,1856

(Water low,100's of bu.of grain in
mill waiting to be ground. Several
wagons left. Col.Webb was there (at
Father's) he and I had some hard words.
He accused us of hiring men to let off
the water from the upper lockes. I told
him it was false.(see above) Just as I
was eating my supper,John Peyton came
down by here as hard as he could go on
horseback. He said Sam Stanley had shot
his wife. Doct. McCullough soon passed &
we all prepared ourselves with arms to
take Stanley. Bob & I started on
horseback up to Mat Butcher's
ascertaining they had all gone out, Bob
turned back home, I went on to the house
& saw Stanley's wife. She is Mat
Butcher's daughter. The ball entered
from behind & passed through the thigh
bone & has lodged some where in the leg.
Doct.McCullough returned home just at
dark. I walked down having let Jim
Cowens have my horse and pistol to join
in the hunt.

Real hassel over height of
water in river

Sam Stanley shot wife

man hunt for Stanley

Mat Butcher's daughter

Saturday August 2,1856

No one has been able to see any
thing of Sam Stanley yet. Soon after
dinner, Mat Butcher,Dick Lunsford, and a
lot of others came down here and I drew
up a subscription paper for them
offering a reward for any one to deliver
Stanley to the sheriff of this county.
There was nearly $150 subscribed right
around here and they went on to Town
with the paper. Just at dark Mat & Jeff

neighborhood raised reward

Butcher, Rains and Perry Peyton stopped
here a few moments.
Jeff Butcher borrowed Charley's
yauger. They started up to Jim Morrises
to watch there for Sam Stanley if he
should attempt to cross there.

yauger=gun
everyone got his gun
river ford

Sunday Aug.3,1856

Soon after breakfast, I went up to
Sam Childers & got my revolver. Soon
after Jeff Butcher sent down for it.
Charley re-loaded it and I started to
Mat's with it. Met Jeff coming after it
and gave it to him.

Monday Aug.4,1856

Harvey Smith helped me run two
stones on corn. Did not grind any wheat.
Three wagon loads of wheat came here
towards night & they had to go to the
Steam Mill at Guyandotte.
Smith and another man staid
there(at mill) all night.

Tuesday Aug.5,1856

Smith started the corn stone
running. I then started the burr on
corn. Sam Childers & John Dick commenced
shingling the grist mill.
The Logan mail went down about four
o'clock.

Wednesday Aug.6,1856

The water rose considerable in the
road caused by letting the water out of
the ponds above.
Intelligence was heard of Sam
Stanley and about noon a party started
out to see if they could take him. The
Logan mail went up this morning.

finally enough water
to grind

Thursday August 7,1856

Was summoned with rest of the lodge
to attend the funeral of Brother Henry
Clark at Guyandotte tomorrow(Fri.Aug.8)
morning.
Charley & Robert returned early
this morning with the rest of the party
that was out all night. Hunting Sam

death

Stanley. They did not see or hear anything of him.

Doctor McCullough came here and told us that a Dr.Williams had just come to Roffe's with the intelligence that a Sam Stanley had been taken in Boone County. The sheriff jerked his rifle off his shoulder when Sam ran and he shot him through the thigh very near the same place he shot his wife. Daniels,Jim Cowens and I started right up to Butchers with the news. Found Mat home and a number there all of whom were pleased but afraid the news was too good to be true.

Stanley shot same place he shot wife

Friday Aug.8,1856

About six o'clock Charley & I started in our wagon for Guyandotte to attend Henry Clark's funeral. Stopped at Barboursville a few moments. They had nearly all gone from there. Tom Thornburg rode down with us. When we gone to Clark's house, the committee in charge of the body hailed us & we stopped and accompanied the corpse to Guyan,took it to the Lodge room. There was a good many there, the Lodge from Sandy and some from Ohio. We dressed in full regalia. I was one of the Pall bearers. We marched in procession to the grave yard just below Col.Everett's. Brother Thornton performed the cermony after which, we filled the grave & marched back to the Hall. There Thornton delivered a short address and we adjourned. I was around Guyandotte most of the afternoon waiting for Charley who was in the Chapter.

cemetery on Everett farm 1m S of Guyandotte has been removed

Gave Wheeler an advertisement to put in his paper for a Fillmore Ratification meeting here next Saturday.

Guyandotte Herald

Jim Cowens and Dick Lunsford started to Boone County this morning to see if the report we received last night about Sam Stanley being taken was true.

Saturday Aug.9,1856

There was meeting in the School House in the afternoon.

Sunday Aug.10,1856

There was preaching in the School
House in the forenoon.
Jim Cowens returned from Boone
County just at night and confirmed the
report of Sam Stanley being taken and
shot in the same hip about the same
place & with the same gun he shot his
wife with.

Monday August 11,1856

Just before noon the cattle man
came here again.(They offered us $10.00
a head. We could not trade.)

Wednesday Aug.13,1856

Alex Samuels and Oscar Mathers came
up here. I went with them down to see
McCullough and made arragements for our
Fillmore meeting next Saturday.

Thursday Aug.14,1856

The drover(cattle buyer) paid me
$19.00 for Bowman's cow. Father received
the $85 for the three steers he sold.

Friday Aug.15,1856

The Dutch Butcher came up from Town
early and I bought a quarter of beef of
him. In the afternoon,McCullough,
Charley & some others fixed up tables up
in the School House for our dinner
tomorrow.

Aug.15,1856

Ambrose Doolittle died today.

Saturday Aug.16,1856

Raised our flag about nine o'clock.
About Ten, there was several wagon loads
of men came up from Guyandotte to attend
our Fillmore meeting. This afternoon
they all had Fillmore flags flying.
About noon Roffe,McCullough, Father & I
sent what we had prepared up & I fixed
them on the table. There was no else
sent a single thing. The meeting

Doolittle death
owned mill 2nd falls Mud
(later Howell's Mill)

commenced about Two O'clock. There was a
great many here. Charley,Briant,Father,
and two others played several tunes.
There was two fiddles,Flutes, and
Father's bass viol. Father delivered the
first speech. There was several others
spoke. Then they adjourned to dinner
after which there were some resolutions
passed and some more speaking. Robert
fired the cannon every once in a while.
The meeting adjourned about four
o'clock. Charley Morris paid Father $100
account of rent for the mill. Sam
Childers returned with the mail about
midnight.

political meeting
music & speaches

Sunday Aug.17,1856

Father received a Fillmore paper
called the AGE from Uncle Playfoot,New
York. Sold four bu. meal to a man who
came 25 miles for it.

Uncle Playfoot NY

Monday Aug.18,1856

(Paid Fred Miller our taxes,
licenses,fines,etc. $131.96)
We received news this morning that
Sam Stanley was dead, and in the
afternoon he had escaped. The last
report,we think is true.
Old Webb was here about noon
looking around with Tom Turner.

#982 Turner

Tuesday Aug.19,1856

I settled with Emberson Turley.
Paid him $12 bu meal which balanced
accounts.
Charley & I went to Guyandotte in
the Buggy. Bob Allen rode down with us
on horseback. the Chapter met in the
evening. I took three more degrees
making me a Royal Arch Mason. When we
got through the chapter,Charley,Allen &
I went to Moore's Hotel where we had a
cold lunch & retired.
I sent a letter to Uncle David
containing $1.00.

Moore's Hotel

Uncle David more money

Wednesday Aug.20,1856

Jim Cowens Hauled me a load of
wood.

Thursday Aug.21,1856

I pulled a tooth just at night for
Dave Kyser for which I got half a
dollar.

Saturday Aug.23,1856

(Went to B'ville) Went up to the
Court House and heard a Democratic
Speech made by Col.Hays. It was a poor
thing. He was answered by J.W.Laidley,a
Fillmore man whose speech was nothing
extra either. They raised a pole and
Buchannan flag in Barboursville
yesterday.

Sunday August 24,1856

Anna started on horseback about
eight o'clock with Sam Childers & his
daughter up to the association just by
Salt Rock. Juda went down to Roffe's in
the afternoon.

Monday Aug.25,1856

Tuesday Aug.26,1856

A young man named Bowen stopped
here with the gravel. In great pain.
Dr.William & McCullough soon came.
While the doctors was here, word
came that one of the Hez Swann boys had
got nearly killed in cutting a tree. We   #314 Swann on Tom's Ck
started up there.
The Logan mail carrier went down
this afternoon. Some hands went to work
here for the company to make repairs on
the dam and Locke.

Wednesday Aug.27,1856

Logan mail came up early.
(Cynthia sick) Soon after dinner,
she was so much worse I had to call
Dr.Moss. He soon came and said she had   Cynthia has typhoid
typhoid fever & that it is in very   3 doctors
dangerous condition. Moss came to see
Cynthia again. I told him that I had
spoken to McCullough to assist him. He
objected to him bringing Williams with   doctors fighting
him. Soon after Moss left, they came and

objected to the way Moss was treating
her. He soon came after they left & I
told him of their objections. He then
agreed to see McCullough here, and about
Ten O'clock, I went down to his house
and brought him up. They had some pretty
hard words in the store & nearly came to
blows but at last came to a good under-
standing. Moss agreeing with McCullough
to associate with Dr.Williams.

Thursday August 28,1856

(All doctors came to see Cynthia.
She was better.)

Friday Aug.29,1856

I drove to Barboursville. Cynthia
had a bad spell just as I started.
Mr.Newton of the Kanawha Repulican
came here this morning and I paid him
three dollars, the amount we owed him
for his paper this year, and some
advertising he did for us. Cynthia quite
easy.

Kanawha newspaper

Saturday Aug.30,1856

(I was in Barboursville to court) I
got a piece of beef of Fridle(Feasle-CE)
some sugar of Bloom,molasses of Allen.
Lawyer English rode home with us to
spend the night with Father.
Mat Butcher came here this eve &
borrowed my revolver & Charley's short
rifle to go on the hunt for Sam Stanley
again. English slept in the store with
Charley & Robert.

Stanley got lose

Sunday Aug.31,1856

Dr.English was at Father's all day.
I let Dr.Williams have some lemon juice
for Fetter's wife in Barboursville.
Mrs.Daniels and Swann stopped in a few
moments to see Cynthia.
English was in the store with
Charley & Robert .Staid all night.

Monday Sept.1,1856

Soon after breakfast, Father and I
drove to Barboursville in the buggy.

Charley followed on horseback. We all
went to the Court Room. I had a
conversation with Webb about our suit
with the Guyandotte Navigation Co. I
told him Moore agreed with me to leave a
level mill yard if I'd let him have the
rock in front of the mill. He said he
would be dammed if he would move the
dirt left from the blasting for $1000.
Charley had suit for $3.00 with Parish.
                         before Sam Childers.
Took our dinner at Bloom's.H Henry
Stewart's suit against us laid over till
tomorrow.

    Cynthia worse(Her fever turned to
flux).

    Cynthia much sicker

        Tuesday Sept.2,1856

    (Father agreed to lay over suit
with Guyandotte Nav.co. & let Laidley,
Samuels & English-the lawyers-act as
arbitrators. Took dinner at Bloom's.
Suit of Henry Stewart tried-"We cast him
without any trouble."
    The Logan mail went down this
afternoon.

        Wednesday Sept.3,1856

    (Cynthia about same. Dr.Wms.
stopped. English rode home with me from
Court.) I received a Fillmore song book,
his likeness and some addresses from New
York.(English staid all night.)

        Thursday Sept.4,1856

    We went up to Chap Maupin's to
assist in raising a Fillmore Pole. (FL-
About 7 miles above B'ville) English
came soon after we gor there. McCullough
& Dr.Williams was there.(Pole not ready,
we all came home.)

    Maupin #2
raised political pole in
each community

        Friday Sept.5,1856

    I received a note from Beekman (FL-
Lewis ?) Guyandotte to come there at
three today, and attend a meeting of the
Chapter.
    There is a Methodist Conference in
Guyandotte, and a great many preachers
there.

    Methodist Conference
at Guyandotte

Allen,Moore,Beekman,Collins,Sam
Johnson met in the Hall, & waited there
more than two hours. Not having enough a
Royal Arch lodge,we dispersed to meet
again Monday night. Allen & I went to
Moore's Hotel. He's not to charge us any
bill.

At this point in ledger-Lambert has
copied the diary onto records of the
pigs he kept in 1923. CE

Saturday Sept.6,1856

Allen & I left Guyandotte as soon
as we could get the horse and buggy.(Fed
horse & got breakfast at Allen's in
B'ville) Drove up to Mrs.Jones in the
upper end of town and brought her up to
Mrs.Bowman's. Cynthia quite smart. Came
down stairs to her meals.

Sunday Sept.7,1856

Soon after breakfast,Mother,Sam and
Susie started in the Buggy to Guyandotte
to Church. Mrs.Jones with her twin
babies came in the morning staid to
dinner & a part of the afternoon. Just
before dark,Anna put the side saddle on
the mare and took Caley behind her &
Sarah in her arms, and rode up as far as
Mat Butcher's & back.

Monday Sept.18,1856

Recd a letter from Aunt Lucy(NY).
Charley & I started in the Buggy to
Guyandotte. Allen & Lattine had gone
down. We caught them just below the
Widow Holderby's. Went to the Masonic
Hall. the Chapter had a meeting. We gave
a gentleman named McCade from Sandy the
most excellent degree. Charley, Lattin
& I went to   ----   .

Lattin #219

Tuesday Sept.9,1856

Took our breakfast at Moore's then
went to the wharf boat & bought & paid
for $1.00 some sugar & coffee.
Father employed Little Jackie Smith
yesterday to finish his well, Fielder

having given up the job. Mat Butcher &
Dave Stanley help ed him all day.

Went down to Father's and heard the
music. Mr.& Mrs.Roffe & a lot of young
folks were there singing & playing.

Logan mail went down this afternoon

Wednesday Sept.10,1856

The Logan mail passed up about
eight o'clock. Bowman grinding wheat.
Smith,Dave Stanley & Mat Butcher worked
all day at the well. About eight
o'clock, there was a man came from off
Hurricane in a buggy to mill. He staid
there all night.

Aunt Nancy passed us going down to
a party at Mrs.Roffe's. They wanted us
to go along but we had no invitation.
(Later Robert brought up an
invitation,but they would not go.

The Logan mail passed up about
eight o'clock.(Smith,Stanley & Butcher
worked all day in the mill.)

*refused to go to party
thought they were snubbed*

Thursday Sept.11,1856

(Allen & I went to Guyandotte. I
took tea with him. Put up at Moore's.)

Bob Allen & I went to the Chapter.
Found Comps Moore,Miller,Johnston,
Ricketts,Laidley,Beekman,Wellington,
Anderson & a stranger from Ohio there.(I
was app't secretary, Collins away.)
P.H.McCullough's petition accepted. Bob
& I went to Moore's.

Friday Sept.12,1856

I arose, went to the wharf boat and
got me $1.50 worth of sugar. Got to
Barboursville little after seven
o'clock. I stopped,had my horse fed &
took breakfast with Bob.

Harvey Smith was here in the
morning to see about hiring the double
house up the road.(FL-Probably the John
Gothard House up hollow above Lewis's)

*Bob-brother ??

another house to rent

where was Lewis' ??*

Saturday Sept.13,1856

I lent Jeff Butcher my Revolver to
take another hunt for Sam Stanley, he
having heard where he is. Jake Smith,

Butcher & his son worked at Father's all
day. Drove to Barboursville (to Lodge)
     There was a Committee there from
Guyandotte consisting of H.H.Miller,
Beekman,Sam Johnston,A.Laidley & Mason.
We worked until nine o'clock, then
adjourned to Bill Merritt's and had a
fine supper. Assembled again about Ten
o'clock.

          Sunday Sept.14,1856

     There was meeting in the School
House this morning. Anna went. Dr.
Williams came home with us,took dinner &
staid part of the afternoon.

          Monday Sept.15,1856

     H.Smith moved in the double log
house.

          Tuesday Sept.16,1856

     About eight o'clock,Charley and I
started in the buggy to Charleston,
Kanawha Co. We stopped in Barboursville
a few moments, none being ready to start
there, we drove ahead, the roads are
awful dusty and the sun shone scorching
hot we got to old John Morris' little   at Mud Bridge ??
after eleven o'clock where we stopped to
dinner, our horse had the scours very
bad. We had not been there very long
before three more buggies came along
containing Billy Miller,John Samuels,
Henry Miller,John Everett,Mat Thompson
and William Merritt. After we all got
our dinner about half after one
o'clock,we again started. I paid 25ct at
the first toll gate & 65 cents for our   James River Turnpike toll
feed at Morrises.
     We stopped a while ar Mr.Conners
and had our horses watered, also at
Lewises just this this side of Coal
River. Paid another 25cts for toll just
before we got there. About five o'clock,
we stopped at a Public House two miles
beyond Coal kept by a Mr.Wilson &
concluded to stay all night. I had an
awful head ache. We had not been there
long before Bob Allen and Bill Seamonds
drove up and stopped. I had such an
awful head ache, I could not eat any

supper. Took a cup of coffe and went
right to bed. The evening was beautiful,
warm,clear,and moonlight. Billy and
Henry Miller slept in the same room with
Charley and I. Billy was very restless.
He complained of bed bugs biting him, so   bed bugs sent him to floor
he took to the floor.

Wednesday Sept.17,1856

Arose about three o'clock. Had to
harness our own horses and then wait
over half an hour to get Wilson up to
settle our bills. Allen would not wait
but started off without paying his. I
paid him 75cts. for Charles and I. Got
to Kanawha River opposite Charleston
just after sunrise. Allen and Seamonds
was crossing in the ferry boat. Paid   toll for road-toll for ferry
25cts. toll and 25cts for crossing the
ferry. The most of us put up at the
Kanawha House kept by Mr.Wright.

Soon after we got our breakfast, we
commenced a review of Charleston. The
day was beautiful and clear but the sun
shone awful hot & the roads awful dusty.
There is many fine residences and the
people appear to live very fast.

About ten o'clock,we started on
foot to the grove where the great   Big political rally
Fillmore and Donalason meeting was being
held. It was a mile and a half from our
Hotel & a very hot and dusty walk we had
of it. We were very much disappointed in
not hearing the speakers we left home on
purpose to hear. They were the Messers.
Botts,Flourney & Carlisle,none of whom
were there. There were several pretty
good speeches we heard made. A Mr.
Jackson from Wood and Dr.Parks spoke
very well. The dinner was a wretched
affair. There was nothing but some dry
bread and pieces of meat strewed along   did not like speaches
in piles on the table. We had to play   did not like food
the grab game to even get any of that.
There was a great many people there. I
should think upwards of 2000, about a
quarter of whom were ladies. There were
many fine horses, carriages, and
buggies. I saw Dr.Williams there. He
started up the same morning we did and
drove through that day. Charley left the
meeting some time before I did. I left
just before the meeting broke up, and

went to our Hotel. Strolled around town
until night. Evening clear and mild.
Moon rose about eight o'clock. Just
after dark there was quite a large torch
light procession headed by a band of
music. Soon after supper, we paid our
hotel bill which was $2.50 for us both.
Then just before nine o'clock, Charley
and I, Ira McGinnis, and Victor
Letulle, Dr.Laidley, and Henry Everett
started home in our buggies. Charley
paid 25cts. for our ferriage. All gone
to bed at the toll gate so we passed
without paying. We got down to Lewises,
two miles below Coal River just before
midnight where we stopped and remained
the rest of the the night.

Thursday Sept.18,1856

Arose just at sun up Weather clear
and cool. The sky was clear all forenoon
and the wind blew a gale. The dust blew
terribly. Soon afternoon the sky became
cloudy and there was a slight shower.
Cloudy by spells until night. Charley
paid one bit for lodging,breakfast,and
horsefeed, then we started again for
home. Just below John Morrises,Charley
stopped to see a fellow by the name of
Handley who owed him for watch work. The
other fellows passed us. We had to go
back to Joe Morrises & then Charley did
not get the money. Stopped in
Barboursville a few moments, got my
mail,and then arrived home a little
after one o'clock pretty well smothered
by the dust. Charley paid 50cts for two
toll gates coming down.

Susey has very sore eyes a complaint
she has caught over to school.

pink eye or
Scarlet fever ??

Friday Sept.20,1856

Robert starting to school in
Marietta tomorrow morning. Trade awful
dull in the grist mill. No meal selling
at all.

Marietta College

Saturday Sept.20,1856

Robert started to school today.
(They will go in buggy to Oakhill,about
30 miles out in Ohio where he can get a

river low traveled to
Oak Hill, OH to catch train
for Marietta

46

car to Marietta. Boats not running.
Water too low.)
I was told this afternoon that   manumited slave
George Kilgore today set free the nigger
woman he paid $1600 for last fall.

Sunday Sept.21,1856

There was Sunday School in the
School House.
Judy went ot Barboursville this
morning. She returned just at dark.
Thompson from Guyandotte stopped
here and I got a 50cts bottle of
Gargling oil. He had been to the Falls
with a four horse wagon load.

Monday Sept.22,1856

There was great many passed here
going to court. Charley returned from
Ohio about eleven o'clock. Robert was to
leave ther this morning.
I drove Jack to Barboursville. I
went right in the Court House & heard
John S. Carlisle deliver a Fillmore
speech,Then Governor McComas spoke in
favor of Buchanan & Carlisle answered
him, using up the Democrat party
entirely. He is a beautiful speaker.
Rec'd a letter from Uncle David.

Tuesday Sept.23,1856

Allen has not returned yet(from
Charleston)

Wednesday Sept.24,1856

Dr.Williams stopped to see Father
and Mother. Frenchman sent me a shoulder
of bacon I bought of him yesterday.

Thursday Sept.25,1856

Jim Cowens,Harvey & Dave Smith
commenced cutting corn. (not ripe
enough) Soon after dinner Charley
started to the Academy on the Ohio River   Marshall Academy
to attend an exhibition.
I went over to Charley Morrises to
see his little boy who is very sick.

Friday Sept.26,1856

Charley returns about noon(from
Academy-Ohio River) The two young
Briants came with him to see Father
about getting a place to put up a
wheelwright shop.
There was preaching in the School
House by Mr.Finandan(?) this afternoon.
Susie's eyes about the same.

Saturday Sept.27,1856

Jim Cowens & Harvey Smith cutting
corn at 5cts a shock-12 hills square.
Our case with Roland Bias again put off.
Sam Childers held (magistrates)Court

Sunday Sept.28,1856

There was Sunday School and Prayer
meeting in School House this morning.
Sent a letter to J.F.Brennan,
Louisville,Ky.,with $1.00 for a Ticket
and chance to draw Masonic Library.
Dr.Williams staid in the parlor with
Anna until about nine o'clock when he
left.

Monday Sept.29,1856

Col.Webb stopped here in the
afternoon.Susie's eyes about the same.

Tuesday Sept.30,1856

After dinner, I sent quite a large
mail down by Peter Love.(FL-Often sent
it by neighbors,etc.)
The Logan mail passed down soon
after, Love returned just at dark with
my mail.

Wednesday Oct.1,1856

Snowed this morning. The Logan mail
passed up early. Bill Fielder & Dave
Smith went over to the Widow Lusher's to
find some of our hogs.(Returned 11
o'clock without finding them.)

Thursday Oct.2,1856

Just before breakfast, I bought some beef of Jenkins. Soon after, the butcher in town sent me some.(Simmons & Morris settled rent for mill-$140 due us after deducting $35 for sawing for us. Gave up mill & all. Their contract expired today.)

I gave Harrison Peyton a bad $3.00 bill I got of him some time since. He told me before Pat Thompson that he had not another now but might have when he returned from town, if not when he came down again & that it was the same bill he gave me. Susie went to school.

$3 bill legal currency

Friday Oct.3,1856

(Went to Guyandotte & saw John W.Hite about $101 we owed Butler & Co., Cincinnati & on which he ordered suit. He wanted me to pay $5.00 lawyer fee. I refused. Execution had not been ordered.)

Saturday Oct.4,1856

(Rode to B'ville) I expected to meet David Clark there, but he did not, as he promised, come up from Guyandotte in the stage this morning. I went to old John Samuels and offered to pay him the amount of Butler's claim. There was two suits commenced by Hite against Father and the costs in each including attorney's fee is $4.60. I offered to pay the money and the costs of one suit but he would not take it. I then got some sugar of Bloom and came home.

Did not want to pay lawyer

The water was nearly all drawn off from the Pond last night & this morning for the River Company to fix the Locke. We could only run the corn stones and the very slow all day. They stopped the the water running off before noon.

Sarah was quite sick all day with dysentery.

Sunday Oct.5,1856

I ground a turn of corn for Em Turley. I went to Bill Fielder"s house. He was not home. I then crossed the

river and went up on he bank of the
"Rich Bottom" to get chestnuts. (Gave
Simmon's little nigger a quarter for
about a gallon.

When I got back, Cynthia had gone
up to the School House to hear Mr.
Vanerden preach. Judy also went. Bob
Allen and his daughter came up. He went
to church, and she staid here with Susie
& Anna. They left right after church.
(Father very sick. We got Dr. Williams &
also Dr.McCulloough. He has dysentery &
is broke out with rash.) Sarah not much
better.

1m S-present site
Esquire Golf

Monday Oct.6,1856

David Clark came here. He
breakfasted with me. Just before noon
Bowman stopped the mill & Clark with
Sam Childers commenced fixing the wheel
gates.

Tuesday Oct.7,1856

Montague McComas stopped here
drunk, and I pulled a tooth for him. The
Logan mail went down this afternoon. I
sent my quarter returns by it.

Wednesday Oct.8,1856

(Went to Charley Morrises to get
some wheat to sow. He was down on the
river nearly to Warren Roffe's trying to
dig a red fox out of a hole the dogs had
run him into. Mat B. came down. We
failed & left about noon.)

Thursday Oct.9,1856

(Went to chapter at Guyandotte with
Dr.McCullough. took tea at Moore's.
Reassembled. Gave Mr.Amis,Dr.McCullough
& John Everett each the mark & Past
Master's degree, went to Moore's & had a
lunch.

Friday Oct.10,1856

(When I got home) Lucian Wolcott
and his wife were at Mother's.
Charley and I went over to where
our land joins on Mrs.Blake's. Some one

Guyandotte merchant

had been cutting & hauling hoop poles on our land.

Jim Cowens went to Royal Childers today with the cattle and wagon & hauled us ten bushel of apples.

#85 Childers

Saturday October 11,1856

(Went to B'ville to Lodge) There was considerable business done. John Tessen was initiated and Green Harrison passed. About 4 0'clock, we had supper at Bloom's.(Adjourned past midnight) (Paid Thos.Thornburg $25 on note of Graham's against Father).

Sunday Oct.12,1856

I shot a duck just below thew dam this morning.

There was meeting in the School House after dinner. Sam was here awhile. Then Cynthia and Susie went home with them. They soon returned.

Monday Oct.13,1856

(Water rose about 2 ft. in Pond because water let off from Smith Cr.)

Tuesday Oct.14,1856

The Logan Mail went down about the millde of the afternoon.

Wednesday Oct,15,1856

The logan mail went up about nine o'clock.

Thursday Oct.16,1856

Agricultural fair at Barboursville tomorrow. I took a barrel of flour(FL-279lbs wheat made 231lbs. flour.) Daniels took a new wagon of his make down.

fair at B'ville
Daniels entered wagon

Friday Oct.17,1856

Charley & I drove in the Buggy to Barboursville to attend the fare. I took down a bottle of my blackberry wine. So awful stormy there were few people

there. We took our dinners at Bloom's. I
with Bob Allen & Charley Everett was a
committee to award premiums on fruit and
vegetables. We was in the cattle shed
part of the time. Then we went to the
Court House where the Ladies dep artment
was. There was few out, the day was so
disagreeable. I was awarded the Premium
on home made wine and Father for the
best barrel of flour. We staid until the
mail came in. When I got mine we started
home about 5 o'clock.

best flour
best wine

Saturday Oct.18,1856

Jim Butcher was all the forenoon
fill in gravel in front of the mill.
Judy left me this afternoon, her year
expiring today.

Sunday Oct.19,1856

There was Sunday School in the
School House. Towards night,Thorn and
his little boy Frank came up here, but
they only staid a few minutes. I wrote
for Cynthia to Aunt Sally.

Thorn & son Frank

Monday October 20,1856

Rec'd a letter from Uncle Playfoot.
About nine o'clock, Charley & I took our
rifles & went on the River Ridge to
shoot some squirrels. We returned
through the hollow back of Bill
Fielder's where we each shot one.
Daniel's moved to Barboursville today.

Tuesday Oct 21,1856

The Logan mail went down about
three o'clock. I paid the carrier my
last quarter's account amounting to $4.
Soon after he left the Steamer Adrian
came up here, but the water is too low
for her to get any further. Judy came
here and got some of her clothes. She is
living at McCullough's. Judy came here
with two of Roffe's niggers & took away
the balance of her clothes. The Steamer
Adrian laid here all night. Caley went
to school and staid all day with Susey.

Wednesday Oct.22,1856

(River falling. Adrian here yet &
will be.) The Logan mail came up about
eight o'clock. Caley went with Susie to
school.

Thursday Oct.23,1856

Friday Oct.24,1856

The Steamer Adrain still laying
here. Caley went to school with Susey.

Saturday Oct.25,1856

The Steamer Adrain went through the
Locke this morning and is lying by Sam
Childers awaiting for our Pond to fill,
so they can get in Smith Creek Locke.
(Went to Magistrates Court).Roll Bias
put off his case again on account of his
witness not being there. I bought nine
fine chickens this morning for $1.10   12@ a chicken

Sunday Oct.26,1856

Emily Harrison & Mrs.Cowens took
dinner here. I wrote a letter to Uncle
Francis.

Monday Oct.27,1856

(Went to Court. Many there. We took
dinner at Bloom's.)
There was a nigger woman sold that   slave sale
belonged to John Heath. She only brought
$382. Harshbarger bought her. There was
quite a lot of livestock sold. Water in
the Pond rose a little. Steamer Adrian
started up the river.

Tuesday October 28,1856

Mrs.Moss and Miss Ball was here
most of the afternoon to see Cynthia.
They staid to tea & left soon after,
Charley & Anna going over home with
them.

Wednesday Oct.29,1856

Let Mr.Roffe run some hominy
through our fan mill.   fan mill for
                                             hominy-boiled corn

Thursday Oct.30,1856

(Roffe wanted to saw a lot of logs
at 50cts a hundred. We asked 60cts) They
were most of the day putting one Locke
full(of timber) through.

Friday Oct 31,1856

Hinchman brought up my mail.   Hinchman Bend of Guy. R.

Saturday Nov.1,1856

(Rode to Barboursville) Got some
sugar and coffee of Eggers. Then wnet to
John Millers and got a pair of shoes for
Sarah for which I am to pay him seventy
cents.
        Ben Swann received a letter from
Butcher Davis in Missouri informing us
of the marriage of Lee Bowman the on the
5th of September last(1856).

Sunday Nov.2,1856

There was Sunday School in the
School House in the (morning).

Monday Nov.3,1856

Went to Fetters and got him to fix
our harness a little. Charley bought a   harness made for
set of new harness of him, one he made   someone else
for Mathers. He is to pay him $25 in
flour for them($6.50lb).Left the new
harness until tomorrow.(Considerable
wheat to grind but very little corn.

Tuesday Nov.4,1856

I raised our Flag soon after
Breakfast this being the day of the
Presidential election.(Buchanan &
Breckenridge elected.)(They voted for
Fillmore & Andrew J.Donelson-American
Party)(Freemont & Dayton-Black
Republicans). Sent a letter to J.F.
Brennan(St.Louis ?-FL) containing Two
dollars for Sam Childers and my
subscription to the American Free Mason
for the coming year.

Wednesday Nov.5,1856

The Logan mail went up this
morning. Charley & I made some ink this
morning. Bob Allen had a raft of timber
loaded with coal put through the locke.
Judy was here. Judy & Charley left
about nine o'clock.

Thursday Nov.6,1856
Charley started in the buggy to
Marietta with Robert's things.
The Steamer Adrian came down with a
couple of small boats loaded with coal.
I tried to get some but could not. There
was a large flat boat of coal went down
about noon. I was over in Dave Stanley's
cornfield this morning.

Friday Nov.7,1856

Saturday Nov.5,1856

The Masonic Lodge met. There was a
good deal of business to do. We had a
fine supper about nine o'clock at Bill
Merritt's. Meyer was initiated. Tessen
passed and Green Harrison raised. Past
midnight when we adjourned. McCullough
and Simmons rode home with me. Past 2
o'clock when I got in the house.

Sunday Nov.9,1856

There was preaching down at Bowman's
house. Anna went to church this morning.

Monday Nov.10,1856

I was most of the time cutting out
some stamps for stamping date on
letters.

made his own
"rubber stamps"

Tuesday Nov.11,1856

Started Sam to town with the wagon
to get some barrels.
I paid Mrs.Moore's nigger Sip $5.00
on account of Judy's wages.
Mother received a letter from
Harriet McKibby.

Wednesday Nov 12,1856

(Several hands cutting wood)

Thursday Nov.13,1856

I bought a new saddle of Fetter fro
which I am to pay him $19.00. Started to
Guyandotte---Put our horses up at
Moore's. I was in Henry Miller's store a
while. Chapter met. We gave Shaw and
McCullough the council degrees.

Friday Nov.14,1856

Received a letter from Uncle Cale.
Took breakfast at Moore's then I went to
Nat Adams' house, and saw him about a
situation as clerk on a steam boat. He
has the disposal of it,if he does not
take it himself. He told me he had
promised it to John Everett and if he
did not go, I should have it.
McCullough,Lattin and I started home
about ten o'clock. I stopped at John
Everett's. He promised to let me know on
a day or two whether or not, he should
go on the boat. Jim Cowens and Bill
Fielder got the saw mill started. They
were all day sawing an oak log of
Morrises that was on the carriage. They
had to stop every little while to fix
something. They had to make a new box
for the Pittman, then take off the cap
of the bull wheel and get out a chunk.
The Steamer Adrian passed up by here
this morning with some flatboats in tow.

Uncle Cale

#778 Adams
Wm.F. applied for job
on River boat

Saturday Nov.15,1856

The saw mill does not run very
well. Only sawed 1625ft in the
afternoon. Sam went to Barboursville
with the cattle and wagon. He took two
barrels of flour to Fetter at $6.50, and
one to Mr.A.Holderbees.

Sunday Nov.16,1856

Aunt Nancy went to Sunday School
down to Bowman's.

Monday Nov.17,1856

John Hibbens came up and we settled
accounts, He owes us #4.67. Charley

returned from Marietta. He left there
last Saturday.
    I sent our cannon to Billy Miller
to shoot in honor of Buchanan's
Election.
    I bought 31lbs. of beef of George
Dolen just at night.

Tuesday Nov.18,1856

    Toward night Jim and Bill Fiedler
hauled 25bu. coal for Charley. He
borrowed it of Bill Fielder.
    The Logan mail went down this
afternoon.

borrowed coal !!

Wednesday Nov.19,1856

    (Put our corn in the old carding
room.) The Logan mail carrier went up
this morning.

Thursday Nov.20,1856

    (Cynthia took supper at Mrs.
Bowman's) I sent one of the Buggy wheels
down to Hibbens and Daniels to be
repaired.

Friday Nov.21,1856

    Hands all working the road. Just at
noon, David Clark from Guyandotte, came
up here. He and Father partly came to an
arrangement hiring him the saw mill one
year for $500, Got a letter from Uncle
Francis(FL-New York)

Saturday Nov.22,1856

    (Went to Magistrates' Court. Role
Bias put off his case again.) Got 2
1/2yds. of red fannel of Billy Miller at
50cts. a yard.

Sunday Nov.23,1856

    Sarah Childers was here in the
afternoon a short time. Lawyer English
came here just at dark and staid all
night with Charles in the store.

Monday Nov.24,1856

(Went to Barboursville. Served on a jury.) English and I drove home just at dark.

Tuesday Nov.25,1856

English and I drove to Barboursville. I took dinner at Merritt's. The grand jury brought un two indictments against Billy Miller. Mat Thompson, Alex Samuels,Henry Miller, John Morris, and others for betting on the election. English and I drove home just at dark.
I paid Hite $113.68, Butler & Co. claim of Cincinnati.

Wednesday Nov.26,1856

English and I drove to Barboursville. In Court House awhile. Got my dinner at Bloom's. I was around town a while looking at a shooting match between Wash Hensley & George Kilgore. George beat him.
English & I drove home.

shooting match

Thursday Nov.27,1856

English was here all day. He, Father, and Charley took dinner with me. English took tea with me. None of my family without a grunt.(FL-Sick, I suppose.)

Friday Nov.28,1856

Lawyer English was here until near noon, when he left for Guyandotte to attend a Democratic supper there tonight.
I lent Sam Childers my revolver this morning.

Saturday Nov.29,1856

English returned here just at noon, took dinner at Father's, then left for home.

Sunday Nov.30,1856

Thompson, the wagoner from
Guyandotte, stopped here as he was going
to the Falls with a load, and I let him
have a barrel of flour for the coal
agent by the orders of David Keenan,
price $6.50.(Mrs.Swann stopped to see
Cynthia. Both went to Mrs.Smith's a
while.)

Monday Dec.1,1856

I bought a pair of venison hams
this morning for $1.25. They weighed
27lbs.

deer meat

Tuesday Dec.2,1856

Cowens & Wm.Fielder commenced to
sawing some boat lumber for McCullough.
The Logan mail went down this
afternoon.

Wednesday Dec.3,1856

The Logan mail went up this
morning. Flours(Ezra Flowers-?-FL) from
Guyandotte came up about noon to examine
the saw mill for Clark, but the water
was too high. (Ohio River up Large
Steamboats running.)

#781 Flowers-lumberman

Thursday Dec.4,1856

Cal Swann stopped here and handed
me a letter. It was from Harriet McKibby
who is in Guyandotte and has been there
since last Monday. The news occasioned
considerable of a frustration with
mother.

4 days befor she
sent letter

Friday Dec.5,1856

(Went to Guyandotte) Thorn took the
meal at 60cts a bushel. I went to
Moore's Hotel and saw Harriet McKibby.
Then I went to Lucien Wolcott's store
and bought a box of seegars at $1.50 per
100.(Brought Harriet home.) got me a new
hat of Henry Miller for $3.00.

meal $.60 bu
flour $6.50 bu

Saturday Dec.6,1856

(Went to Lodge) Stopped for
McCullough and he rode down with me.

there was good attendance. Dr.Ricketts
and Beekman up from Guyandotte. We had a
fine lovely meeting.

John Tessen was raised the
conferred some side degrees. Adjourned
about midnight. The Dr. & I rode home
together. The Lodge had refreshments at
Bill Merritt's.

Sunday Dec.7,1856

Aunt Nancy and Susie went to Sunday
School.

Monday Dec.8,1856

Jim Cowens,Fielder, and I went up
to Butcher's then with him out in the
woods to find our hogs.(Found them near
night.)

Soon after Tea, I went up to Ben
Swann's to pull a tooth for his wife,
but Moss was passing & she had got him
to pull it.

The Steamer Adrian passed through
the Locke about nine o'clock with a coal
boat in tow.

Tuesday Dec.1856

Jim Cowens and I started out to
hunt the hogs. We stopped at Butchers a
while to warm,where we found Bill
Fielder. Staid there about half an hour,
ThenJim and I with Mat,his son, and Bill
Fielder took to the woods. Dave Stanley
went along to hunt his own. Jim and I
separted from the rest. We started up a
deer, but could not get a shot at it.
Jim saw it. Mat then came to us and said
he had found the hogs. I staid on the
ridge and the rest started the hogs.
They ran like deers in all directions. I
kept the ridge back toward home. All but
Mat & Fielder soon caught up to me and
said they had lost all track of the
hogs. As we came out on the road, we saw
Fielder who had managed to get one of
the shoats -- & in a pen with assistance
of his dog. As Jim and I was coming
through the pasture home, we saw a lot
of the hogs we had been after just goin
g into the cow yard where we fastened

them. They had struck a straight course for home when we started them.

(David Clark here from Guyandotte, but we could not come to an agreement about the mill.)

The Logan mail went down this afternoon. I was down to Father's a few moments, then went out to Smith's and got him to saw tomorrow.

Wednesday Dec.10,1856

The Logan mail went up this morning. Cowens & H.Smith ran the saw mill. Bill Fielder,Mat Butcher and his son commenced killing hogs about nine o'clock.(They killed 7)

Thursday Dec.11,1856

Bill Fielder and Mat Butcher did not get to killing hogs until after nine o'clock(killed 8 for me,1 for Father in forenoon. Killed for Bowman in afternoon. I shut up six hogs in my pen to fatten more. Charley Morris and Bowman heard the evidence in the case of the disputed hog between Father and Roffe. they both claim the hog, and Roffe had marked him. There was several witnesses. After dark when they got through, the verdict was that neither had proved owenrship and that the hog be killed and divided between them, which I thing was wrong as Father clearly proved the hog was his.

Friday Dec.12,1856

Lattin came here for me to go with him & survey a piece of land I am about entering.(On upper end of Smith Cr.)

Saturday Dec.13,1856

(Went to B'ville in buggy)Got measured for a pair of pants at Mathers. I left the stuff there some time since. Got a ball of wick of Bill Millers which I did not pay for.

Lee Hinchman died tonight. He had been sick but a week.

Hinchman died

Sunday Dec.14,1856

Sam and Harriet staid all night at
Mr.Holderby's in Barboursville.(They got
there at dark and raining.)
There was preaching down at
Bowman's this morning but not many was
out. Aunt Nancy went.

Monday Dec.15,1856

Lee Hinchman's corpse was taken up
home this morning by Hibbens.
Cynthia all day frying out lard,   killed hogs
making head cheese & sausage meat.

Tuesday Dec.16,1856

The Logan mail went down this
afternoon.

Wednesday Dec.17,1856

The Logan mail carrier passed up
soon after breakfast. He had not much
mail for me.

Thursday Dec.18,1856

(Sawed the small hickory we cut for
sled runners.)
Charley & I each bought a bu. of
dried apples of Ruel Porter.($1.25bu.)
Dave Stanley helped Sam haul wood.

Friday Dec.19,1856

(Webb sawed wood all day for me
Cynthia gave his wife some spare ribs.
They are very poor.)Cynthia and I
gathered up a lot of rags to take to
Guyandotte to sell.

Saturday Dec.20,1856

Charley got the cattle and with
Bill Fielder went up the road opposite
the house where Dave Stanley lives, and
hauled an old black walnut log down to
the mill. sawed it up in the afternoon.

Wrote to Uncle Cale & Uncle Francis

   Monday Dec.22,1856

(Cold.Saw mill not running. Court
day. Few there acct. cold.)

   Tuesday Dec.23,1856

River frozen over below & above
dam. Logan mail went down about four
o'clock.

   Wednesday Dec.24,1856

The Logan mail went up about nine
o'clock. Soon after Burt Hensley's son
brought me fourteen turkeys that I
bought of him at 50cts a piece. I was
thirty years old tonight.(b 24 dec 1826)
(sold rags 85lbs to Thorn at .03 a lb.)
I stopped at Hiltbruners & got a parlor
stove for Roffe. Stopped at Roffe's to
take out the stove, but the devilish
niggers was so long taking it out of the
wagon, the horses started and the stove
fell to the ground breaking it so it is
almost runined.(Got 75cts for part of
turkeys.)

Wm.C.'s birthday
sold rags for$25.53
(used to make paper ?)

   Thursday Dec.25,1856

Gave Bowman & Jim Cowens each a
turkey. Had one for dinner.

   Friday Dec.26,1856

Charley and Anna went over to
Charley Morrises to a party.(Anna came
home about 9 o'clock.)

   Saturday Dec.27,1856

Charley,Cynthia,Anna and I began to
fix ourselves to go to Barboursville to
attend the Masonic dinner. Leaving
others at Merritt's, Charley & I went to
the Lodge room.
About three o'clock we marched in
regalia over to Merritts and with our
wives,daughters,and sisters returned to
our hall & the degree of master mason's
wife and daughter on all who have not

before received it. Anna had it
conferred on her. About five o'clock,
the ladies returned to Merritts and we
closed the lodge. Then Charley & I went
in Miller's store where Tom thornburg
tried Father's suit against old Role
Bias. We then went to Merritts. Cynthia
and Anna had concluded with some others
to remain a while to have a dance.
Charley fiddled for us and after several
vain attemps to get through a cotillion
about eight o'clock, we left and came
home.

Sunday Dec.28,1856

Ohio River closed with ice. Charley
couldn't come home.

Monday Dec.29,1856

Webb that lives in Roffe's house
above the Smith shop,helped Sam take the
straw out of the ice house.(About 2 tons
ice still left in it.)

Tuesday Dec.30,1856

Charley & Anna went up to Simmons
to a dinner party. Col.Webb and Cohen,
the coal man, stopped here as they went
down in the afternoon. The Logan mail
went down towards night. Cynthia fried
some lard and made mince and sausage
meal today.

Wednesday Dec.31,1856

Charley brought up a pint of Brandy
from Bill Merritt's.
Cynthia and I staid up until the
old year passed. We had a piece of mince
pie just at midnight.

Index 1856

Note: Blacks(both free and slave) are listed as Dusenberry
referred to them:Nigger.

Adam's Nat 26,55
Allen,Bob 4,7,8,18,20,26,
    30,32,37,39,41,42,43,
    44,46,49,51,54
Amis,Mr. 49
Aunt Nancy 11,15,55,59,61
Aunt,Lucy 11,15,25
Ball,Miss 15,52
Beach,Walden 16
Beekman 22,40,41,42,43,59
Bias,Roland 6,13,22,47,52,
    56,63
Blackwood 32
Blake's,Mr. 49
Blankenship 22,25,26,27,28
Bloom,Evan 12,15,21,22,25,
    26,27,28,32,39,40,48,
    51,52,57
Botts 44
Bowman 5,6,11,16,26,36,38,
    42,49,54,55,60,61,62
Bowman,Lee 6
Bowman,Mrs. 41,23,56
Brennan,J.F. 47,53
Briant 37,47
Bryan 14
Buchanan's 56
Buffington 25
Bumgardners 5,24
Butcher & his son 43
Butcher's 59
Butcher,Ben 14
Butcher,Jeff 11,33,34,42
Butcher,Jim 2,51
Butcher,Mat 7,9,10,12,13,
    17,31,33,34,35,39,42,
    49,59,60
Butcher,Mrs. 6
Butler & Co. 48,57
Calvary 31
Capt.Jack 4
Carlisle 11,44
Carlisle,John S.46
Childers,Royal 50
Childers,Sam (A.)4,6,17,
    21,22,27,32,34,37,38,
    40,47,52,53,57
Childers,Sarah 56
Childers,West 32

Clark 19,24,35,49,58
Clark,David 48,49,56,60
Clark,Henry 34,35
Cohen 63
Collins 41
Conners,Mr. 43
Cook 27,30
Cowens 58,60
Cowens,Daniel 35
Cowens,Jim 1,2,3,4,6,31,
    33,35,36,37,46,47,50,
    55,59,62
Cowens,Mrs. 14,15,52
Cox,Mrs.22
Crump,Mr. 12
Daniels 4,25,29,50,51,56
Daniels,Mrs. 16,29,39
Davis,Butcher 53
Dick,John 4,12,16,17,34
Dides,John 7
Doctor Moss 28
Dodd,John 1,3,4,10
Dodd,John 10
Dolen 1
Dolen,George 56
Donalason 44
Doolittle,Ambrose 36
Dusenberry,Louisa 16,17
Dusenberry,Thorn 16,17,19
Dutch Butcher 8,36(Espy)
Eggers 25,53
English 13,15,17,39,40,56,57
Espy,Godfrey 10
Everett,Charley 22,29,51
Everett,Col.35
Everett,Henry 45
Everett,John 22,43,49,55
Fetter's 25,39,53,55
Fielder,Bill 1,2,6,11,
    12,13,15,23,30,31,32,
    38,41,47,48,51,56,58,
    59,60,61
Fielder,Jim 56
Fielder,John 6,13,18
Fillmore 44
Finandan,Mr. 47
Flourney 44
Flours 58
Frank 51

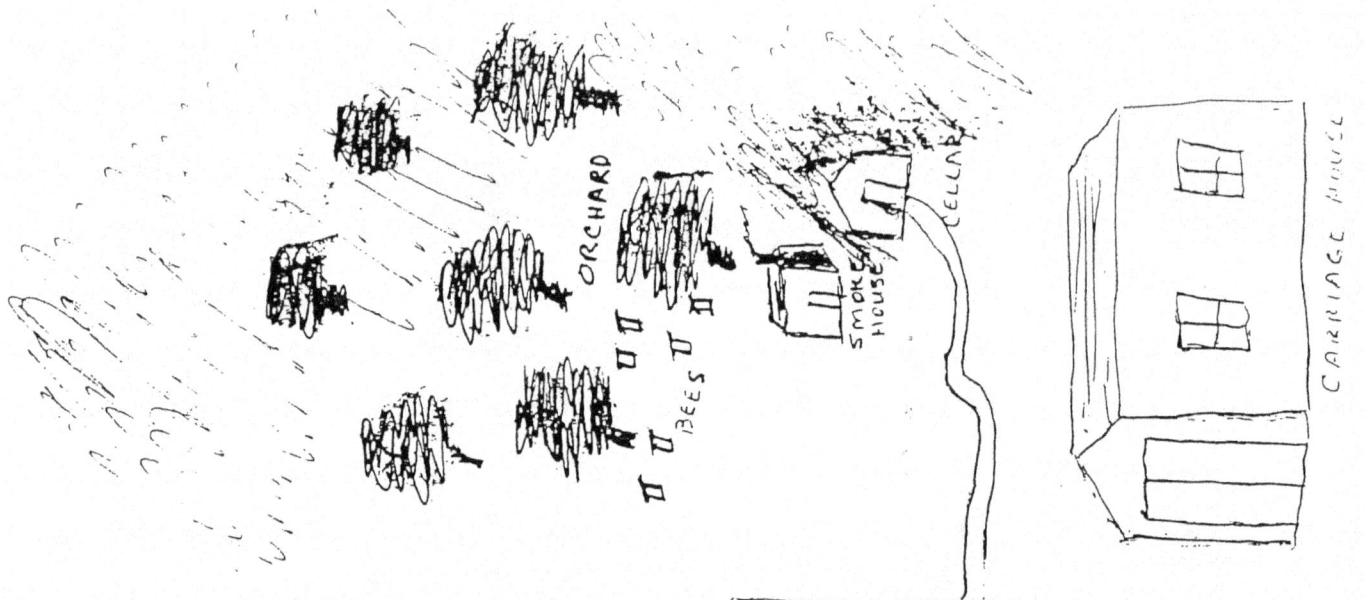

The 1869 Diary follows 1856 and is in same book, but Lambert makes no comment concerning the missing dates. Nothing is known concerning their orginal existance or if they were copied.

DUSENBERRY DIARY 1869

Jan.1,1869

I am now residing in the Town of Guyandotte,West Virginia. My family consisting of myself,my wife,my daughter,her husband Roland Clark,their infant son,my son Caleb,daughter Jessie, daughter Sallie who is lying very low with spotted fever, and my Father's sister Nancy Dusenberry. My occupation U.S. Assistant Assessor Internal Revenue.

baby FRANK

measles or chicken pox ??

Friday Jan.1,1869

Sallie not any better. I sent over for Dr.Ricketts but he was not home. I sent for Dr.Ginnis. He and Hysell came together. They seemed alarmed at Sallie's back set & ordered medicine to be given.(Gave her quinine pills.)
Sallie being so sick casts a gloom over us all here & makes this a very dull,gloomy New Year's Day to us. Roland was up at my new building until night.
Hysell did not come at all.

Dr.Ricketts
Dr.McGinnis
Dr.Hysell

Saturday Jan.2,1869

All three doctors here in the forenoon. I let Hysell know I did not like the way he neglected Sallie yesterday. Roland was out with a serenading party.
Mrs.Bonner was here awhile in the eve.

Sunday Jan.3,1869

Hysell sent me word by Ryan to get some one else to take care of the case.

Monday Jan.4,1869

I paid $2.00 Bridge toll for the Normal School Exe.Committee. I went over to Charles and got a small bottle of his wife for Sallie. She is resting easier.

Caley went over to King's to stay all
night.

Tuesday Jan.5,1869

Roland helping to load the Barber
mill in a boat. I paid D.d. smith $5.00
and Ryan $10.00 Schmidt & Berger came
this afternoon. I pulled a tooth for
Burt Russell.

Wednesday Jan.6, 1869

Roland went with the boat
containing Barber's saw mill down to
Holderby's Landing. Then they hauled it
out to Peter Buffington's place I was
about my office and town during the day.   death-Taylor
Taylor's child was buried yesterday.

Thursday Jan.?,1869

Ricketts said Sallie was so much
better there was no need of his coming
any more unless sent for. Helped Roland
lath some.

Friday Jan.8,1869

I got six yards of domestic of
D.D.Smith. Toward night a nigger woman
named Clara came here to work.   hired negro servant

Saturday Jan.9.1869

I got 3lbs. Tea & a small ham at
the Comissary, I attended Lodge.

Sunday Jan.10,1869

Got an orange off the Fleetwood for
Sallie.Paid 15cts.
John T.Hibbens was on her going up
the river.

Monday Jan.11,1869
Tuesday Jan.12,1869

Susie and Roland and baby went to a
dance at Hiltbruner's. About 11 o'clock
I went and brought Susie home. She
nursed the baby, and then I took her
back & returned home.

3

Wednesday Jan.13,1869

(Aunt Olive died in New York)   death-Aunt Olive
Susie,Roland,and Caley came home
from the dance 1/2 after 2 o'c.
Jim Wright and I up to my building a
short time.

        Thursday Jan.14,1869

    Roland all day up to my house
lathing.

        Friday Jan.15,1869

    Caley went to a party up to Widow
Stewart's.

        Saturday Jan.16,1869

    I started to Barboursville in
Ryan's skiff with Dunlevy and another
man from Cincinnati. Got Jewell and John
Foster roused up. I had a suit before
Sam Childers. M.Stewart & Co. sued me
for about $12(I confessed judgement
$1.25.) Ryan hauled me load of lath from
my stable. I paid Dunlevy & Co. $47.65
(FL-I presume from Cincinnati) amt. of
grocery bill.

        Sunday Jan.17,1869

    Dr.Ricketts & McGinnis here to see
Sallie.

        Monday Jan.18,1869
        Tuesday Jan.19,1869

    Susie's baby so sick Sallie had to
go see it.

        Wednesday Jan.20,1869

    Mark Henderson, who is on the Kate
Henderson, left me a bottle of sweet
oil.
    I bought of Bill Wright a pair of
pants $5.00. Holley paid his licenses
$15.

Thursday Jan.21,1869

Bob & Sam came down about 3 o'c. (Aunt Olivia Playfoot, mother's last surviving sister died Jan 13th.

Aunt Olive Playfoot was mother's sister

Friday Jan.22,1869

Ryan hauled me three rock for my portico steps.

Saturday Jan.23,1869

(Caley bought a Pea hen for me over in Ohio for $1.00.) Sallie Boggs came to work for us this morning.

Sunday Jan.24,1869

The Annie Laura went down this morning before day. The Fleetwood went up just at dark.

Monday Jan.25,1869

(About my office and town during the day) Jim Sedinger & Latulle commen--

Sunday Jan.26,1869

I paid E.A.Smith $5 for 50lbs. of nails and 9lbs. calico I got yesterday. I went down to the landing of the Fleetwood.

Wednesday Jan.27,1869

Sedinger & Letulle lathing. Wright & Gullion finished portico.Ryan hauled my sand. Robert let me have $200. He went home this morning.

Thursday Jan.28,1869

A drover landed a lot of horses here last night. This morning one of them had his leg broken by being kicked. It was given to John Laidley.(He wanted me to feed & cure if for half. I refused. Dr.McGinnis agreed to.) I paid George Laidley $10 balance due on the corn I bought of Womeldoff.

Friday Jan.29,1869

Sallie had a very high fever.

Saturday Jan.30,1869

I paid Blankenship $10 for seven
Bls. of line yesterday.
I attended a meeting of the
Guyandotte Bridge Co. this morning. I am
one of the Directors on the part of the
state. I paid Jim Wright $15 on account
of work.

Sunday Jan.31,1869

Mrs.Price in to see Sallie in the
afternoon.

Monday Feb.1,1869

I was up to my building fixing to
make mortor. Gullion there at work.
Roland and Thornburg hauled some water
from the branch in the afternoon. Miss
Young here awhile.

Tuesday Feb.2,1869

I paid D.I.and D.D.Smith $6.25.

Wednesday Feb.3,1869

Dr.McGinnis vaccinated the children
including Susie's baby. Paid Douthat
6.63 for 26 1/2lbs. lard. Also
Blankenship 3.25 for freight bill.
Thornburg hauled some more lumber.

Thursday Feb.4,1869

Paid Lieut.Wearing $5 for something
I got out of the comissary. I went to
the Fleetwood and got two oranges.

Friday Feb.5,1869
Saturday Feb.6,1869

I pulled a tooth for Big Jim Wright
this afternooon. He paid me 15 cents and
a fine comb.

Sunday Feb.7,1869

Gen.Enochs & other Lawyers came today to attend the called court that commences tomorrow.

Monday Feb.8,1869

I started on my mare to Barboursville. Rode up with Hagan & Lou Burks. Took dinner at Hatfields. Was there offically engaged. Called Court for trying the West boys for killing W.B.Moore, also some other prisoners. C.B.Webb & Ike Bloss came up about noon. Ferguson on the bench.
    I paid Bright 50cts for Seidlitz powders got for me. I was in town a while. Paid Hysell 25 cts for whisk--- and chimney.

murder trial

Tuesday Feb.9,1869

Paid Hysell 30cts.for medicine also Tom Cook 25cts.for chicken for Sallie. Hugo Dietz came here ahile. I went with him to Hayslips.

Wednesday Feb.10,1869

I sent my report to Thornburg by Howard. I went to the wharfboat & saw Hugo Dietz who was on the ------------
    Dobbins returned here on the Edenburg which landed just after the Hudson.

Thursday Feb.11,1869

The West boys were acquitted today of murder in killing Wilson B.Moore. Burt Chambers came here with five skiffs to sell. Henry Carter & Chambers here. The latter staid all night.

Friday Feb.12,1869

(Chambers hauled & stacked his skiffs on my lot. I tried to trade him a sewing machine for one. Chambers & Carter went home on the Victor.

Saturday Feb.13,1869

Silas Clark hauled some manure(for me). The Steamer Golden Eagle came up & I with Doc.Hysell and Jum Ferguson started to Wheeling. Paid $6.00 fare.

Sunday Feb.14,1869

Hysell,Ferguson & I was all day on the Steamer Golden Eagle on our way to Wheeling.Arrived at Parkersburg just at dark.
   (FL-Some dates left out)
   Thursday Feb.18,1869
   Friday Feb.19,1869

Intense exciment in town. Mr.Bukey has the small pox,so pronounced by Drs. McGinnis,Hysell and Ricketts. The town council ordered fences to be built across street each side of the house which was done & small pox signs put up. All communication forbidden-nothing but small pox talked of. Robert came down in the afternoon. He bought a mare to Mr.Clerighton. Paid $126 for her and bridle.

small pox-quarantine

Saturday Feb.20.1869

The excitement still great about the small pox. Reported that two of Able Clark's children has it. I paid John Joseph 1.00. Paid Silas Clark for 500 brick and hauling them($3.00). Dobbins left on a Pittsburg boat towards night.

Sunday Feb.21,1869

Small pox excitement not abating any. Some horses and carts for the Railroad came in on the Fleetwood. Also Ingle & Ingraham's wives.

Monday Feb.22,1869

(Jim Wright & Henry Campbell worked at my building.)

Tuesday Feb.23,1869

(Jim Wright and Henry Campbell
working again at my building.)

Wednesday Feb.24,1869

Roland and Jim Wright went out on
Four Pole to hold an inquest on a man
named Bowden who was killed by a tree   death from fallin tree
falling on him.

Thursday Feb.25,1869

Caley went over in Ohio to a school
exhibition.

Friday Feb.26,1869

I paid Frank Joseph 25cts. for
wheeling the dirt away.(John Joseph had
worked for him.)
(Robert's wife Mary Ann confined
with a boy.)   brother Robert's baby

Saturday Feb.27,1869

There is a rumor this afternoon
that the soldiers will leave here soon.
I attended Lodge. Hayslip went to
Wheeling and I acted as secretary.

Sunday Feb.28,1869

Sergent Reitzheimer & I was up to
my house in the afternoon a while.

Monday March 1,1869

I helped Campbell set the pillars
for back porch.

Tuesday March 2,1869

Sallie went over to Thornburg's
today.

Wednesday March 3,1869

Sallie went over to Anna's. Wright
& Campbell working on back porch & paid
J.B.Hite 2.90 for hair & 5.00 for flour.

Thursday March 4,1869

There was festival of the sewing   festival
circle over to the church. Two quilts
were drawn, one for Mrs.Bonner &
Mrs.Ritzheimer the other.(Grant &
Schuyler inaugurated today.)

Friday March 5,1869

Lew Peters brought me two grates
from Cattlettsburg.(I decided to keep
one & send the other back.)

Saturday March 6,1869

The Steamer Golden Eagle came up
just before night & left off a cake for
each Doc.Hysell,Chubb Scott and myself
as a present. It caused considerable
excitement.

Sunday March 7,1869

Fleetwood came up about 4 o'c.
Alford & Hayslip came from wheeling
about 3 o'c.

Monday March 8,1869

(Took grate to Crossley(Steamboat)
to send back to Whitman at Catlettsburg)
Reported that Press Bukey has the small
pox.

Tuesday March 9,1869

The soldiers received orders to
leave by today's mail.
Roland helped Wright & Campbell
weatherboard the privy.
The soldiers packing to leave
Friday. I sent $17 to Henry Miller to
pay for lime,cement and plaster he sent
me.

Wednesday March 10,1869

I paid Hysell $50 on account of
glass and paint. I attended the auction
sale of the soldiers. I bought a stove
at $6.25 also some other things. Paid
them $4.00 for 6lbs. of Tea.

Thursday March 11,1869

I paid the Major $13.35 for flour,
sugar,coffee and oven & also $7.00 to
Lieut.for stove,etc.I bought yesterday.
Fleetwood passed up just before
dark. The soldiers packing up to go down
on her tomorrow. Roland out serenading
until after midnight.

Friday March 12,1869

Towards night, the Fleetwood came
down. The soldiers all got on board and
most of their stores on to leave,when
the mail came bringing orders to the   soldiers finally leave
Major to remain here until further
orders. They then took their things off
the boat & returned to their quarters. I
sent my pipe over to let them use my
stove. Sergt.Ritzheimer took supper
until us.

Saturday March 13,1869

Bought some fruit trees of Sam
Hayslip for $1.00.(paid by order on
A.G.White) Put them in a row on my lot.
I lent H.H.Wood $1.50.Soon after
dinner,Caley rode the mare up to the
mill.
The Major received orders to report
his company at Louisville. They leave
Tuesday.

Sunday March 14,1869

The Fleetwood came up just before
night.
I wrote a letter for Cynthia to her
sister Jane.   Nagle
Aunt Nancy over here a while.

Monday March 15,1869
Tuesday March 16,1869

Major Kreutenger and his company
left on her(Fleetwood) for Louisville.
there was a noisy time at the Wharf
Boat. Jim Wright,Jim Sedinger,Irving
Smith,Chubb Scott and several others
were about half tight & Billy Rodgers
and Sam Johnston raised the mischief
until near night.

Wednesday March 17,1869

Jim Wright commenced putting up a
house for himself next to the church
yesterday.
Roland all day taking down the
oven. I bought of the soldiers &
cleaning the brick. Ryan commenced
taking down the quarters.

Thursday March 18,1869

Nothing much going on about
Town,but ball playing.

Friday March 19,1869
Saturday March 20,1869
Sunday March 21,1869

The Fleetwood & Telegraph landed
nearly at one time.
Bonner came home yesterday & told
us that Robert & Sam had another house
of tobacco burned Friday night.
I went to the M.E.Church and heard
Mr.King preach his last sermon.

Monday March 22,1869

Jim Sedinger & Letulle commenced
plastering my house. Roland mixed the
mortor and Gates carried it up.
Mr.&Mrs.King and their two boys took
supper here. Then they went to the Grant
(House)to wait for a boat. They move
from here tonight. The Templers have an
anniversary Supper tonight.

Tuesday March 23,1869

The Annie Laurie landed here this
morning. I got a bale of hay off the
Victor.Paid $3.70.

Wednesday March 24,1869

Gates went off and I had to get the
black man,Doss,to carry the hod for
Sedinger & Letulle.

Thursday March 25,1869

Friday March 26,1869

Children over at Anna's sewing
carpet rags.

Saturday March 27,1869

I paid the man Gates $1.50 for
carrying the hod. Caley went down to
Henry Russell's and brought up my cow.
        In the afternoon, The Guyandotte
Base Ball Club had a match with the
Normal Club. The Guyandotte Club beat.
        I attended the Lodge. Jacob
Hiltbruner initiated. Pollard(?) took
second.

baseball match between
Guyandotte & Marshall ?

Sunday March 28,1869

I pulled a tooth for Blankenship's
daughter. Tom Thornburg came down this
morning & left for Philadelphia on
Fleetwood.

Monday March 29,1869

I paid George Holderby $15 on acct.
of rent for Mrs.Chapman(to Mrs.C.) Role
& Cale went down to Henry Russell's this
morning & brought the cow & calf up.

Tuesday March 30,1869

I pd Chs.Ryan $20. I paid Bill
Wright $3.50 for a pair of boots for
Cale. The new Steamer Ohio No.4(here)

Wednesday March 31,1869

Paid E.A.Smith 90cts. for 3lbs.
butter.

Thursday April 1,1869

Mr.Schmidt came down here. He dah a
barge load of lumber, came down just
after dark.(He expected to have Tow Boat
take it to Pittsburg.Took tea with us.

Friday April 2,1869

Schmidt went down the river on the
Fleetwood.

Saturday April 3,1869

Dobbins household fruniture was sold this morning. Most of it brought more than they can be got new. In the afternoon, the lumber about the mill was sold. Price buying most of it.

Sunday april 4,1869

Ohio No.4 went down. Fleetwood went up.

Monday April 5,1869

Roland and Cale went across the Guyan River at the mouth and got some sand in Price's boat.Thornburg hauled it in two loads. I planted my early Goodrich potatoes. The tow boat hauled here for Schmidth's barge load of lumber. Roland was there with it all night.

Tuesday April 6,1869

I found the tow boat Tigress aground on the flat just below the Bridge.
Role was at work on her. The Kenton & Crosley pulled at her last night, but could not get her off.(I) arose just at daylight. The Tigress was whistling for help. Just as I got out, the tow boat came to her assistance and pulled her off.

Wednesday April 7,1869

Roland finished digging our cistern. Tom Thornburg returned from Philadelphia on the Golden Eagle. Got Freutel's(FL-Julius ?) boy to haul some water in the afternoon.

Thursday April 8,1869

I set out some onions. Newt.Bonner helped Role. robert & his nigger William staid last night at Hiltbruner's. He concluded to take his tobacco(down) on the Fleetwood this afternoon & I lent him my mare to go back home and return by three o'clock.(Too late.Fleetwood

14

went an hour earlier than usual.) Roland arching cistern.

Saturday April 10,1869

Robert's Black man William was here & staid.

Sunday April 11,1869

Colored William here to breakfast. Robert came down about 10 o'clock & concluded to ship their tobacco to Bodman. A Mr.Ford from that house was waiting for him here(From Cincinnati) After dinner Telegraph came down(& they & tobacco went.)

Monday April 12,1869

Towards night,Mr.William Morris from Hurricane Bridge came here . He took supper and staid all night with us.

Tuesday April 13,1869

Cynthia bought 26yds rag carpet for $13.00

Wednesday April 14,1869

Miss Young left for Missouri today.

Thursday April 15,1869
Friday April 16,1869

Roland & Cale fixing calf pen & bee house. Major Weimer's Steamboat went to Barboursville.

Saturday April 17,1869

Roland & Wiliam returned from Cincinnati. They have not done very well with their tobacco. Only sold two hogsheads.

Sunday April 18,1869

Fixed myself to go to Charleston to attend U.S.Court. About 3 o'c, the Fleetwood came & I with Tom Thornburg,Albert Laidley,Burnett,Bill Wentz,Fuller,Ben McGinnis,Peter Holryde

& Newcomb all went on board arrived at
Gallipolis just after dark. We
immediately went on the Kanawha Steamer
Mountain Boy, & tried to get rooms,but
could not. Webb,Ramsdell,Bloss, and
others also came up.

Monday April 19,1869

Webb & I got room together at the
St.Albert. The Court organized after
dinner

Tuesday April 20,1869

I was called before the Grand Jury,
but indicted no one. The assistant
assessors had a meeting and agreed to
present Oley & Thornburg with a silver
mounted cane each.
I got Wentz,Fuller,Holryde,and
Newcomb released & paid by the Marshall.
I got $14.50,just enough to pay my fare
and Hotel Bill.

Wednesday April 21,1869

(Our party left Charleston at 9:30
on Steamer Kanawha Belle,landed at
Pt.Pleasant about 6 o'clock. Took Golden
Eagle home.)
My family had moved in my new
house. I had to inquire where I lived.

Thursday April 22,1869
Friday April 23,1869

Oscar Mathers was here today. he
told me he had recommended (Frank)
Lesage for my position as Asst.Assessor.
He offered me the Clerkship. I told him
I wanted to take charge of his office
for $800 a year.

Saturday April 24,1869
Sunday April 25,1869

Fleetwood went up, Ohio No.4 went
down.

Monday April 26,1869

Paid Peter Holryde #.50 for work on
our stable.

Tuesday April 27,1869

The Barboursville Brass Band came
down this morning & played around town
until the middle of the afternoon,when
they returned.

Brass Band

Wednesday April 28,1869

Black William brought me some
strawberry plants from Roffe's.

Thursday April 29,1869

Holryde here all the forenoon
puttin locks on my doors. Frank Hite
came here a while.

Friday April 30,1869

I mailed my April Account to
Thornburg.(Sallie staid all night at
Hiltbruner's acct.storm.

Saturday May 1,1869

Caley took the mare and put her in
John Everett's pasture this morning.
Rodolph Dietz's daughter & Got(Gov.)
Jewell was married this morning.
     I pulled a tooth for Pres.Bukey
this morning and one for his father this
afternoon, Role,Susie and the children
all went to meeting.

Deitz m Got Jewell

Monday May 3,1869
Tuesday May 4,1869

1/4 to 6 o'c, the little steamer
Hunter came along. Roland and I got on
her for Barboursville to attend Court.
He on jury. Arrived there little before
nine o'clock. I paid our fare 5cts each.
     Took dinner at Hatfield's. bought a
hat for Sallie of Tom Thornburg. Paid
him $5.00 on account. Role & I started
home on the boat(at 1/4 till 6). About a
hour coming down.

fare to B'ville 5¢

Wednesday May 5,1869

(Went to Court on the boat.)

Thursday May 7,1869

Rivers rising. A lot of timber came down Guyan.

Friday May 7,1869

About 1/2 after 6 went to Barboursville on the Steamer. Took dinner at Hatfield's.

Saturday May 8,1869

A large number of rafts came down guyan. About 5 o'c, the steamer came from Barboursville.

many rafts

Sunday May 9,1869

Mr.& Mrs.Hayslip,Charley,Annie, & others here while I was gone.

Monday May 10,1869

(Pacfic R.R. completed today.) I rode to Barboursville & back home by noon. Lou Dusenberry,Mrs.Ong & Stewart was here to see Cynthia in the afternooon.(Last nail on the Pacfic R.R. was laid at noon today.

Tuesday May 11,1869

Paid D.I.Smith $2.00 for Dad Russell.

Wednesday May 12,1869

Towards night Lesage came to my office as Asst.Assessor Internal Revenue over to him.(I refused as neither he nor I had orders to turn over the books & papers to him.)

Thursday May 13,1869

Mathers went up by here. He offered me $600 a year to clerk for him.

Friday May 14,1869

Rec'd a note from Mathers to turn over the books & papers belonging to my office to Lesage.(My offical career

expired yesterday.)Caley was down to the
Rebel Church festival.

Saturday May 15,1869

Bob Allen returned my latern. Caley
was down to his temperance Lodge until
ten o'clock.

Sunday May 16,1869

Mrs.Frank Hite here a while in the
afternoon. Children all went to the
meeting.

Monday May 17,1869

(Lesage came about 6 o'c & I turned
over books & papers---"which office I
ceased to hold this day."

Tuesday May 18,1869

(Pd.E.A.Smith $4.00 for a
20lb.middling of bacon.)

Wednesday May 19,1869

Bill Worden came this morning and
commenced cutting the stone to go under
my front porch. Roland helped All White
raft logs in the afternoon.

Thursday May 20,1869

Roland helping All White raft.

Friday May 21,1869

Roland rafting during forenoon.

Saturday May 22,1869

There was a dancing party went from
here this morning on the Victor 4.
Black William down from the mill.

Sunday May 23,1869

Black William went to Cincinnati on
the Ohio about noon. Mr.& Mrs.Ryan,Sue
Barber,All White & Dept.Marshall Slack
with Jackson & Marcum from Wayne Co.was
here this afternoon.

I went up to Frank Hites a while.

Monday May 24,1869

Roland rafting.

Tuesday May 25,1869

Roland started down the Ohio with
All White on timber.(rafting)

Wednesday May 25,1869
Thursday may 26,1869
Friday May 27,1869

Sallie & Cale went to a Festival
down to Peter Buffington's.(Back after
midnight.)

Saturday May 29,1869

I got Ryan's black horse & about 7
o'clock, Doct.Hysell & I started out to
Barbours school house. Had a trial there
with Bill Turner on a note for $25.
Col.Carroll attended to it for me.

Sunday May 30,1869
Monday May 31,1869
Tuesday June 1,1869
Wednesday June 2,1869

Great preparation making by the
Rebels for a festival in their church   festival
tonight. The Hunter came from
Barboursville towards night bringing the
band and lots of ladies. Capt. Mann the
U.S.Collector, came this afternoon to
collect here. I was at Bill Wright's
with him most of the afternoon. Black
Wm. came down and went up the river on
the Hudson.

Thursday June 3,1869

I was in town awhile. made
arragements with Dave Thornburg to go up
to the mill in the morning with some of
the jury summoned to condemn our mill
privilege.

Friday June 4,1869

About 7 o'clock, Thornburg came
along with his hack containing
Newcomb,Hayslip, and Ben McGinnis.
(Started to our mill.Stopped in B'ville
a while. Freutl & Silas Clark rode up on
horse back). Kline(FL-attorney T.B.) was
there for the company & Ricketts & Ben
McGinnis appeared for us. The Deputy
Sheriff,Henry Harshbarger swore the jury
who were T.J.Hayslip, Silas(Mac)Clark,
Newcomb,Freutel,Jim Baumgardner,Salmon,
Dave Harshbarger,Hinchman,Chas.Hall,
Turley,Sampson Handley & John Merritt.
The lawyers stated the case for
both sides, Then Lev Swann & Bill
Rodgers examined as witnesses.(Jury gave
verdict for us for $3000, after short
time out) After which, the jury took
dinner with us prepared by Robert. Sarah
was there helping Mary Ann(Robert's
wife) (Bought 2 lamp chimneys of
Hackworth at 20cts each) Got some hen
eggs of Bob Allen.

condemed mill $3000

Saturday June 5,1869

Bought & paid Wright & Co. $1.00
for sugar and $1.50 for stockings.

Sunday June 6,1869

Robert expected to go to the
mill,but could get no conveyance.
Expected Sam & Sarah down but they did
not come.

Monday June 7,1869

Roland went up to the mill on the
steamer Hunter to work for Schmidt.
Girly Hite staid all night with Sally.

Tuesday June 3,1869

There was a Mr.Norton here
inquiring into Dobbins affairs.(He had
had several suits against him) The
Steamer Fleetwood left off a cake for
the M.E.Sunday School festival Thursday
night. I paid Dr. McGinnis $12.40
balance in full for rent due Mrs.Chapman

for the house we lived in.(Pulled a
tooth for Peter Baker.

Wednesday June 9,1869

Helped the girls some fix for their
festival tomorrow night. Their
strawberries,ice and lemons came. The
Steamer Fayette gave them a fine cake,
and the Victor No.3 gave them $10.00.
(Caley got Pete Baker's horse to ride to
B'ville for the mare at Hatfields)
Hatfield made her back sore.

Thursday June 10,1869

Cynthia and Susie fixing for the
Sunday School childern's festival tonight. I was at the Festival. Children
all there. Aunt Nancy came up and staid
with Cynthia. I attended the door. A
good many there.(Closed at 10 o'clock.

Friday June 11,1869

Just at night,Charles & Anna was up
here for a short time.
Paid Bill Wright $6.75 for barrel
of flour, and we wheeled it home in the
wheel barrow.

Saturday June 12,1869

Paid E.A.Smith $1.75 for coffee,
Butter, and soda. The children gave the
minister the plate of honey we sent to
the festival.

Sunday June 13,1869

Children went to meeting in the
forenoon.

Monday June 14,1869

In the afternoon,Col.Carroll & Doc
Hysell came here after the mare.(Let
Carroll take her to sell at $130, or
return her in as good order as he takes
her.)

Tuesday June 15,1869
Wednesday June 16,1869

Thursday June 17, 1869

Sallie made up a bunch of Flowers &
when the Fleetwood came, took it down
and presented it to Capt.Halloway.

Friday June 18, 1869
Saturday June 19, 1869

(Roland came from the mill. He rode
Hatfield's horse.)

Sunday June 20, 1869

Baker & Holdryde was here this
morning.

Monday June 21, 1869

I went down with Hysell, Sedinger,
Jim Wright, Brother Charles & some
other. About 7 o'clock. We fixed
platforms & seats for the speaking at
the laying of the corner stone by the
Masons on the 24th. About 2 o'c., we all
came up on the Victor NO.3.

Tuesday June 22, 1869

Womeldorff and Jennie Hite was   marriage Hite to Womeldorf
married this morning. Fanny,Ed, & Girley
Hite was here a short time.

Wednesday June 23, 1869

In the afternoon, Mr.Moore from
Cincinnati & Hubble from Galipolis
stopped off the Ohio to attend the
laying of the cornerstone tomorrow. They
came up to the house with me and had   corner stone for new lodge
some honey.
Roland came bringing
Sarah, Bro.Sam's wife & baby with him.
The Golden Eagle came down about 9
o'clook bringing about thirty masons.
Hysell and I attended them to the
Hotels.

Thursday June 24, 1869

J.M.McWherter came up here early
and insured my house. Then we went down
& took a policy on P.S.Smith's house and
stock of goods.

Then the Hunter coming down from
Barboursville. Doc.Hysell,Scott,
Sedinger, & I, the committee escorted
what few Masons came down to the Lodge
room. About 10 o'clock, the steamer
Fayette came with our band and the
Masons from Portsmouth. we escorted them
to church. Then the Dexter came with
Catlettsburg & Wayne Lodges. We also
escorted them up,and then with our lodge
formed in procession at the church and
marched up one street and down the other
to the Boats. Little after 11 o'clock,
the two boats took us down to Holderby's
Landing. None of my folks got ready on
time to get on the boat. Marched direct
from the Landing to the College.
Dist.Dept.G.M.H.J.Samuels then laid the
corner stone & then we marched to the
Grove where Prof.Thompson read a short
address, and Charley Moore made a short
speech,after which they all adjourned
for dinner.

real celabration

corner stone laid at
Marshall

I got Joe Stewart's horse & wagon &
sent Caley up for Susie and Sall. They
came after all was over & while I was
finding them, the Band and Masons went
on the Boats and returned to Guyan
leaving Sedinger & I with a few others
behind. We were surprised at their going
and taking the Band as the expectations
were for them to play for a dance. About
4 o'clock, the Fleetwood came and
Susie,Sall,and I with about 300 others
returned to Guyan on her. The Capt.would
not take any fare.

        Friday June 25,1869

I bought a calico dress(in town)
for Sarah at Bill Wright's($1.22.) I
also got three yards green calico.

        Saturday June 26,1869

Towards night, young Stewart
commenced plowing my corn, but horse
broke down so much he quit.

        Sunday June 27,1869

Bro.Sam and Sarah went home.

Monday June 28,1869

Caley helped Baker harvest in the forenoon. Sall went down to the temperance lecture & after ten when she returned. I retired.

Tuesday June 29,1869

Caley helped Baker harvest.

Wednesday June 30,1869

I was in town a few minutes(FL- He must have lived out of town.)

his farm was about 3 blocks from the main business district

Thursday July 1,1869
Friday July 2,1869

I took a couple pieces of honey down to the <u>Fleetwood</u> for Holloway and Simmons. Hovey(Tom Thornburg's son-in-law) put off a patent gate. I helped him set it up in front of the Drug Store.

Saturday July 3,1869

Col.Carroll came here about 9 o'clock. I made off his report for him as Asst.Assessor. Int.Rev.for the month of June. Then I went in Town. Newcomb holds court & he has several cases. Sedinger came up & got 60cts. from Carroll and I for a distressed mason. Roland and Bonner brought down Schmidt's boat with the mill on it.

Sunday July 4,1869

Hovey & Lew Peters up here a whiloe in the afternoon. The <u>Steamer Ohio No.4</u> & <u>Fleetwood</u> was all dressed off in flags today.

Monday July 5,1869

I pulled a tooth for Tom Tucker's wife. She did not pay anything.

Tuesday July 6,1869

Robert came down in a boat this morning with two small hogsheads of tobacco. Roland came down with some logs

for Schmidt about the middle of the
afternoon.

Wednesday July 7, 1869

A part of the Chesapeake & Ohio
R.R. Co. passed here going to Ceredo.
They had come through viewing the line
of the road. Albert Laidey was with
them. I lent him $2.00.

Thursday July 8, 1869

I sent the cane to Oley by the
Fleetwwood to H.R.Howard, Point Pleasant.
Paid for the canes $16.00. had to put in

Friday July 9, 1869

Roland and Boner working on
Schmidt's mill boat. Caley went up to
Rece's in the skiff & got 21 Turkey(18
little ones two hens & a gobbler) I
bought a Woodrum for $5.00.

Saturday July 10, 1869

Sent a package by Steamer Golden
Eagle to the West Virginia Insurance
Co., containing O.J.Smith's & my
applications for insurance & $56.14 amt.
of our premiums. Paid C.B.Scott $5.00.
Got a pair of boots of Bill Wright am to
pay $7.00 for them. Roland and Bonner
working on the mill boat.

Sunday July 11, 1869

Ed Hite was here a while.

Monday July 12, 1869

Schmidt sent word last night for
Roland to come up to our mill & work on
the barge. he went up with Thornburg
this morning.(Dusenderry was having
several bee swarms.

Tuesday July 13, 1869

(Roland brought a Mr.Peters home
with him.)

Wednesday July 14,1869

Caley went to the Brick Yard at the College to work this morning.

Thursday July 15,1869

All White came for Roland soon after breakfast to go down river on timber with him & about 10 o'clock they started. I was down town a while. Got 20lbs. of sugar of All White. also accep[ted Jim Wright's order on White for $50.00. Cale wnt to Brick Yard again to work.

Friday July 16,1869

I hired a skiff to Crump.

Saturday July 17,1869

I let Geo.Price,Joe Hysell and some others have to(the ?) skiff Dove(?FL) Paid Bill Wright 85cts. for a Pr. of hoops for Sallie.

Sunday July 18,1869

Just as we were taking breakfast, word came that Schmidt's mill boat had caught out on the bank and was sinking. (She sank. I immediately sent word up to Schmidt & Bonner. I tried all afternoon to get some one to help raise her,but they said they would get nothing for it.) river fell of course. I got help enough to put ropes on the cabin to keep her from going over. Oley Smith staid all night (acct of rain).

Monday July 19,1869

There was a man with an organ had singing in the M.E. Church. The children all went.(Schmidt & Bruce Wolcott came & commenced getting the loose things off her.(They blame me & say they left her in charge of Roland.) Bonner came down in the afternoon.(River rising & they can not raise her.)

Tuesday July 20, 1869

There was singing in the Baptist Church. The children all went.

Wednesday July 21, 1869

There was singing again in the Baptist Church. I was in town a while. Stopped at Bro. Charles.

Thursday July 22, 1869

I pulled a tooth for Talt Everett's little girls. Mrs.Ryan here in the afternoon. (Children all singing at the Baptist Church.)

Friday July 23, 1869

Hight's(Hite's-FL) & Joseph's little boys found a swarm of bees hanging on a paw paw bush on the hillside back of my house. Mrs.Hite & Fanny was out there. Children at the singing.

Saturday July 24, 1869

I paid Freutel 20cts. for 3/4lb butter.

Sunday July 25, 1869

Mrs. Rece & Hite here just at night.

Monday July 26, 1869

Children fixing for the Baptist Festival to-night.(I was appointed to keep the door.) Singing fine but there was a poor turn out(acct of storm)

Tuesday July 27, 1869

Roland came home (from Louisville) on Steamer Ohio. Went ot helping Bonner & Schmidt raise the mill boat.

Wednesday July 28, 1869

Cale & Sall was invited to help sing at the Rebel Church festival. They

went to practice this evening when
Oley,Dietz, the Blankenships & others
objected to an Yanks having anything to
do with it so Cale & Sall came home.

Thursday July 29,1869

Ed Hite,Caley & I put up a
swing(PM)

Friday July 30,1869

I paid Joe Hysell 75cts. for 3lbs
butter from Wilson. There was another
Festival at the Baptist Church.. The
children went. Mrs.Skelton died about
one o'clock this morning. The church
bells tolled.

death Mrs.Shelton

Saturday July 31,1869

Mrs.Skelton was taken to
Barboursville early this morning and
buried. Just as the funeral passed here
little Frank fell down the cellar
stairs(Didn't hurt himself much.()

Sunday Aug.1,1869

I lent Bias the skiff in the
afternoon to go over the river with his
sons's child.

Monday Aug.2,1869

Roland working on the mill boat.

Tuesday Aug.3,1869

Col.Carroll took supper here.

Wednesday Auf.4,1869

Soon after breakfast, I started to
Barboursville on foot. About Rece's, the
Barboursville Hack that came down this
morning came along and I rode the rest
of the way up in it.
(Took Tom Thornburg's cane to him)
Caley & Clay Hite came up in the skiff.
I took dinner at Hatfield's. Got some
lard,sugar. I, Hayslip, and Bonner came
down in the skiff.

Thursday Aug.5,1869

Was told the Grand Jury indicted
our dam today, as an obstruction to the
river.

Friday Aug.6,1869

I walked to Barboursville to court.
Caley,Alex. Clark & Bert Ong came up in
the skiff. About 4 o'clock,we started
home bringing Ben Hanley(what was
crippled by jumping out of a Buggy
Wednesday) his wife & Newt.Keenan with
us.

Saturday Aug.7,1869

Arose early. Weather clear & cool
most of the day. some clouds. About 5
o'clock, there was an Eclispe of the
sun. It was not quite total. My chickens
and Turkeys went to roost.

Sunday Aug.8,1869
Monday Aug.9,1869

I paid Tom Thornburg $1.00 for
5lbs. butter & left it to be sent down
in the hack.
Roland started to Cincinnati on
timber, but it got on the bar at the
mouth of the creek & he returned home.

Tuesday Aug.10,1869

(Went ot B'ville) The dam question
was brought up and laid over until after
dinner. Took dinner at Hatfield's. Found
the Judge was not going to allow the
amt. of finding of the Jury for damanges
so we got Suydam & agreed with him that
the Company should pay us $2500 for
taking out our dam, which amount the
Judge accepted and awarded us that
amount of damage. I got some goods for
Susie of Schmidt. Rode home in a buggy
with Ben McGinnis & Ricketts.

$2500 damages

Wednesday Aug.11,1869

Towards night Robert & Sam(who had
come down) Started to Sam Johnstons

intendening to go home by the other
road.

Thursday Aug.12,1869

About noon, the threshing machime
came to thresh Baker's wheat(I helped
him as he was short of hands. I filled
and carried sacks. Hot work. They put
two of their horses in my stable.)
Alice Wilson,old man Douthat's   death Alice Douthet Wilson
daughter, was brought home a corpse
about midnight. She died back of
Maysville. had been sick some time.

Friday Aug.13,1869

Pulled a toothe for Spicer's
wife(50cts) Alice Wilson was buried this
morning. I went to the funeral.

Saturday Aug.14,1869
Sunday Aug.15,1869
Monday Aug.16,1869
Tuesday Aug.17,1869
Wednesday Aug.18,1869

Caley went to Barboursville to try
to get H.H.Woods buggy

Thursday Aug.19,1869
Friday Aug.20,1869

Robert's nigger Harrison came down
with the wagon.

Saturday Aug.21,1869

Mr.Frank Hite came from Lincoln
towards night. I attended Lodge. Raised
J.C.Baker.

Sunday Aug.22,1869
Monday Aug.23,1869
Tuesday Aug.24,1869

Caley took Wood's buggy & Robert's
horse home and returned in the hack.

Thursday 26,1869

There was a circus came here this
morning. About noon Charley came up here
and said I ought to collect license. I

went down but Hayslip had collected it.
Children all went to the circus. They
cam home by ten o'clock. Caley went home
with Girly Hite. (FL-John Calvin)Rece
was there marring Fanny to Billy Church.

Friday Aug.27,1869

Roland making a cider press.

Saturday Aug.28,1869

Towards night Role and I gathered
about a bushel of peaches off my trees
in the mill lot.(Made 5-6 gal.cider.

Sunday Aug.29,1869

Bill Church and his wife (Fannie
Hite that was) was here part of the
afternoon.

Monday Aug.30,1869

Made about 15 gals.cider.

Tuesday Aug.31,1869

(Price came here,got a drink of
cider & shook a lot of apples from his
trees & gave them to me for cider.)
Black William who used to work for
Robert came here and staid all night.

Wednesday Sept.1,1869
Thursday Sept.2,1869
Friday Sept.3,1869

Sent Caley up to the mill after a
horse. I went to my trees in the mill
lot & took off the peaches as Joseph's
children are stealing them. I started
down to see Hysell & Baker about going
to Wayne C.H. in the morning to assist
the Masons there in laying the corner
stone to their Masonic Hall. Met they &
they said we would start at 3 o'clock in
the morning. Baker met me at 2 o'clock.

Saturday Sept.4,1869

Baker called me quarter to one
o'clock this morning. Blankenship came
and I lent him a spur at 2 o'clock.

Blankenship,Sedinger,Doc Hysell, Irving Smith,Witcher,Chub Scott,Baker and I started to Wayne C.H. to assist in laying the corner stone of the Masonic Hall there. We got there at 6 o'clock and put up at Col Carroll's who has lately moved there & open a HOtel. We were about here all the forenooon. NOne of the Masons there welcomed or paid any attention to us at all. Soon after dinner, there was addresses in the Court House by a Mr.Johnson & Medley. A good many people there not liking the way we were treated, not even being invited in the Lodge,about 2 o'clock, we started home (after paying our Hotel bils 80cts.

Sedinger remained to go to the Association on Mud River. We stopped at Sam Blankenship's and ate some watermelons. Got home at sun down.

Sunday Sept.5,1869

Children went to meeting.

Monday Sept.6,1869

Roland working for Jim Wright.

Tuesday Sept.7,1869

The Dobbins Mill was to have been sold today. But sale was postponed until the 29th. Black William came from the mill.(Staid all night.)

Wednesday Sept.8,1869

Paid the Steamer Crosley $1.50 for towing coal boat. Lou Burks paid me $6.40 amt.due me from Laidly'e estate.

Thursday Sept.9,1869

Roland working on Jim Wright's Boat.

Friday Sept.10,1869

Roland working on Wright's boat.

33

Saturday Sept.11,1869

Before noon Caley & Freutel's boys started to Dutch Town in the Skiff. Robert came down and went with the wagon to Sam Johston's for his Evaporator.

Sunday Sept.12,1869

Ohio River hugh.Guyan backed up above Barboursville.

Monday Sept.13,1869

I was about home all day drying fruit.Caley returned home from Dutch Town bringing----

Tuesday Sept.14,1869

Roland working on boat.(Jim Wright's)

Wednesday Sept.15,1869

Cynthia made peach butter in the wood house.

Thursday Sept.16,1869

Roland working on boat. There was an exbition at the Rece Church.

Friday Sept.17,1869

Saturday Sept 18,1869

Burt Chambers came and took his (two) shiffs away. Roland bought the Sallie for $10.00. He took supper with us and home on the Victor No.4. Roland working on boat. Chambers here a while.

Sunday Sept.19,1869

Children all attended meeting.

Monday Sept.20,1869

Caley with some children started to the State Normal School. They returned early in the afternoon. They charged $4.00 a month which is too high and they

concluded not to go. Mr.Schmidt and
another Dutchman from Pittsburg wad here
a while.

Tuesday Sept.21,1869

Fannie Hite and her sister was here
a while in the afternoon.
(R.D.)Bright was married in
Barboursville to Lafe Samuel'd daughter
& they went to Cincinnati this
afternoon. Roland worked on Wright's
boat.

Samuels to R.D.Bright

Wednesday Sept.22,1869

Cynthia(and children) made
applebutter(about 17 gallons.) I paid
50cts. for use of kettle.

Thursday Sept 23,1869

Sampson Simmons and Miss Ruffner
was married in Barboursville Church.

Ruffner to Sampson Simmon

Friday Sept.24.1869

Roland working on boat.

Saturday Sept.25,1869

Roland working on boat. I attended
Lodge.

Sunday Sept.26,1869

I read the account of the Woodall
Mine Horror by which 108 miners lost
their lives on the 6th inst.

Monday Sept.27,1869

I was down in town. Paid Keenan
$2.00 for sugar & coffee.

Tuesday Sept.28,1869

A Mr.Vosberg was here most of the
afternooon. He came to bid on Dobbins
mill tomorrow. Remained here till after
supper. About 8 o'clock, I went down to
the Hotel with him. Roland working on
Boat.

Wednesday Sept.29,1869

About noon, Kline(F.B.) and the
sheriff came down to sell the mill. They
waited until the Steamer Mounatin Bell
came up thinking Mr.Selden from
Erie,Pa., as Mr.Vosberg said he was
certainly on the road. He not coming,
the sale was put off until tomorrow.
There was several bidders here. Vosberg
went up the river on the Mountain Belle.

Thursday Sept.30,1869

Mr.Selden and his wife arrived here
this morning.(They came to my house.)
About 2 o'clock, the sheriff came and
sold the mill. Mr.Selden bought it foe
$1550. Price,Witcher,White and Selden
were the bidders. Mr.Selden & wife took
supper here.(I gave them some
strawberries.) Col.Witcher came just
before night.(He took $12.00 insurance
on the mill to secure the last
payments.) After supper ,I went down to
Witcher's with Selden. He topok his wife
to the Hotel. I lent Witcher $1100 to
make change to Sheldon in making payment
on the mill.

Friday Oct.1,1869

A wagon came along with Chickens.
Cynthia bought 2 doz. for $4.00

Saturday Oct.2,1869

Dan Rice's Circus landed here about
9 o'clock on the Steamer Willis Hay. she
landed at the grade. I went on board and
saw Dan Rice. Then according to his wish
I got a lot of Masons & we all went and
called on hi. I collected a corporation
license $40. He passed me in the circus.
Jessie went to the circus in the
afternoon. Roland,Susie,Sallie and I
went down to the circus. Dan Rice passed
Sallie & I in. He promised to call up &
see us tomorrow. Caley was also there,
so I came home just as the performance
commenced.

Circus

Sunday Oct.3,1869

Dan Rice called on us in the
afternoon. He was here quite a while.
rode one of his trained horses here.
Just before night his boat left for
Point Pleasant. Mr.Schmidt was here a
while in the afternoon.

Monday Oct.4,1869

Roland worked on the boat most of
the day.

Tuesday Oct.5,1869

Roland working on steam boat. The
Ohio No.4 went up this afternoon.

Wednesday Oct.6,1869

Roland working on the steam boat.

Wednesday Oct.6,1869
Caley went down to Coles early to
gather apples. Roland working on boat.
Engaged 3bbls.russet apples of Dr.Tuning
for $1.25 & I find the barrel. Role & I
took the barrels down to Deed Smith's
for Tuning.

Thursday Oct.7,1869

I went hunting with Pete Baker.

Friday Oct.8,1869

Old Mrs.Shelton died today.   death-Mrs.Shelton (twice??)

Saturday Oct.9,1869

Roland and I went over to the mill
in Proctorville & got my flour. Albert
Laidley stopped here at noon and took
dinner. Paid Keenan $1.00 for sugar.

Sunday Oct.10,1869
Monday Oct.11,1869

I went with Caley back of the house
and shot four pigeons. Roland was out
most of the day and shot Twelve pigeons.

Tuesday Oct.12,1869

Roland commenced sawing for
Schmidt. I bought a pair of boots for
myself of Mr.Douthet, price $5.00.

Wednesday Oct.13,1869

Roland working on saw mill. Just at
noon Robert & Sam came down here. After
dinner, they went down town and returned
with Charley. We signed an agreement
with Albert Laidley to sell the estate.
Caley went up to Stewart's in the
afternoon. Cynthia and children up to
Mrs.Hites.Paid Keenan $1.00 for coffee.

estate sale

Thursday Oct.14,1869

Roland sawing all day.

Friday Oct.15,1869
Saturday Oct.16,1869
Sunday Oct.17,1869

Mr.Berger was here a while in the
forenoon. Anna and her children came &
staid to supper. Roland,Susan,Cale &
Sall went to meeting.

Monday Oct.18,1869

Mr.Bolt's child died last night.
Hysell & Scott came by the house about 9
o'clock & got me to go to the Grave Yard
with them and pick out a place to bury.

death

Wednesday Oct.20,1869

Caley & I went up to the Graveyard
soon after breakfast to see if there was
any water in the Bolts child's grave.
Found that it was dug in the nigger part
of the grave yard. Then got Lou Peters
and we selected another place & got
Thompson to dig it. Lou, Cale and I cut
a road way to it. The funeral took place
about 3 o'clock. No ladies attended.

Thursday Oct.21,1869

Roland sawing.

Friday Oct.22,1869

Sal & Jessie was down to singing school. Cale went over the river to a Temperance meeting.

Saturday Oct.23,1869

I attended Lodge. Pollard was raised. Gave $1.00 to send representative to G.L. Home.(Horne ?)

Sunday Oct.24,1869

I went up to the graveyard with Mr.Bolts.

Monday Oct.25,1869

Roland sawing.

Tuesday Oct.26,1869
Wednesday Oct.27,1869

I went to John Everett's. He was not home.

Thursday Oct.28,1869

Dutch Schmidt licked his wife this evening.

Friday Oct.29,1869

The children went to singing school.

Saturday Oct.30,1869
Sunday Oct.31,1869
Monday Nov.1,1869

George Price was married yesterday and brought his wife home today. He married Mather's daughter. Susie & Cale at the Temperance Lodge. Sall at Singing School

Tuesday Nov.2,1869

Flower's house caught fire this morning. It was soon extingtished. The children commenced going to school.

Wednesday Nov.3,1869

Fult Tucker and I went over to the Coal Boat wreck in the forenoon, and got two skiff loads of coal.

Thursday Nov.4,1869

Blew & rained hard.

Friday Nov.5,1869

John Douthet and I walked up to court. We got there just behind the Hack. I took dinner at Hatfield's.(Our dam case laid over.) I rode home in the Hack. Paid 50cts. A tow boat with some barges stuck on the bar this afternoon. Roland went over and sent word home he should remain there all night helping them.

Saturday Nov.6,1869

In the afternoon, I collected some freight bills for Blankenship($30.35) I paid it over to him. Did not charge him anything. Children went to the temperance Lodge.

Sunday Nov.7,1869
Monday Nov.8,1869

Silas Clark & I walked to Barboursville. I paid Harshbarger $7.00 on my taxes. Rode home with Doc,Hysell & Ed Smith.

Tuesday Nov.9,1869

I rode up to court with Dave Thornburg, leaving the horse for Roland and Susie to come up in Claughton's buggy. I walked home.

Wednesday Nov.10,1869

I borrowed the Florence Sewing Machine Agent's wagon to go up to our mill in tomorrow.

Thursday Nov.11,1869

Fanny Hite was here a while. She came to Borrow.

Friday Nov.12,1869
Saturday Nov.13,1869

Vincent came here to look at my sewing machines. I want to trade them for his wagon. I got a pair of shoes of Douthet for Jesse.

Sunday Nov.14,1869

Charley Ryan here to dinner.

Monday Nov.15,1869

Silas Clark's team hauled my slabs from the mill yard.

Tuesday Nov.16,1869
Wednesday Nov.17,1869

Got a bbl. of flour of Bill Wright. Robert's nigger staid at Bukey's.

Thursday Nov.18,1869

Young Carter took dinner with us. My cow got in George Laidley's smoke house and ate about 1/2 bu. of shorts.

Friday Nov.19,1869

I paid D.I.and D.D.Smith $12.15(amt. I owed them) I commenced collecting corporation taxes.

Saturday Nov.20,1869

Trying to collect Crop. Taxes, but made a poor thing of it. I attended Lodge. Initiated Mr.Steel.

Sunday Nov.21,1869

Young Rickets came from Ohio. Came home to dinner with the children. Sall & Jessie did not come home for supper. They came down to meeting.

Monday Nov.22,1869

The children (went) to school.

Tuesday Nov.23,1869

Roland commenced sawing for
Schmidt. Just after dark he(Robert) left
on the Victor 3 for Ironton.

Wednesday Nov.24,1869

I was negotiating with Blankenship
for half of the Wharf boat.

Thursday Dec.2,1869
Friday Dec.3,1869

I bought half of the Wharf Boat of
E.D.Blankenship. Hayslip drew up the
contract and holds it. In the afternoon,
I paid Blankenship $350.00 and took
possession.

Saturday Dec.4,1869

I was at the Wharf Boat all day(and
till 9 P.M.

Sunday Dec.5,1869
Monday Dec.6,1869

Tom & Carey Hayslip & Black here to
supper & spent the eve.

Tuesday Dec.7,1869

Boys let the boat get on the bank
again last night.(The Crosley pulled her
off. The Hunter borught down a wedding
party. George Thornburg married Miss
Wilson.

Wednesday Dec.8,1869

Roland Rafting. Hunter did not come
from Barboursville.

Thursday Dec.9,1869
Friday Dec 10,1869

The Ohio came very late & put off a
tremendous lot of freight. They landed
George Thornburg and his wedding party
at the grade.

Saturday Dec.11,1896

Sunday Dec.12,1869
Monday Dec.13,1869

Caley & Robert started to Cattlettsburg in the shiff. Enoch & Jerrard went there this morning. The Webb on the Boat with me.(?) I paid Hayslip $1.00 for coffee & Douthet $2.70 for Jessie' shoes & a broom.

Tuesday Dec.14,1869
Wednesday Dec.15,1869

Roland working on boat repairing damages done by Fleetwood & Crossley. Dolen brought my desk from mill.

Thursday Dec.16,1869

Had my supper sent down. Weaver & Hersey took supper at house. Staid all night on boat with Cale.

Friday Dec.17,1869
Saturday Dec.18,1869

Cale & Burks staid with me (on boat)

Sunday Dec.18,1869

Fleetwood came up about 3 o'clock.

Monday Dec.20,1869

A lady staid at Wharf waiting for steamer.

Tuesday Dec.21,1869

Bro,Sam came down with sheriff and laid an attachment on the Tob Factory (Tobacco ?) for aunt. Porter's not $500. Cale staid with Blankenship. I came home (at 10).

Wednesday Dec.22,1869

Thos.Webb & I staid all night on the Boat.

Thursday Dec.23,1869

Thursday Dec.23,1869

About noon Blankenship & McGinnis
had a fight at Ed Smith's store. Paid
W.O.Wright $2.70 for sugar.

Friday Dec.24,1869

Caley went to the mill this morning
on the Steamer Hunter.

Saturday Dec.25,1869

Aunt Nancy,Charles & his family
took dinner with us.

Sunday Dec.26,1869

The St.Charles went down as also
did the Annie Laurie in the afternoon.
The Fleetwood up about 1/2 after one
o'clock & Ohio 4 down 1/2 after two
o'clock.

(All this was   Monday Dec.27,1869
nearly faded out   Tuesday Dec.28,1869
but I could read   Wednesday Dec.29,1869
it.It was of no   Thursday Dec.30,1869
importance.FL)
          Friday Dec.31,1869

A good many tight about town today.
The Ohio 4 brought me coop & returns for
my turkeys.(14cts a lb.)

The record for 1870 is in this
volume but I don't have room for it in
this book.--F.B.Lambert

(Part of the Lambert Collection Marshall
University,Huntington,WV.-Reprinted with
permission.)

Alex 29
Alford 9
Allen,Bob 18,20
Aunt Nancy 10,21,43
Aunt Olive 3,4
Baker 22,24,30,31
Baker,J.C. 30
Baker,Peter 21,36
Barber,Sue 19
Barbours 19
Baumgardner,Jim 20
Berger,Mr. 37
Bias 28
Black 41
Blankenship 5,12,28,31,
    39,41,42
Blankenship,Sam 32
Blankenship,E.D. 41
Bloss 15
Bloss,Ike 6
Bodman 14
Boggs,Sallie 4
Bolt,Mr. 37,38
Bonner 11,24,25,26,27,28
Bonner,Mrs.1,9
Bonner,Newt 13
Bowden 8
Bright,(R.D.) 34
Buffington,Peter 2,19
Bukey,Mr.7,40
Bukey,Press 9,16
Burks 42
Burks,Lou 6,32
Burks,Lou 6
Burnett 14
Calvin,John 31
Campbell 9
Campbell,Henry 7,8
Carroll 22,24
Carroll,Col. 19,21,24,
    28,32
Carter,Henry 6
Carter,Young 40
Chambers,Burt 6,33
Chapamn,Mrs.12,20
Childers,Sam 3
Church,Billy 31
Clara (nigger 2)
Clark,Able 7
Clark,Roland 1
Clark,Silas 7,20,39,40
Claughton's 39
Clerighton,Mr.7
Cook,Tom 6,27,30

Crump 26
Dietz 28
Dietz,Hugo 6
Dietz,Rodolph 16
Dobbins 6,7,13,20,32,34
Dolen 42
Doss,(black)11
Douthat 5,30,37,40,42
Douthet,John 39
Dunlevy & Co.3
Dusenberry,Lou 17,
Dusenberry,Mary Ann 20
Dusenberry,Mary Ann 8
Dusenberry,Nancy 1
Enoch 42
Enochs,Gen.6
Everett,John 16,38
Everett's,Talt 27
Ferguson 6
Ferguson,Jim 7
Flower's 38
Ford,Mr.14
Foster,John 3
Frank 28
Freutel 13,20,27,33
Fuller 15
Gates 11,12
Grant 9
Gullion 5
Hackworth 20
Hagan 6
Hall,Chas. 20
Halloway, 22,24
Handley,Sampson 20
Hanley,Ben 29
Harrison 30
Harshbarger,Dave 20
Harshbarger,Henry 20
Hatfield 6,16,17,21,
    22,28,39
Hay,Willis 35
Hayslip 6,8,9,17,20,
    28,41,42
Hayslip,Carey 41
Hayslip,Mrs. 17
Hayslip,Sam 10
Hayslip,T.J. 20
Hayslip,Tom 41
Henderson,Mark 3
Hersey 42
Hibbens,John T.2
Hight's 27
Hiltbruner 2,13,16
Hiltbruner,Jacob 12

(The following diary entries came to
light in 1990 in an antique shop in west
Huntington. They were found in the back
of an obvious "Fred Lambert" ledger. The
ledger was loanded to Marshall Special
Collections for copying by Rick Whisman.
1870 was entered before 1862.

W.F.Dusenberry's Diary for 1870

Saturday Jan.1, 1870

Caley & I remanined all night on
boat.

Sunday Jan.2,1870

The Annie Laurie came down about 3
o'clock & laid here until daylight on
account of the storm. Fleetwood ran in
at the grade & put off a wagon and some
horses. The Ohio did not go down.

Monday Jan.3,1870
Tuesday Jan.4,1870

The R.C.Gray went up. Role helped
Hugo Dietz kill hogs. Mrs.Peters &
Mollie at house for dinner.

Wednesday Jan.5,1870

At boat until about 9 o'c.

Thursday Jan.6,1870
Friday Jan.7,1870
Saturday Jan.8,1870

Blankenship got half of Boat
released from Holly's deed of trust & I
paid Ball $300 & took in my note.
Blankenship sold his half to A.G.White.

$300 for half boat
wharfboat was used as
a dock for unloading

Sunday Jan.9,1870

The Annie Laurie landed about 3 0'c
and said ice was coming and we had to
move the boat round in the creek.
Fleetwood up and Ohio down. Tho.
Webb & Bill Hiltbruner staid on boat.

Monday Jan.10,1870

River falling & full of ice. No boats but Crossley & Victor 3. A.G.White took possession of his half of the Wharf Boat this morning. Evening clear & cold & moonlight. Quite a number here until the Crossley came at 10 o'c when they left. Caley remained on Boat all night.

Tuesday Jan.11,1870

The Crossley & tow boats-Charley Bowen(?) and Webster up in mouth of Guyan. (River full of ice.(All White made arrangements with Roland to stay at Boat in his place. A Mr.Peters took supper with us. Fleetwood down Ohio up.

Wednesday Jan.12,1870

The same boats here as yesterday. Fleetwood & Annie Laurie up,Ohio down.

Thursday Jan.13,1870

River raising. Annie Laurie left here before daylight. The tow boats went out today.(Ice getting thinner.) The two Victors(3&4) went down. The Fleetwood up

Friday Jan.14,1870
Saturday Jan.15,1870

Anderson & Charmer broke the lower end of boat loose just at night.

Sunday Jan.16,1870

Roland & I at boat all day.

Monday Jan.17,1870

(River rising) The two Victors all the boats that passed.

Tuesday Jan.18,1870

River rising. Getting in the cellars. Jim Hayslip moved in the store on the point. The Fleetwood & Victor 3 only boats that passed.

Wednesday Jan.19,1870

River too high for the Steamer
Hunter to come below the Bridge. Cale
went to the Hunter and had some oysters.

Thursday Jan.20,1870

River lacked about 4 ft.of being on
the bank at the end of Guyan Street.
Aunt Nancy & Amanda Smith at our house.

Friday Jan.21,1870

The Ohio came up just at night.
Role,All,Cale & I went to the Hunter &
had some oysters.

Saturday Jan.22,1870

Hunter can not get below the bridge
yet. Annie Laurie came just at midnight.
I did not go to bed until she left

Sunday Jan.23,1870

Fleetwood up and Ohio down. Old man
Baker married Miss Butcher.

Monday.Jan.24,1870

Hunter came under the Bridge and
took freight off the Wharf Boat. Robert
came down early this morning and went to
Ironton on the Crossley .Steamer
R.C.Gray landed. Robert returned on the
Crossley and staid with me. Cale started
to the college.

Tuesday Jan.25,1870

Cynthia in town visiting the sick
in the afternoon. Cale at school.

Wednesday Jan.26,1870

I paid Dr.McGinnis $10.

Thursday Jan.27,1870
Friday Jan.28,1870

Frank Hersey & I staid on the boat.
did not get much sleep.

marriage- Butcher to
"old man" Baker

Saturday Jan.29,1870

Cale & I at the boat all night.

Sunday Jan.30,1870

This morning little Ed Smith died.
The bell tolled.

death of child

Monday Jan.31,1870

Hersey & I at boat all night.

Tuesday Feb.1,1870

Role & I went on the <u>Hunter</u> took 2
cans of oysters & had them cooked. I
then took one home.

Wednesday Feb.2,1870

The <u>R.R.Hudson</u> put off a large
amount of freight and in backing tore
off the guard,half the length of the
wharf boat. Midnight before I laid down.

Thursday Feb.3,1870

Got Noah Wellington and Roland to
repairing the boat. Ann up to the house
today.

carpenter

Friday Feb.4,1870

I paid Weimer 50cts for Logwood.
Staid on boat.Weimer with me.

Saturday Feb.5,1870

Wellington(Noah) working on quard.
The <u>Arlington</u> & the <u>Anderson</u> passed up
about breakfast.

Sunday Feb.6,1870

Cynthia,Sall, and I went to Charles
a while. Mr. & Mrs.Weld & Mrs.Botts was
here.

Monday Feb.7,1870
Tuesday Feb.8,1870
Wednesday Feb.9,1870

Bonner returned home.

5

Thursday Feb.10,1870
Friday Feb.11,1870

   Dolen came down with a load in his
boat. A Mrs.Peters came down from
Roffe's with him. Role was here ans took
her up to our house where she remained
all night.

   Saturday Feb.12,1870

   Mrs.Peters at the house until after
dinner when she went to the house on
Victor 3. Charles Burkes here waiting
for Annie Laurie.

   Sunday Feb.13,1870

   Three o'c this morning when Annie
Laurie came. Charley Burk's wife came &
he took her home. Fleetwood came up
about one o'c.

   Monday Feb.14,1870

   In the afternoon,Lawson set out
some trees for me.
   There was a R.R. transfer steamer
going to Omaha. Laid here all night.

   Tuesday Feb.15,1870
   Wednesday Feb.16,1870

   Mrs.James Wilson died last night.   death-Mrs.Wilson
About midnight, the Mountain Belle came
up & laid here until nearly daylight.

   Thursday Feb.17,1870

   The Mountain Belle left about
daylight. The J.C.Crossley brought us a
skiff.

   Friday Feb.18,1870

Hersey & I on boat.

   Saturday Feb.19,1870
   Sunday Feb.20,1870

Fleetwood up.

6

Monday Feb.21,1870

    A R.R. man named Emmons & a
Mr.Wm.Grey of Richmond was here a while
in the afternoon and eve.

        Tuesday Feb.22,1870

    I was at Boat all day. Mr.Emmons &
Grey here at times.

        Wednesday Feb.23,1870

    Robert & Sam down & took dinner
with us. Emmons,Grey,Laidley & Samuels
here awhile and then went down the river
on the Anderson.

        Thursday Feb.24,1870

    Fleetwood passed up about 2 o'c.

        Friday Feb.24,1870

    Mr.Emmons returned on the Ohio.
Hunter brought down 228 sacks of wheat
for John Miller.

        Saturday Feb.26,1870
        Sunday Feb.27,1870

    Loaded a boat with Justice goods.
Fleetwood & Ohio landed. Weed took 3
head of cattle down on Ohio.

        Monday Feb.28,1870

    Considerable excitement about town
about the sell of property. Doc.Hysell
sold his house & lot(dwelling) for $1000

        Tuesday March 1,1870

    Role put new skiff in and took two
men to Indian Guyan making $2.00. Emmons
left tonight on Charmer.
Sall & Cale at a party.

        Wednesday March 2,1870
        Thursday March 3,1870

    All White started down river with a
fleet of timber. I went to the
Photograph boat and set for some

pictures. The <u>Victor 4</u> brought me 2 cans
oysters & 2 Pair stockings for Sallie.

Friday March 4,1870

Went home & helped eat the oysters.

Saturday March 5,1870
Sunday March 6,1870
Monday March 7,1870

<u>Ohio No.4</u> did not go down until 3
o'c. An old man named Irvin at ? died
this morning.

Irvin -death

Tuesday March 8,1870

The children had a party home.

Wednesday March 9,1870
Thursday March 10,1870

Baker & Bill Church both very sick.
I was at boat until after 9 o'c then
home after going with Scott to get
Charley to set up with Baker. Got a
barrel of flour of Bill Wright this
morning for $6.50.

Friday March 11,1870

All White returned home on the
<u>Ohio</u>. Bro.Sam came down just at night
with a raft of pine timber.

Saturday March 12,1870
Sunday March 13,1870
Monday March 14,1870
Tuesday March 15,1870

The Steamer <u>Reindeer</u> took the
Bar ge out the creek. We had $41 charges
on it. I tried to stop them but no use.
They went off. Blankenship's daughter
Lizzie was married this morning to Isom
Adkins. Was up to see Bill Church. He is
some better.

Lizzie Blankenship
m Isom Adkins

Wednesday March 16,1870
Thursday March 17,1870
Friday March 18,1870

Cale went down on the <u>Crossley</u> this
morning to school. As she was landing a

8

pig Jumped off her, and swam over below
Guyan. I got Frank Joseph to go & get
it. Gave him 50cts.

        Saturday 19,1870
        Sunday 20,1870
        Monday 21,1870

    Roland took a runner down to
Burlington in our skiff. Brought it back
on the Victor with two of the seats out
& one oar broken.

        Tuesday March 22,1870

    The Hunter returned here this
morning and went up to the dam.

        Wednesday March 23,1870

    I paid Limon(Lyman)Clark the
balance I owed him for work on the house
$21.50

        Thursday March 24,1870

    The Hunter moved Rev.Mr.Steele up
to the dam. Role took a man down the
river in our skiff.

        Friday March 26,1870

    I paid Sheriff over $6.00 taxes.

        Saturday March 27,1870

    Susan & Cale came home on the
Hunter.

        Sunday March 27,1870

    Pulled a tooth for Baker's wife.

        Monday March 28,1870
        Tuesday March 29,1870

    I pulled a tooth for Alice White.

        Wednesday March 30,1870

    Role took a lot of passengers to
Barboursville in the shiff making over
$5.00. (River falling.Chilly & showery.

runner=racehorse

Thursday March 31,1870

Hunter went to Barboursville today.

Friday April 1,1870

I was at boat until after 9 o'c.
when I went home. Role remaining all
night.

Saturday April 2,1870
Sunday April 3,1870

I was at the boat assorting freight
until after 9 o'c, then went home and
soon retired.

Monday April 4,1870

Elected corporation officers.
Mrs.Calvin Rece and Mrs.Frank Hite at
the house for dinner.

Tuesday April 5,1870

I paid Prof. Thompson $3.65 on
Caley's schooling for this quarter.

Wednesday April 6,1870
Thursday April 7,1870

Thornburg commenced plowing my lot.
Guyan River full of timber.

Friday April 8,1870
Saturday April 9,1870

Robert came down this morning with
Boat stove,skiff and hoop poles.

Sunday April 10,1870
Monday April 11,1870

Frank Hersey & I on boat all night.

Tuesday April 12,1870

Bob Allen came down, and I rode his
horse up and put him in my stable.

Wednesday April 13,1870
Thursday April 14,1870

Jennie Douthet and Miss Lickey took
supper at the house. I pulled two teeth
for each Jane and ----Letulle. The
Fleetwood came up 1/2 after 10 and put
off a big lot of R.R.stuff.

Friday April 15,1870

Hunter did not go today. Ohio late
coming up. All White came on her. Newt
Keenan married yesterday and brought
wife home.

marriage

Saturday April 16,1870

An awful gale of wind commenced
about eleven and lasted until 3. The
Anderson landed at the time, broke our
stone and spring chain. Role and all had
gone to Barboursville on the Hunter & I
had an awful time getting boat in to
bank again. Robert was here a while. He
went up and told them to sent me some
dinner.

Sunday April 17,1870

Fleetwood came very late 10 o'c in
the evening. Put off large lot of R.R.
stuff.

Monday April 18,1870
Tuesday April 19,1870
Wednesday April 20,1870
Thursday April 21,1870

Guyan running out strong.

Friday April 22,1870

Cynthia took Mr.Blair to board.
Hunter not running & boat full of goods.
All White went to Sandy & hired another
wharf boat at $50 a month.

Saturday April 23,1870
Sunday April 24,1870

Fleetwood came about 6 o'c & put
off a large lot of R.R. stuff. Went home
& bed about 9 o'c. Soon after heard the
Hudson come.

Monday April 25,1870

The Steamer Crossley brought up the Wharf boat we have rented.

Tuesday April 26,1870
Wednesday April 27,1870
Thursday April 28,1870

Boat on the bank. We had to get some Logan men to help off with it. Crossley tried and tore half the guard off.

Friday April 29,1870

Got our Boat round in the mouth of creek & moved my office in the other.

Saturday April 30,1870

Hunter went home. cale staid with me.

Sunday May 1,1870

Fleetwood put off a lot of R.R.stuff.

Tuesday May 3,1870

Robert came down just as the Fleetwood landed here before dinner & went to Cincinnati with 2 Hds & 2 boxes tobacco.

Wednesday May 4,1870

Pete Baker & Mary Stewart married.   marriage

Thursday May 5,1870
Friday May 6,1870

Roland(Robert) returned from Cincinnati.

Saturday May 7,1870

Role & Bonner caulked our boat.

Sunday May 8,1870

Blankenship's Stea mer Yanthe came up last night & went to Barboursville today.

Tuesday May 10,1870

The Tow Boat Sam Erwin landed here
with a lot of lime and cement. they left
1000 barrels here,346 on the bank and
854 in a barge. 200 of the 1000 is lime.
The tow boat with two more barges of
lime & cement went up the Kanawha.
The Yanthe went to Barboursville.

Wednesday May 11,1870

Alford's suit against me for the
piano I bid for Jim Ferguson was tried
yesterday. I went to Barboursville on
the Yanthe to see about it.

Thursday May 12,1870

Got all the cement off the bank in
the Wharf boat except 62 barrels the
Hunter took to Barboursville this
morning. Both boats went up.
Roland bought a horse of the
Frenchman McLaughlin(?). Paid him $200,
$100 cash & his & my note for $100 at 60
days. Mr.Weed's raft got loose above the
grade & we caught it at the Wharf Boat.

May 13,1870

Roland came about 11 o'clock on
Mountain Belle bringing a dray and
harness for which I am to pay $61. Susie
remained at Mr.Daniels.

May 14,1870

Al White went to Cincinnati on
Charmer Sunday morning the 15th.

The water in Guyan getting so low
neither of the Steamers went up on 21st.
(FL-? wrong date)   (Sun.22)

Monday May 23,1870

The Yanthe started to Gallpolis
this morning . Bias and Cockings took
two lads in lighters to Barboursville.
Noah Wellington,Garland Flowers &
Leve(?) Tucker at work repairing our
wharf. Just at night Wednesday, the Tow

boat Sam Irwin landed here and commenced
rolling cement throught the Boat on the
bank. They were all night at it. Left
soon after day. Bonner & Al White
commenced putting up our warehouse on
the point. River rose fast all day, and
at night getting up to the cememnt and
rain began to fall, had to get a lot of
hands & roll it up on the bank. The
Fleetwood pushed the Wharf Boat up on
the bank this afternoon made her spring
a leak, had hard time shoving her in.
Thursday night at Wharf with 6 or 8
hands rolling cement & pumping boat.
Everything went well until about 3 o'c
Friday morning (27th) when the wharf
boat sprung a leak & sunk in less than
3/4 of an hour. Got most of the freight
out on the inside guard. some little got
damaged. All day Friday getting freight
in our wharf boat and warehouse. Butcher
& Wright dropped in to the foot of the
street with their wharf boat.

Monday May 30,1870

Moved our boat out in the Ohio
above the sunken boat & below the Wright
boat.

Tuesday May 31,1870

Hunter went to Barboursville
brought back Bbl. of Kline's rice
spoiled by being wet.

Wednesday June 1,1870
Thursday June 2,1870

I made contract with Burt Russell
to raise the Wharf Boat & put cargo box
back on her all right for $2.25. The
Fleetwood & Mountain Belle lands all
their freight on the other boat. Bonner
came home on Fleetwood

Friday June 3,1870

Russell at work on the sunken boat.
Started the saw mill again today. The
Ohio came up.

Saturday June 4,1870

The opposition boat make business dull.

Sunday June 5,1870
Monday June 6,1870
Tuesday June 7,1870
Wednesday June 8,1870
Thursday June 9,1870

Sall,Cale & Blair with a lot of other youngters went to Cattlettsburg on <u>Hudson</u> this afternoon.

Friday June 10,1870

Business so dull White told Roland he could not keep him at the Wharf any longer.

Saturday June 11,1870

Paid <u>Annie Laurie</u> $80 and <u>Crossley</u> $50. Frank Hersey staid with me.

Sunday June 12,1870

Paid <u>Mountain Belle</u> $45.15. Frank Hersey & Dolen staid on boat.

Monday June 13,1870

White made arrangements with Sam Hayslip to stay on boat if he would keep sober.

Tuesday June 14,1870

Sam here part of time drunk. Frank Hersey run the <u>Hunter</u> to Barboursville.Cale drove the dray.

Wednesday June 15,1870

Sam here a while drunk.

Thursday June 16,1870
Friday June 17,1870
Saturday June 18,1870

Roland running on the <u>Hunter</u>.

Sunday June 19,1870
Monday June 20,1870

Roland now working on river boat-he did most everything

Tuesday June 21,1870

Steamer Ohio 4, smashed in against
cargo box of the sunken wharf boat &
washed it down.

Wednesday June 22,1870

Roland still running on the Hunter.

Thursday June 23,1870

Hunter not running. Roland draying.

Thursday June 23--28, 1870
Wednesday June 29,1870

A good many here waiting for boats
& I was up all night.

Thursday June 30,1870

Dropped our boat down out sideof
the sunken boat. The other boat followed
us right down. Midnight when Fleetwood
came up.

Friday July 1,1870
Saturday July 2,1870
Sunday July 3,1870
Monday July 4,1870

Had my flag out on boat. The new
Steamer James Fisk Jr. went up this
afternoon.

Tuesday July 5,1870
Wednesday July 6,1870

Thursday July 7,1870

River still rising. had to move the
boat above the sunken one. The Fleetwood
in landing, ran her prow into Butcher &
Wright's Wharf Boat clear into the hull.

Saturday July 9,1870

Snyder here waiting Annie Laurie to
go down to Cincinnati on his way home.

Sunday July 10,1870

Synder left on <u>Annie Laurie</u> about 3
o'c. This morning.

Monday July 11,1870
Tuesday July 12,1870

Sall & Mollie Peters went to
Petersburg on <u>Belle</u> this morning. I gave
Sall $2.00.

Wednesday July 13,1870

Sall & Mollie returned home on
<u>Belle</u> from Petersburg.

Thursday July 14,1870

Mr.Duncan took dinner & tea with
us. Cale went with him to Barboursville
in a buggy.

Friday July 15,1870
Saturday July 16,1870

Sunday July 17,1870

Role,Susie & Jessie returned home.

Monday July 18,1870

Steamer <u>Piketon</u> came to run from
here to Gallipolis.

Tuesday July 19,1870
Wednesday July 30,1870

Blair's school closed today.

Thursday July 21,1870

One of Snyder's hands & young
Welshman about 19 named David Isaac was
found drowned this morning opposite my
house. Had a coroner's jury. Clothes
found on bank. Supposed he went in to
wash last night, got in deep water &
drowned as he could not swim. His two
borthers brought him to he boat and
waited most of the afternoon for the
<u>Fleetwood</u>. Blair left on the <u>Fiske</u>. He
went off mad because we charged him
$4.00 a week board. Evening raining
after dark when the <u>Fleetwood</u> &

death-David Isaac

<u>Henderson</u> came. Corpse taken up on
<u>Fleetwood</u>.

July 22--26,1870-

Wednesday July 27,1870

Synder returned here.

June 28,29,1870
Saturday June 30,1870

Pulled a tooth this afternoon for
Kate Hite.

Sunday July 31,1870

Al White came up for me about day
light to come to the boat as the river
was raising so he had to move the boat.
Sunken wharf boat all afloat. Sunken
boat floated down about 50 feet & we got
Wharf Boat into the bank. Synder went to
Charleston. Sall,Cale, & Alice Daniels
went to Portsmouth on the <u>Mountain
Belle</u>. They were invited by Clerk on
some excursion.

Monday Aug.1,1870
Tuesday Aug.2,1870

Miss Daniels went to Barboursville.

Wednesday Aug.3,1870

<u>Hunter</u> took load of goods to
Barboursville.

Thursday Aug.4,1870

I went to Barboursville on the
<u>Hunter</u>. At court. took dinner at
Hatfield's. Role brought a load in the
wagon & I went back with him. We rented
Wright & Butcher's boat for one year at
$50 a month. Took possession today.

Friday Aug.5,1870

Moved office on the new boat.

Saturday Aug.6,1870
Sunday Aug.7,1870

Monday Aug.8,1870

We dropped the boats down. Bought 126 melons at 25cts. each. Bob sent a horse by John Douthit for me to come to court on tomorrow.

Tuesday Aug.9,1870

I rode to Barboursville in Hack. Paid $1.00.

Wednesday Aug.10,1870
Thursday Aug.11,1870
Friday Aug.12,1870

Circus came this morning. A good many in town. (Circus) left about midnight.

Circus

Saturday Aug.13,1870

Dolen & a lot of Logan fellows here some of them pretty noisy.

Sunday Aug.14,1870

Hudson went down about 8 o'c.

Monday Aug.15,1870
Tuesday Aug.16,1870

Lot of timber ran out of Guyan. A lot of White's.

Wednesday Aug.17,1870

Snyder here awaiting Annie Laurie to go up Kanawha. She did not come.

Thursday Aug.18,1870
Friday Aug.19,1870

Sarah & Becky Bukey went down to Ironton early this morning.

Saturday Aug.20,1870

Bruce came in te afternoon to help in White's place. Lots of niggers going on boat to Association at Gallipolis. Caley went to Ironton on the Florence.

Negro Association
meeting-Gallipolis

Sunday Aug.21,1870

Bruce staid on boat.

Monday Aug.22,1870
Tuesday Aug.23,1870

Snyder returned on <u>Fleetwood</u> from Charleston.

Aug.24-Aug.27,1870
Sunday Aug.28,1870

The Tow Boat <u>Sam Ervin</u> landed here with lime and cement. Put off 200bbls. cement & 100 barrels lime for Snyder.

Monday Aug.29,1870

At boat until after 9 o'clock. The Lytle(?) and I went home together.

Tuesday Aug.30,1870

Bro.Robert brought a Hhd.of tobacco down about noon. He took dinner with us. Sam Childers here awaiting for a boat.

Wednesday Aug.31,1870

Ball in Leckey's new house.   Ball
Susie,Roll & Cale there.

Thursday Sept.1,1870
Friday Sept.2,1870

Susie,Role,Frank,Cale & Jessie went
on <u>Victor 4</u> to Fair at Ashland. Bruce &   Fair
his wife also went .

Saturday Sept.3,1870

Got news that the Prussians had taken Louis Napoleon and the French Army.

Sunday Sept.4,1870

Mrs.Lytell quit work for Snyder.(I was)at the boat with Snyder & Lytell. Snyder & I soon went home . Left Lytell waiting for the boat.

Monday Sept.5,1870

Lytell left on the Hudson last
night.

Sept.6,7,1870
Thursday Sept.8,1870

Mountain Belle came off the docks
this afternoon and went on to Ironton.

Monday Sept.12,1870

Cale & Sanford Keenan went to the
Handing Rocks this morning to help
E.Ward.

place on the river

Tuesday Sept.13,1870

Several waiting for boat. They all
came late.

Wednesday Sept.14,1870

Snyder returned from Charleston.

Sept.15,16,1870
Saturday Sept.17,1870

Synder returned from Chaleston.

Monday Sept.19,1870

Bruce at his coal boat.

Sunday Sept.25,1870

Boats very uncertain.River low.

Monday Sept.26,1870

America came up. Could not go over
the bar.Put off about 50 tons of freight
for up the river, then went on up.

Tuesday Sept.27,1870

The Florence took up the freight
the America left.

Thursday Sept.29,1870

No boat here but the Crossley today
& every thing getting awful dull.

Saturday Oct.1,1870

Water too low for most any of the boats to run.

Monday Oct.3,1870

Cale went to college. River still rising. Raising to two boat, Little Condor, that has been on the bar for three weeks floated off and went up the river.

Tuesday Oct.4,1870

The school teacher Lewis struck Sall with a stick in school this morning which made some excitement. I took her from school.

teacher used stick

Wednesday Oct.5,1870

Fisk up. The only boat. I paid another $10 on sewing machine making $41.

Monday Oct.10,1870

Mr.Snyder returned home(FL on margin"Snyder returned here".

Tuesday Oct.11,1870

The Baptists have a festival in the church.

festival

Wednesday Oct.11,1870

O'Brien's Menagerie came this morning & showed afternoon & Eve. A great many here to see it.(Gen.Lee died today.)

menagerie

Thursday Oct.12,1870

Mr.Paden came up last night & staid at Put Smith's. He was robbed of $150 and his watch,don't know by whom. A Mr. Staunton came here making a Republican speech. Put Smith hit Steve Hilbruner with a brick.

Thursday Oct.20,1870

The Steamer James Fisk came down.
Snyder came home on her. I started on
her to Portsmouth.(Snyder had been to
Charleston.) I arrived at Portsmouth
before day. Did not charge me any fare.
Went with Dutch Milkes(Wilkes ?FL) and
got my breakfast. Got measured at----
for a suit of clothes. About 2 o'clock,
the Mountain Boy came up and I started
home on her. The sheriff brought Henry
Smith up on the Crossley. Some
excitement here.

Saturday Oct.22,1870

Henry Smith was tried and acquited.

Thursday Oct.27,1870

Election today. Much excitement on
account of niggers voting. About 1/2
doz. voted here.

Friday Oct.28,1870

Cale at boat waiting for Belle to
go to Portsmouth.

Saturday Oct.29,1870

Irvin Smith elected sheriff,Hyslip
recorder,County gone Democratic. Witcher
beat. Snyder here waiting for boat to go
to Portsmouth on his way home.

Monday Oct.31,1870

Both boats crammed full of freight.
Judge Smith moved here & Dolen took his
furniture to Barboursville.

Tuesday Nov.1,1870

About nine o'c. Charley,Cale & I
drove up to Barboursville in my wagon.
Had Ward's horse. Our farm was to be
sold today. Had dinner with Hatfield's.
Paid 50cts. after which Tom Kline tried
to sell some of Roffe's land, but the
bids were so low, he postponed the sale.
Then Jeff Samuels tried ours, but my bid
of $6,000 was the only one & we

sell of farm & mill
why ?

adjourned it until Friday. Then we drove
home.

Friday Nov.4,1870

Court commenced. I rode up to
Barboursville with Thornburg. Court
commenced. Our land not sold. Rode home
by dark.

Sunday Nov.6,1870

The Fleetwood came just at dark.
Cynthia's sister,Jane Nagle & her
daughter came on her. We were surprised
to see them.

Saturday Nov.12,1870

Sent Cale to stay with Bruce at
Boat.(I was lame in the thy.)

Sunday Nov.13,1870

Frank Fessler here to see Sall.

Tuesday Nov.15,1870

Cale went to a dance at
Hiltbruners. Fessler went with Sall.   dance

Friday Nov.18,1870

Fleetwood went down.

Saturday Nov.19,1870

May Anderson put off 220 Bbls. Lime
for R.R. Co.

Sunday Nov.20,1870

Frank Fessler took supper with us
then he & Sall went to meeting. Jane &
Roland also went.

Sunday Nov.24,1870

The Ohio No.4 came down. I went
back. Cale came down with Sall & we went
on board for Cincinnnati. All day on
board. Mr.Damels & his daughters came on
board to see us.

Monday Nov.25,1870

Arrived in Cincinnati about 3 o'c.
I was all day running about the city.

Tuesday Nov.29 & 30,1870

I was all day on Steamer Ohio No.4
coming up the Ohio River.

Wednesday Nov.30,1870

Irving Smith and Fred Miller's
daughter was married and went down on
Ohio No.4.

Miller mIrving Smith

Thursday Dec.1,1870-2,3,4

(My rhumatism troubling me.) Got
Ward's Magic to doctor my ankle. Johnson
& his Jerr hung my blinds & nearly
furnished my smokehouse. Last week, I
paid him $10.00.
Conwellzie Simmons was buried
today. A number of the Mason's from here
went up.

death-Conwellzie Simmons

Wednesday Dec.7,1870

Brother Robert & his wife Mary Ann
came down here today. Took dinner.

Dec.13-17th,1870

Bro.Sam and his wife Sarah and
their two children came down & staid all
night with us.

Tuesday Dec.20,1870

Sarah & the children went home in
the Hack this morning.

Wednesday Dec.21,1870

Bruce & I would of got Wharf boats
in Guyan R. had not Thacker dropped a
raft there and said he would run it out
in the morning.

Thursday Dec.22,1870

The raft frozen in the mouth and we could not get the wharf boats in. Ice running in the Ohio River.

Friday Dec.23,1870

Much worried at not getting boats in Guyan. Ohio full of ice. The Fleetwood went down and the Ohio up about 9 o'c.

Saturday Dec.24,1870

I wanted to cut the ice in mouth of Guyan & get the boats in,but Bonner persuaded White there was no use.

Sunday Dec.25,1870

Ice running so thick & hard against boat, I had to have more planks on gunnels(FL-gunwalls.)

Monday Dec.26,1870

Had men cut a channel to get the boats in Guyan, but could not move them as the ice has blocked up solid under them. Several putting up ice all day.

Tuesday Dec.27,1870

The river has fell so the boats are above the water on a bank on a bank of ice,out of the way of running ice.

Wednesday Dec.28,1870

The Masons went from here up to Cal Swann's funeral. Boats lodged some and the ins ide gunnel cracked in the center. Both boats high up above the water. Cale & Sall went to a dance. Dick Hersey went with Sall.

death-Cal Swann

dance

Thursday Dec.29,1870

Jane & her child,Sam,Jessie,Cale,& Roll all went to the festival at the Northern M.E.Church.

church festival

Friday Dec.30,1870

Roll,Cale & Sall went to a dance.

Saturday Dec.31,1870

   Ice gorged this side of Gallipolis.
Sall & Role did not get back from the
dance until after 3 o'clock.

The next enteries follow those for 1870
in the Lambert ledger and are limited to
one week.(Lambert makes the
comment"Following in Book for 1870 &
erased. Probably in another book".

The next enteries follow those for 1870 in the Lambert ledger and are limited to one week.(Lambert makes the comment"Following in Book for 1870 & erased. Probably in another book".

Sunday Jan.1,1871

The Steamer Mountain Belle came up.

Monday Jan.2,1871

Susie sick all day. About nine o'clock, Roll went for Dr.McGinnis & about 11 o'c,she was confined with a boy. About midnight,Dr.Bell,Jane & I had some oysters.
Settled with Al White by paying him $300 for the bal. of his share of te profits to Jan.1.

Tuesday Jan.3,1871

Susie & baby smart.

Wednesday Jan.4,1871

The Ohio 4 came down & put off some freight. Mountain Belle came up.

Thursday Jan,5,1871

The Mountain Belle went down early this morning.

Friday Jan,6,1871

Mountain Belle came up & returned.Crossley came up and (I) went to Ironton. A ferry boat moved a shoemaker here from Pomeroy. She returned there.

Saturday Jan.7,1871

Settled with Butcher & paid him for rent.

This next section for 1862 is found in
the same "Lambert Ledger" after 1870 &
1871. No comment is made.

Jan.1,1862

Bloomingdale,Cabell Co.Va.

I am still at this place with my
family consisting of my wife,four
children,my Aunt Nancy Dusenberry &
Thorn's Nigger Ann. The Civil War now
distracting our beloved country has
ruined our business and is causing
everything along the border here to be
destroyed. Being a Union man, I do not
know what moment I may be stripped of
everything and driven from my home. My
greatest wish is that before this day
1863,peace and harmony will be restored,
and we will be united & happy people
again.   William F.Dusenberry

fear

Wednesday Jan.1,1862

About 10 o'clock, I went over to
Morris & got him to bring over Rodgers
dun horse. Then rode to Barboursville,
only stopped there a few moments to get
a pass, then rode down to the Widow
Shelton's where I found Rodgers. I took
dinner at Shelton's & talked with
Rodgers until 2 o'c. I left the dun and
got another horse of Rodgers. Charles &
I got home about dusk. Rodgers & George
ran the saw mill most of the day &
Nicely the grist mills. Rogers & Robert
ran the saw mill awhile.

Thursday Jan,2, 1862

The Zouves brought our wagon home
this morning also my lantern. They also
brought me a pork bbl. & two sterene
candles. Rodgers & Smith ran the saw
mill all day. Nicely went home about the
middle of the afternoon to prepare for
moving. The Zouaves handled three loads
of lumber from the mill. I sold them 5
doz.eggs. Rodgers sons came here with a
lighter and took away some lumber.

Friday Jan.3,1862

Nicely moved in the LLoyd house today. Called up by the Zouave Pickets little after five o'clock. They came in and sat by the fire until daylight when we had breakfast. They left soon after. (It was freezing cold.) H.Smith took our wagon and cattle up to move Nicely down.

About ten o'clock, Mrs.Scales came up here for me to go town with her to see about her horse. Elijah Adkins and several other Adkins came in and gave themselves up. Cap.Shaw took me to Bukey's to dinner with him. Sweetland, Love,Mrs.Roffe & Miss Brown came out as I did. Nicely moved in the house where Lloyd lived. The Zouave Pickets came in and warmed & then got my latern to make fire in the house by the bridge.

Saturday Jan.4,1862

The Zoaves hauled a load of lumber. About 11 o'clock, I walked to town with Farley, met Sam coming home. I took a little bite of dinner at Hatfield's. Runnels,Parish,Everett & some other secession Prisoners returned from Columbus this afternoon. I got a paper of the second Inst. Just before night. Sweetland,Love,Farley and I walked out home. George Moore took supper with me.The Zouave's picket came out, one of them came in and got some fire to start one in the house by the bridge.

Sunday Jan 5.1862

Smith,George,Sweetland and Cowens came in about ten o'clock. About noon just as Smith and Sweetland left,two officers connected with the quarter-master department of the 34th O.V.U.S.A. cam up here,one by the name of Harris from New York City. The other's name was Taylor. They with Cowens and George took dinner with us. They all left about Two o'clock. Mrs.Mat.Jewell was here in the afternoon. Aunt Nancy and Jessie was down to Mother's awhile in the afternoon. Just before night, I went out to Smith's awhile. George and I went down to Nicely's awhile.

Monday Jan.6,1862

Jim Cowens and Sam Kelly came here
and I walked to town with them. We met
two teams coming up for lumber. I was
around the different quarters. Lieut.
Buttors got me a paper of the 4th Inst.
I got a cup of coffee at Hatfield's. I
was in the Adgts. quarters quite awhile
interceding for old Elijah Adkins.

walked

NOTE:Martha is 3 /12m S of Barboursville
B'ville 6 1/2 mile S of Guyandotte.

The way this diary begins may indicate
that is separate from the others.

CABELL COUNTY WILL BOOKS

Will Bk2-304

In the name of God, Amen, I William Conklin Dusenberry
of the County of Cabell and the state of Virginia being weak
and feeble in body,but a sound mind and disposing memory do
hereby make ordain and publish this my last will and
testament,etc.
1st-After payment of just debts residue of personal
estate to wife Susan Dusenberry.
2nd-1/3 part to wife Susan and sons Robert and Samuel at
age 21 years.
3rd-wife Susan appointed guardian of sons
4th-wife and 4 sons hold rest of estate, if estate is
sold before Robert and Sam reach 21, a trust to be
established.
5th-wife Susan,sons William F. and Charles appointed
executors.
written 19 dec 1857
witnessed
C.L.Roffe
H.L.Samuels   brought to court 5 Jul 1858 H.H.Wood CCC

Will Bk 4-304

Charles O.Dusenberry 9 may 1891
            to court 29 oct 1831
    1. all debts paid
    2. wife Annie F. all real estate
        1/2 policy of Knight of Honor Mistletoe Lodge #466
Htng,WV, also policy on Masons
    3. son William C. policy #2210 Golden Knights and all
watch repair tools
    4. daughter Nellie F. 1/2 policy
    5. wife Annie executor

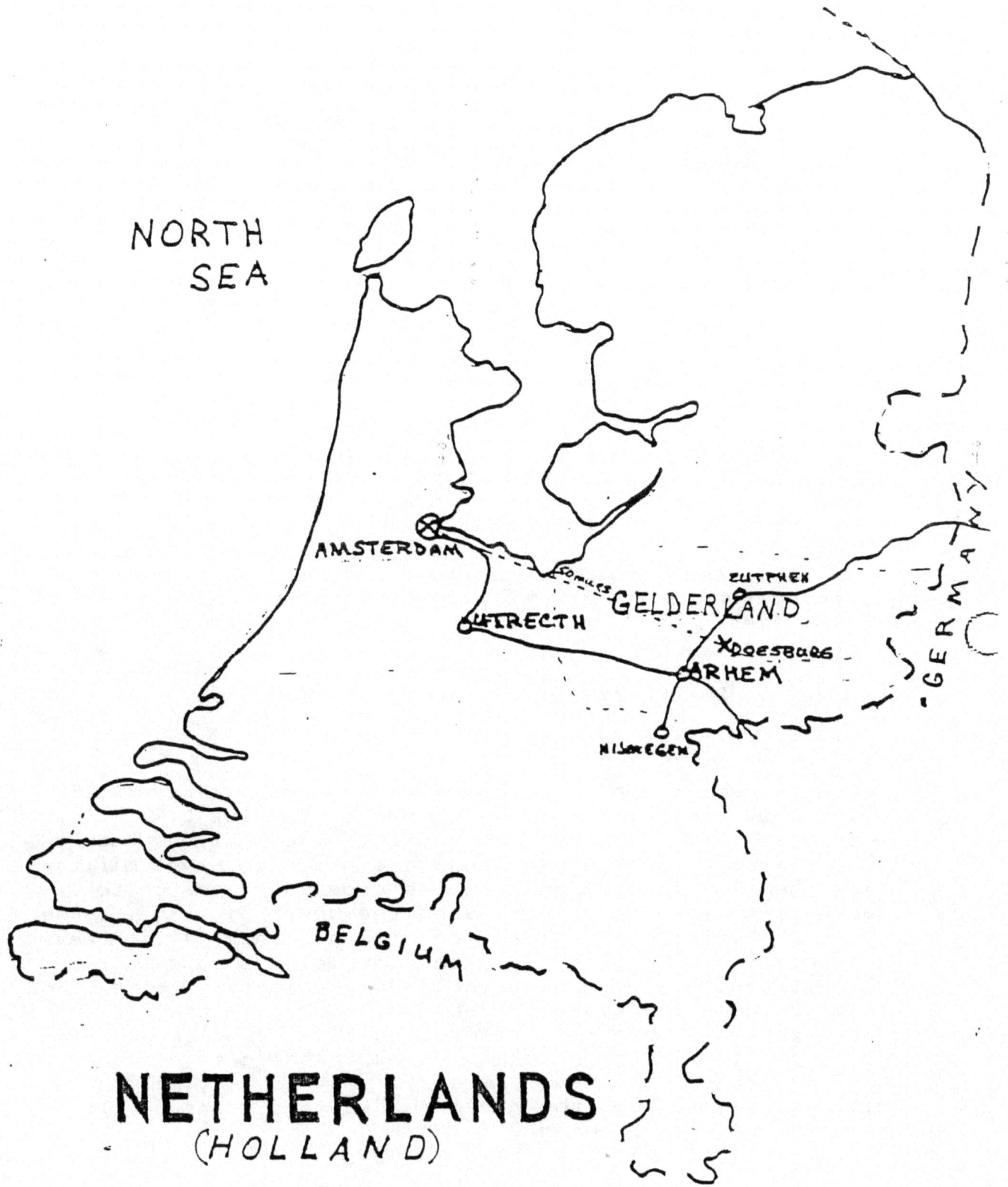

NORTH
SEA

AMSTERDAM

20 MILES

GELDERLAND

ZUTPHEN

UTRECTH

DOESBURG

ARHEM

NISMEGEN

GERMANY

BELGIUM

NETHERLANDS
(HOLLAND)

1 INCH = 20 MILES

Estes to Saunders 8 may 1824 part of 1520 patented b. John
   Fry
deed calls

Begining at 3 white oaks standing on the west side of
Guyandotte just below the mouth of a small run and 32 poles
below a Buffalo lick about 11m from mouth of said river
thence .S45EW 102 poles to a sugar tree the S61 1/4 E about
580 poloes to a large white oak and beech on the bank of
Guyandotte river standing at the foot of the round hill in
the Rich Bottom thence down the said river with its meanders
to opposite a sugar tree marked as a corner just above 3
rock in the river a short distance above the mill thence
across the said river to the sugartree thence a due East
cource to a stake standing in the back line of sais Fry's
survey thence N26W following said back line to two white
oaks,dogwood & hickory standing on the side of a hill in a
corner to Fredrick G.L.Beuhring's land thence with said
Beuhring's line to a sugar tree on the bank of said river
thence down the river & begining therewith to a sugar tree
being one of the corner trees made in the orginal survey for
said John Fry thence crossing said river and down on the
opposite side with its meanders N60W 26 poles west 56 poles
S43W 164 poles S--W 20 poles to a lick in the bank of the
river 48 to a drain and 52 to begining. 700a except 12
square feet in the edge of orchard on the east side of river
a grave yard. EAST--Morris

Sanders to Dusenberry 9-537 1848

tract one 217a

Beging at an Elm on the bank of the Guyandotte River 118
pole below the mill near the corner of Charles L.Roffe' land
thence N73 1/2E 810 poles to a small black oak on Vaugh's
line thence with it S 149poles to a beech on Fry's Military
line thence with it S26E 59 poles crossing a branch to a
buckeye,ash and two hornbeams on the bench of a hill corner
to ---- the Sanders land,thence with his back(?) line West
204 poles to a suger tree on the bank of the said
river,thence leaving said line and crossing said river S36W
80 poles(30) to a stake 10 feet below a box elder S72W 9
poles 20 links to a rock planted in the ground thence N18W
41 poles-21 links to a rock planted in the ground thence
N72E 30 poles across said river to a stake just below the
mill and thence down the river and landing there on 116
poles(?) to the begining 217a.

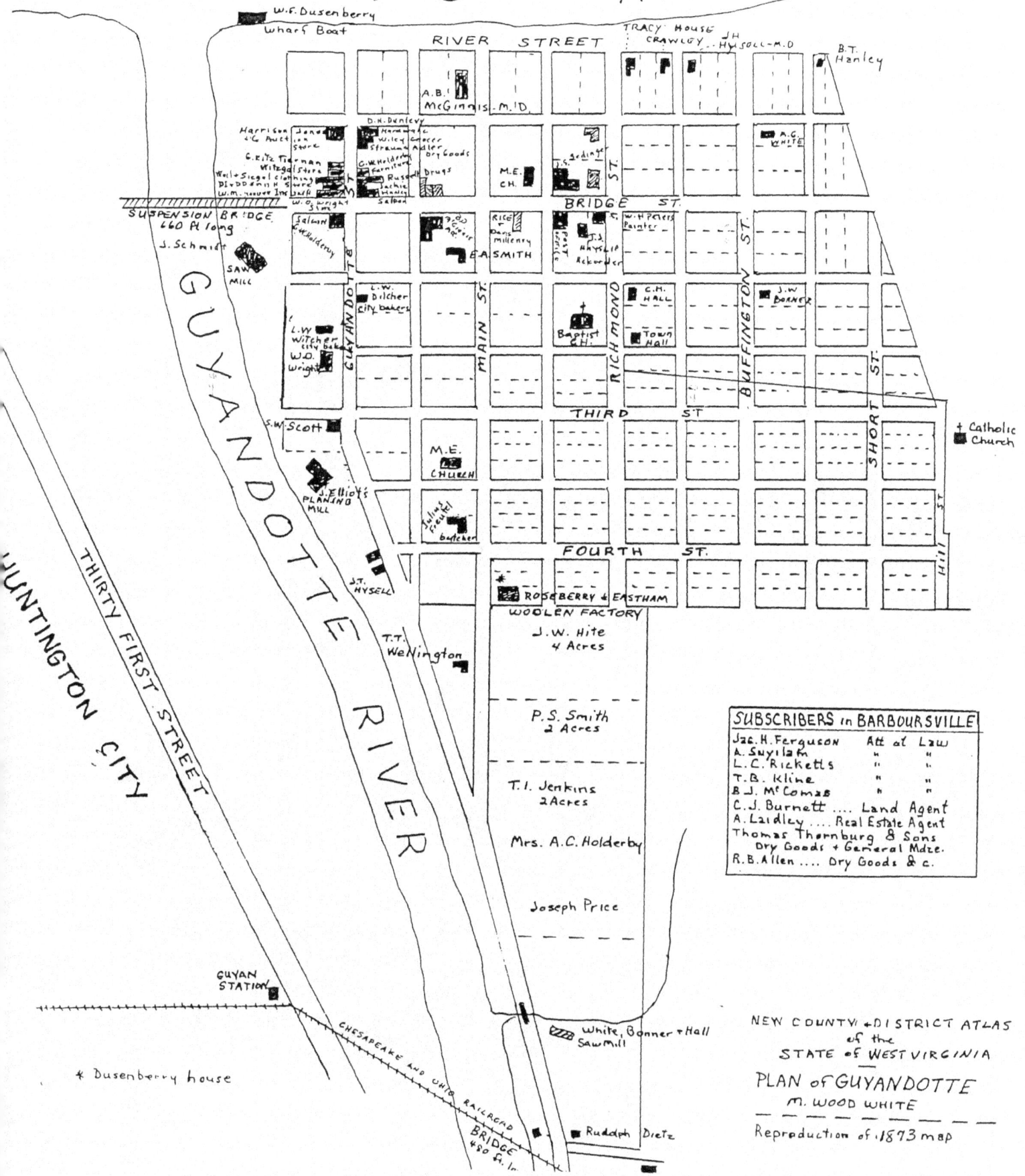

201

O H I O   R I V E R

W. F. Dusenberry
Wharf Boat

RIVER   STREET

TRACY HOUSE
CRAWLEY
JH HYSELL - M.D
B.T. Hanley

A.B. McGinnis, M.D.

D.H. Dunley

Harrison & C. Auction
Jones ion Store
Harpingale
Wiley Grocer
Straum Adler Dry Goods
A.G. White

G. Ritz Tierman
Witzgdl Store
C.W. Holderny Furniture
Russell Drugs
M.E. CH.

Wolf + Siegel clothing
Di DD Smith Store
Jackie Hensley
J.S. sedinger

W. M. Moore Inc Wharf
W. O. Wright Saloon

BRIDGE   ST.

SUSPENSION BRIDGE
660 Ft. long

J. Schmidt

SAW MILL

Salaon
W. Holderny

A.C. Across
Rice & Dans milleney
W. H. Peters Painter

J.J. HAYSLIP Rekorder

E. A. SMITH

GUYANDOTTE

L.W. Dilcher City bakery

C.H. HALL
J.W. BONNER

Baptist CH.
Town Hall

L.W. Witcher city bakery
W.O. Wright

MAIN   ST.

RICHMOND   ST.

BUFFINGTON   ST.

SHORT   ST.

Catholic Church

S.W. Scott

THIRD   ST.

M.E. CHURCH

HILL   ST.

J. Elliot's PLANING MILL

Julius Freukl butcher

FOURTH   ST.

J.T. HYSELL

Roseberry & Eastham
WOOLEN FACTORY

T.T. Wellington

J.W. Hite
4 Acres

GUYANDOTTE   RIVER

THIRTY FIRST STREET

HUNTINGTON CITY

P.S. Smith
2 Acres

T.I. Jenkins
2 Acres

Mrs. A.C. Holderby

Joseph Price

GUYAN STATION

CHESAPEAKE AND OHIO RAILROAD

BRIDGE 480 ft. l.

* Dusenberry house

White, Bonner + Hall Sawmill

Rudolph Dietz

SUBSCRIBERS in BARBOURSVILLE

Jac. H. Ferguson	Att at Law
A. Suylah	" "
L.C. Ricketts	" "
T.B. Kline	" "
B.J. McComas	" "
C.J. Burnett	Land Agent
A. Laidley	Real Estate Agent
Thomas Thornburg & Sons	Dry Goods + General Mdze.
R.B. Allen	Dry Goods &c.

NEW COUNTY + DISTRICT ATLAS
of the
STATE OF WEST VIRGINIA

PLAN OF GUYANDOTTE
M. WOOD WHITE

Reproduction of 1873 map

202

Deaths & Burials
Dusenberry Diary

Thornburg,Squire 17 Jun 1791-30 dec 1854	(slave)Love's
Stanley, son & son-in-law 31 dec 1854	(Slave)McGinnis
Mays,Hamilton (Stanley s/l) 31 dec 1854	(slave)Morris's
Merritt,John bur-18 Jan 1855	Bolt-child
Wintz,Mike & child 23 Jan 1855	Bowden
Thompson,Bill 21 Jun 1855	Clark,Henry
Degra--Mrs.-(Baumgardner)bur-29 Jun 1855	Degra--,Mrs.
(slave)Morris's woman 5 may 1855	Doolittle,Ambrose
(slave)McGinnis's girl 12 may 1855	Gillenwaters
Miller,Mrs.John 4 aug 1855	Hensley,William
Morrison,Anna Scales,Mrs.Patrick 4 aug 1855	Hinchman,Lee
Thompson,child 2 oct 1855 (Sarah J.-stone)	Irvin
Gillenwaters 16 mar 1856	(Mays,Hamilton)
Nagle,Susan 10 apr 1856	Merritt,John
Ward 19 Jun 1856	Miller,Mrs,John
(slave)Love's spring 1856	Morrison,Anna S.
Hensley,William 29 Jul 1856	Nagle,Susan
Clark,Henry bur-8 aug 1856	Playfoot,Lucy
Doolittle,Ambrose 15 aug 1856	Shelton,Mrs.
Hinchman,Lee 13 dec 1856	Shelton,Mrs.
Playfoot,Aunt Olive 13 Jan 1869	Smith,Ed
Taylor-child 5 Jan 1869	Stanley-son
Bowden-@ 24 feb 1869	Taylor-child
Shelton,Mrs. 30 Jun 1869	Thompson,Bill
Wilson,Alice Douthet @ 12 aug 1869	Thompson-child
Shelton,Mrs. 8 oct 1869	Thornburg,Squire
Bolt-child 17 oct 1869	Ward
Smith,Ed 30 Jan 1870	Wilson,Alice
Wilson,Mrs.James 15 feb 1870	Wilson,Mrs.James
Irvin 7 mar 1870	Wintz,Bill &Child

Slaves were buried and then later(often months) there would be a gathering and someone would preach a funeral service.(often Uncle Tom of Everett's)

Wintz died in summer of 1854 near Salt Rock, several months later (January) the bodies were moved down the river to the Merritt Cemetery just north of Barboursville.

Doolittle=Ambrose owned mill(later Howell's)2nd fall Mud River
Gillenwaters=James Revolutionary War 98yr-near Roach
Thornburg=Solomon--west of B'ville and across river

Dusenberry Diary Marriages

(slave)Spencer to Simmon's wench 3 feb 1855
Blake,Martha to Salmon 23 feb 1855
Blackwood,Mary to Peter White 4 apr 1855
Morris,Mary to V.R.Moss 14 aug 1855
Butcher,Sarah to Jim Cowens 13 sep 1855
Butcher,Ella to Charley Shipe 16 oct 1855
--- to Lee Bowman 5 sep 1856 (Missouri)
Dietz,---- to Got Jewell 1 may 1869
Hite,Jennie to Womeldorff 22 jun 1869
Hite,Fanny to Bill Church 26 aug 1869
Samuels,-- to R.D. Bright 21 sep 1869   (Emma)
Ruffner,--- to Sampson Simmons 23 sep 1869
Mather,--- to George Price 31 oct 1869   (Rochylena)
Wilson,----George Thornburg 7 dec 1869   (Nannie)
Butcher,-- to --Baker 23 jan 1870   (Leanna-John C.)
Blankenship,Lizzie to Isom Adkins 15 mar 1870
------- to Newt Keenan 15 apr 1870
Stewart,Mary to Pete Baker 4 may 1870 (Henry Preston)

Male to female

Adkins,Isom   to Lizzie Blankenship
Baker-----   to----Butcher
Baker,Peter   to Mary Stewart
Bowman,Lee   to--------(Missouri)
Bright,R.D.   to   --Samuels
Church,Bill   to Fanny Hite
Cowens,Jim   to Sarah Butcher
Jewell,Got   to ----Dietz
Keenan,Newt   to   -----
Moss,V.R.   to Mary Morris
Price,George to   --Mather
Salmon,---   to Martha Blake
Shipe,Charley   to Ella Butcher
Simmons,Sampson to ---Ruffner
Thornburg,George to --Wilson
White,Peter   to Mary Blackwood
Womeldroff,--to Jennie Hite
(slave)Spencer   to (Simmon's)wench)

Birthdays

William F.Dusenberry 24 dec (1826)
baby Dusenberry 26 feb 1869 (Robert's son)

Masonic Lodge 1855-56
Barboursville

Allen, Bob
Bloom, Ivan
Childers, Sam
Cowens, Ben
Cox, George W.
Daniels
Dirton, John
Dusenberry, Charles
Dusenberry, William
Egger
Everett, Charles
Fetter
Harrison, Green
McCade
McCullough, Dr. P.H.
Meyer
Miller
Moore, A.
Samuels, Jeff
Shaw
Shelton, Jerome
Simmons, Cornwesley
Tessen, John
Thornburg, John
Thornburg, Thomas
Vertigans
Williams, George
Wood

Masonic Lodge 1855-56
Guyandotte

Amis
Anderson
Beekman
Collins
Everett, John
Johnson, Sam
Laidley, Albert
Mason
Miller, H.H.
Moore, Comps
Peters
Rickets, Dr.
Welington

Guyandotte Lodge 1869

Baker, J.C.
Blankenship
Dusenberry, William
Hiltbruner
Hysell, Dr.
Pollard
Scott, Chubb
Sedinger
Smith, Irving
Steel

The Dusenberry Family

        "The Dusenbery Story" by Henry Dusenbery and Jean
Porcaro is an interesting source of information about the
Dusenbery family in America. According to this book the
first member of this family in North America was Hendrick
Hendrickson van Doesburg. Doseburg being the town in
Gelderlandt, Holland from which Hendrickson immigrated. Over
the years the name was changed to Henry Dusenbery(many
spelling variations).
        The original Hendrick Hendrickson van Doesburg settled
on Jamica Road just outside Hempstead, Long Island in New
York state about 1676. The family members owned property
around Hempstead until the last property was sold in 1791.
At this time the family Dusenbery was found in Westchester
County, New York and across the river in Hunterdon County,
New Jersey. The part of the family which moved to Cabell
county is found in Putnam County, New York as early as 1750.
        The following information is from the Dusenbery book.
There is an extensive family with major branches in Ohio and
the Carolinas as well as all points west. The reader should
remember that the numbering system does not necessarily
follow the order of children.

        Hendrick Hendrickson van Doesburg was able to read and
write and he had some money as he was listed as a "Small
Burger". He also held several positions in the Hempstead
government including Town Drummer and a member of the
Rattlewatch(night watchmen). Following is the lineage from
Hendrickson (of Doesburg)to William F.Dusenberry of Cabell
County, Virginia(writer of the diary).

Family genealogy taken from "The Dusenberry Story" by
Henry Dusenberry and Jean Porcaro.

1   Hendrick Hendrickson van Doesburg @1635-@1689
                     b Doesburg,Netherlands
          m Marritjen Hendrick van Haarlem 1655 -7 children
          two sons
1-4   Hendrick b 1658(of Hempstead,Long Island,NY)
              m Mary Thorn (family traced)-will 1742
1-6 *   Johannes b 1666 (b Hemstead,NY)
              m Mary

1-6-1   John @1686
              m Elizabeth Mudge
  6-1-1   Jarvis   * -5 William 1731
    -2   Elizabeth   -6 Henry 1735
    -3   Moses   -7 Jane 1738
    -4   John

1-6-1-5   William 1731-1815 of Putnam Co.,NY(Dutchess Co.)
              m Sarah Lane 1733-1821   15 children

1-6-1-5-1 Benjamin c1750   -6 Fanny   -11 Sally
    -2 Polly   -7 Amaziah   -12 Levisa
    -3 Elizabeth   -8 Margaret   -13 Abby
    -4 Jarvis   -9 Drusilla   *-14 Charles @1772
    -5 William H.   -10 Nathan   -15 Susan

page 173
1-6-1-5-14 Charles Dusenbery @1772 of Putnam Valley,NY
              m 1.Sarah Conklin 6 children
1-6-1-5-14-1 Samuel b1792 Peekskill,NY d Horry Co.SC
        -2 Nancy
        -3 Charles
        -4 Isaac
      * -5 William Conklin 1799-1858
        -6 Mary 1812 m Gilbert Hadden
   -14- Charles m 2nd Elizabeth Hadden -left will Putnam Co.NY
        -7 Justus Thorn 1817-18-- resided Cabell Co.
             m Louisa Moore of Cabell County
        -8 Ann Eliza
        -9 John C. 1805-1813

1-6-1-5-14-5 William Conklin Dusenberry
                b 1799 Putnam Co,NY-d @1858 will in Cabell Co.
                m Susan
   *-5-14-5-1 William F. 1826-1903 d Cabell Co.
                m Cynthia   1826-1886   (both b Spring Hill)
           -2 Charles O. 1828-1891 d Cabell County
                m Anna F.   (Chas.b Spring Hill)
           -3 Robert 1838-1868
                m Mary Ann Wentz
           -4 Samuel 1842
                m Sarah G. Marsh

        William F. Dusenberry is the author of these diaries.
He arrived in Cabell County with his father about 1850 when
father Wm.C.Dusenberry purchased the Saunders Mill from Sampson
Saunders. Saunders was a very wealthy land owner who had also
purchased the mill site.(from Joel Estis 1828.)
        Wm.F. listed members of his family in the diaries and
tells some of their relationships, but he did not identify all
of the people he refered to in the diaries. The book The
Dusenbery Story helps the reader better understand the family.
        William F. and Cynthia( ) Dusenberry had four children.
        1-Susan 1848-1931 m Roland Clark 1841-1884 b Sp Hill
        2-Caleb C.1853-1929 m Anna P.1858-1915   b Sp Hill DAMRON *
        3-Sarah K.1854-1880 m James K.P.Adams d 1926-Sp Hill
        4-Jessie F.1857-1935 m George McMahan d 1884-Sp Hill
              d/o King Solomon DAMRON GREENUP Co.Ky
All of this family is buried at Spring Hill Cemetery,
Huntington,W.Va except Sarah Adams and her grave may be
unmarked as husband is buried here.

Family members from Diary:
        father-Wm.C.Dusenberry
        mother-Susan
        brother-Robert
        brother-Samuel
        niece-Anna Marsh(must be father's niece)
        Anna's Grandmother Mrs.Weimer
        Aunt Nancy-father Wm.C.'s sister
        Aunt Lucy & Uncle John
        Aunt Olive and Uncle -- Playfoot(Mother's sister)
        Uncle David
        Uncle Cale
        Uncle Francis (NY)
        Jane Nagle w/o Joe -Cynthia's sister
        Roland Clark husband of daughter Susan
        Frank Clark-first child of daughter Susan
        Mary Ann Wentz Dusenberry-brother Robert's wife
        Sarah Marsh Dusenberry-Brother Sam's wife
                (Anna's sister ??)
        Thorn Dusenberry-father's half brother
        Louisa Moore Dusenberry -Thorn's wife

Hendrick Hendrickson @1635
von Doesburg
Marritijen Hendrick van Haarlem

Johannes Doesburg   b 1666

Mary

John Dosenbery   @ 1686

Elizabeth Mudge

William Dusenbery   b 1731

Sarah Lane

Charles Dusenbery   b 1772

Sarah Conklin

Wm.Conklin Dusenberry(NY & Va/WV)   b 1799

Susan

William F.Dusenberry   b 1826

Cynthia

Diary

Source:Personal Diary of William F.Dusenberry
and
The Dusenbery Story
by Henry Dusenbery and Jean Porcaro
453 No.650 East
Orem,Utah 84057

GUYANDOTTE HERALD
AND CABELL & WAYNE ADVERTISER
VOLUME 1--DECEMBER 23,1853

GUYANDOTTE HERALD
TERMS

One year in advance $1.50
If paid within 6 months   1.75
If paid within 1 year   2.00
Advance payments will always
receive a preference. We would
much rather have $1.50 at the
beginning of the year than $2
at its expiration.

TERMS OF ADVERTISEMENT

12 lines one month $1.00
12 lines three months   3.00
2 squares,three months   5.00
3 squares 12 months   15.00
    For all Chancery,Foreign
attachment and Transient adver
tisement,advance payment will
be required.

HEAD QUARTERS

FAMILY GROCERIES

J.T.Dusenberry,having bought
out the entire interest of
Wayne McMahone in the firm of
Dusenberry and McMahone is now
prepared to furnish everything
in his line at prices so low as
to defy competition. Thank-ful
for past favors, he hopes by
strict attention to busi-ness
and low prices to merit and
receive a liberal share of
patronage. He has on hand a
large assorment of
    COFFE,SUGARS,TEAS
and in fact every thing in the
grocery line, to which he has
added a superior lot of Boots
and Shoes direct from the
manufactories at prices that
cannot fail to please.
    Call at the old stand of
Dusenberry & McMahon and
satisfy yourself that there's
the place to get your money
back.

GUYANDOTTE DRUG
STORE
Dr.T.C.BUFFINGTON

Would respectfully announce to
the physician and citizens of
Western Virginia, that he has
just received from New York and
Boston and is now opening
    GUYANDOTTE DRUG STORE
a large and well assorted stock
of Drugs,Medicines, &c. which
he offers for sale on as
resonable terms as they can be
purchased in the west-all articles warranted NO.1. Also,
the largest and best stock of
Paints,Oils,Window Glass,Putty
Brushes of every variety and
Dye Stuffs ever offered in this
place, to which he would invite
the attention of
Builders,Painters and county
Merchants before purchasing
elsewhere. Also a fine assortment of perfumery,Sationary and
fancy articles to which he
respectfully asks the special
attention of the Ladies.

WATCH REPAIR & JEWELER

The subscriber at the solica-
tion of his friends, informs
the public that he will devote
more of his time to the above
business at Bloomingdale,
Cabell Co.Va. He flatters
himself from his experience,
(having been engaged in some of
the most expensive manufactories in New York) that he is
able to give entire satisfac-
tion to all that favor him with
their patronage. All kinds of
watches and jeweler made and
repaired in the best manner,
and if worthy, warranted.--
Watch glasses fitted and
spectacle glassed adjusted to
the sight. Cains of any pattern
mounted with gold or silver;
and musical boxes repaired.--
This community need no longer
send their work to Cinncinati
or Portsmouth for repairs.
    CHAS.DUSENBERRY

GUYANDOTTE HERALD
December 23,1853

LAND and MILLS for SALE
I wish to sell my Land and
Mills on Mud River in the
County of Cabell and the state
of Va. 6 miles from the Court
House and one mile from the
Covington and Ohio Railroad.
The tract of land contains 751
acres and 67 poles,150 acres
cleared and in cultivation, the
balance,timbered land.
The improvements on the farm
consist of a two story hewed
log house,frame kitchen and a
frame barn 40 by 60 ft.,two
small frame and log buildings,
for the use of tenants, apple
orchards, and about 100 peach
trees, all of which are bearing fruit the present season.
The mill is a three store frame
building 40 feet square and a
basement of stone. The Mill
runs three pair(4 feet stones 2
pair of which are burrs of the
best quailty. All the shafting
and wheels for running, the
machinery are cast iron. The
saw mill is 22 by 60 feet
long, and can cut 6,000 feet of
lumber in 24 hrs There is also
a building 24 by 40 feet long,
one and a half stories high and
used for a Carding Machine and
cabinet shop; in the cabinet
shop is a good turning lathe
run by water. There is an
immense quality of Iron Ore on
the land, the vein of Ore is
sup-posed to be 20 feet thick,
and said by judges of Ore to be
of a quality that will justify
working. Persons wishing to
purchase such property are
invited to call and see it, or
by addressing me(post paid) at
Cabell Court House,Va., they
may obtain any information they
may desire.
    AMBROSE L.DOOLITLE

SALT ! SALT !
JUST received from the salt Co.
50 bris salt.
    J M & J S Walcott

GUYANDOTTE VARIETY
STORE

The undersigned would respectfully announce to the citizens
of Guyandotte and vicinity that
he has open a --
FANCY GROCERY and VARIETY STORE
in this place, where can at all
times be found a superior assortment od Grociers, Candies,
Preserves, Cigars, Flour, Hareware
and in fact everything appear-
ing in his branch of business,
which he is determined to sell
on the most resonable terms,
and by doing would respectfully
---- the patronage of his
friends and the general public.
N.B.-A fine assortment of
ploughs constantly on hand,
cheap for cash.   S.M.CLARK

HOUSE AND LOT FOR SALE
In Trouts Hill, the county
seat of Wayne County. The
House is a frame----
21 ft by 16 with well finished
rooms. The lot has a good plank
fence around it and on it a
good smoke house and stable.
For further---- inquire of
J.C.Wheeler, General Agent.

T.M.LAIDLEY

PHYSICIAN and SURGEON
office in Hites Building
GUYANDOTTE, VA.

J.C.WHEELER
REAL ESTATE AGENT
Guyandotte, Virginia
Will attend properly all business relating to buying and
selling lands, paying taxes,
redeeming land sold for
taxes, drafting deeds, deeds
of trust &c. Fees moderate.

Dr.J.W.PEYTON
Physician & Surgeon

ON the Taurpike,

GUYANDOTTE HERALD
December 23, 1853

CLOTHING !! CLOTHING !!
THE Boston Clothing Store has
just been replenished with a
stock of Superior Clothing from
the House of J & M
Kornblith, Cincinnati, O.--
The undersigned Agent for the
sale of these goods has made
arrangement with this House, by
which he will be constantly in
receipt of supplies to the
present stock, and will be
happy to wait upon his old
friends and the public gener-
ally, and supply them with
    COATS, VESTS, PANTS
shirts, drawers, and other
articles of clothing selected
by himself with special
reference to the wants of his
customers.   ISAAC ONG

ISAAC ONG, TAILOR
Would return his most grateful
acknowledgements to the public
for their liberal patronage and
announces he still carries on
the Tailoring business, and
will do all work entrusted in
his care, according to the lat -
est style and in the most sub-
stantial manner. He has suppl-
ied himself with a superior lot
of cloths and cassimeres which
he will make up for his
customers.

FALL AND WINTER GOODS
COVINGTON & OHIO RAILROAD DEPOT
at NO.2 Commerical Row
    GUYANDOTTE, VA.
Is now receiving the most
extensive assortment of

FALL AND WINTER GOODS

Ever before opened in
Guyandotte, Va.
    GREAT BARGAINS in
RIBBONS, DRESS GOODS,

PERSONS wishing to purchase
over will do well to call
☞   C.L.ROFFE

W. L. PETERS
would respectfully inform the
public that he is prepared to
do all his line of business on
the shortest notice and at
ruinously low prices. As I work
for amusement there can be no
fear of prices being too
strong.
House, Sign and Ornamental
Painting, Graining, Glazing, Paper
Hanging &c...&c.done in the
neatest style. Any job from
Mosquito to Elephant is grate-
fully received. Paints ready
mixed for sale at any time.

VEGETABLE TONIC ELIXIR

Prepared and sold by Dr.H.Clark
    Guyandotte, Virginia
THE saftest and most valuable
Medicine ever offered to the
public. For the cure of Dyspe-
peia, Jaundice, Liver Complaint,
Consumption in the first magic,
Billose Fever, Fever and Ague
and all diseases arising from
an impure state of the blood.
PRICE 75 cents..............
ANTI-BILLOUS PILLS....25 cents
WORM MEDICINE.........no family
            should be without
Dr.CLARKS LINIMENT   25 cents
The above medicines are kept
constantly on hand and for sale
at his residence in Guyandotte.

BOOT & SHOE MANUFACTORY
WM. EGGERS
MANUFACTURES AND keeps constantly on hand a supply of Boots
and Shoes of the best quality.
he works the best French Calf
skin and Morocco and keeps all
kinds of Find-ings, such as
lining, bindings &c. One door
South of the store of
Wm.C.Miller & Co.

BLASTING POWDER & FUSE CONTRACTORS need send no farther than Guyandotte for their Powder now. Lucien M. Wolcott has the DUPONT AGENCY at this point and can furnish any quantity at DUPONT prices. All the Powder that has been used here this season has cost too much, but the subscriber sells on commission for CASH ONLY for the most extensive manufactory of the kind in the world, and is determined no man shall go further than this place for it.

LUCIEN M. WOLCOTT

LUMBER ! LUMBER !
LAIDLEY having erected one of the very best saw mills in this section of the country 3 miles South of South Landing, Cabell County, Va. in the midst of a large tract of Timber Land is prepared to deliver on the bank of the Ohio, on short notice, to fill any bill that may be ordered for Popular, White Oak, Yellow Pine, Beech or Sugar Tree lumber, at the usual prices.

address A. LAIDLEY

(Ironton Register Copy)
N.B.--Corn will be ground for the neighborhood every Wednesday and Saturday. A.L.

---

40 KEGS Superior Lynchburg Tobacco Just received and for sale wholesale of retail, at prices ranging from 20 to 60 cents per lb.

HITE & CO.

CIGARS ! CIGARS !
FRESH arrival from Baltimore 12,000 Barrios Principle $4 50 boxes Jenny Lind @ $1.50 box 10,000 Half Spanish $4 per 100

L.M. & A.S. WOLCOTT

YOUNG CATTLE
THE undersigned has on his farm in the Mud River valley, 50 or 60 head of lively young cattle which he will sell for a fair price.

GEO. W. SUMMERS

---

clothing ! clothing !
JUST received a large and splendid assortment of clothing, consisting of Coats, Pants, Vests, Drawers &c..which will be sold cheaper than any other house in the city of Guyan-dotte. S.E. corner of Court St. and Guyandotte.
P.S. SMITH

GUYANDOTTE HERALD
AND CABELL & WAYNE ADVERTISER
an Independent Newspaper devoted to the Interests of Western Virginians
Volume 1 --- December 23, 1853
J.C. WHEELER Editor

BIBLIOGRAPHY

Cabell County Cemeteries-Volumes 1,2,3
    Carrie Eldridge Chesapeake,OH 1991

Cabell County Court Records
    Deeds 1824-1850
    Marriages 1809-1870 Cabell County,WV

Community Histories-Cabell County,WV
    West Virginia Extension Service 1925

The Dusenberry Story-Henry Dusenberry and
    Jean Porcaro Orem,UT 1990

Fred B.Lambert Munscript Collection MS76
    Barboursville & Guyandotte Interviews
    Special Collections Morrow Library
    Marshall University-Huntington,WV

Guyandotte Herald- Volume 1 1853 published
    Guyandotte,VA-Editor P.C.Wheeler

New County and District Atlas of West Virginia
    M.Wood White 1873

Guyandotte Herald,

AND CABELL & WAYNE ADVERTISER

J. C. WHEELER, Editor.   AN INDEPENDENT NEWSPAPER, DEVOTED TO THE INTERESTS OF WESTERN VIRGINIA.   C. C. CURTIS,

VOLUME I.   GUYANDOTTE, CABELL COUNTY, VIRGINIA, ...DAY MORNING, DECEMBER 2..., 185...   NU...

1853

Guyandotte Herald,

AND CABELL & WAYNE ADVERTISER.

J. C. WHEELER, Editor. AN INDEPENDENT NEWSPAPER, DEVOTED TO THE INTERESTS OF WESTERN VIRGINIA. C. C. CURTIS, Printer.

VOLUME 1.) GUYANDOTTE, CABELL COUNTY, VIRGINIA, FRIDAY MORNING, DECEMBER 2?, 1853. (NU...

1853

BIBLIOGRAPHY

Cabell County Cemeteries-Volumes 1,2,3
    Carrie Eldridge Chesapeake,OH 1991

Cabell County Court Records
    Deeds 1824-1850
    Marriages 1809-1870 Cabell County,WV

Community Histories-Cabell County,WV
    West Virginia Extension Service 1925

The Dusenberry Story-Henry Dusenberry and
    Jean Porcaro Orem,UT 1990

Fred B.Lambert Munscript Collection MS76
    Barboursville & Guyandotte Interviews
    Special Collections Morrow Library
    Marshall University-Huntington,WV

Guyandotte Herald- Volume 1 1853 published
    Guyandotte,VA-Editor P.C.Wheeler

New County and District Atlas of West Virginia
    M.Wood White 1873

www.ingramcontent.com/pod-product-compliance
Lightning Source LLC
Chambersburg PA
CBHW080418270326
41929CB00018B/3070